Corpora in Language Acquisition Research

Trends in Language Acquisition Research

As the official publication of the International Association for the Study of Child Language (IASCL), TiLAR presents thematic collective volumes on state-of-the-art child language research carried out by IASCL members worldwide.

IASCL website: http://iascl.talkbank.org/

Volume 6

Corpora in Language Acquisition Research. History, methods, perspectives
Edited by Heike Behrens

Corpora in Language Acquisition Research

History, methods, perspectives

Edited by

Heike Behrens
University of Basel

John Benjamins Publishing Company
Amsterdam / Philadelphia

The paper used in this publication meets the minimum requirements of American National Standard for Information Sciences – Permanence of Paper for Printed Library Materials, ANSI Z39.48-1984.

Library of Congress Cataloging-in-Publication Data

Corpora in language acquisition research : history, methods, perspectives / edited by Heike Behrens.

p. cm. (Trends in Language Acquisition Research, ISSN 1569-0644 ; v. 6)

Includes bibliographical references and index.

1. Language acquisition--Research--Data processing. I. Behrens, Heike.

P118.C6738 2008

401'.93--dc22 2008002769

ISBN 978 90 272 3476 6 (Hb; alk. paper)

John Benjamins Publishing Co. · P.O. Box 36224 · 1020 ME Amsterdam · The Netherlands

John Benjamins North America · P.O. Box 27519 · Philadelphia PA 19118-0519 · USA

Table of contents

List of contributors

Shanley Allen
Boston University, USA

Hans Basbøll
University of Southern Denmark

Heike Behrens
University of Basel, Switzerland

Johannes Bertl
Austrian Academy of Sciences, Austria

Morten H. Christiansen
Cornell University, USA

Katherine Demuth
Brown University

Wolfgang U. Dressler
Austrian Academy of Sciences, Austria

Sarah L. Fletcher
University of Liverpool, UK

Daniel Freudenthal
University of Liverpool, UK

Steven Gillis
University of Antwerp, Belgium

Mary Hughes
Boston University, USA

Katharina Korecky-Kröll
Austrian Academy of Sciences, Austria

Sabine Laaha
Austrian Academy of Sciences, Austria

Elena Lieven
Max Planck Institute for Evolutionary Anthropology, Germany
School of Psychological Sciences, University of Manchester, UK

Brian MacWhinney
Carnegie Mellon University, USA

Padraic Monaghan
University of York, UK

Bracha Nir-Sagiv
Tel Aviv University, Israel

Dorit Ravid
Tel Aviv University, Israel

Katja Rehfeldt
University of Southern Denmark, Denmark

Caroline F. Rowland
University of Liverpool, UK

Barbora Skarabela
University of Edinburgh, UK

Agnita Souman
University of Antwerp, Belgium

Preface

The present volume is the sixth in the series 'Trends in Language Acquisition Research' (TiLAR). As an official publication of the *International Association for the Study of Child Language* (IASCL), the TiLAR Series publishes two volumes per three year period in between IASCL congresses. All volumes in the IASCL-TiLAR Series are invited edited volumes by IASCL members that are strongly thematic in nature and that present cutting edge work which is likely to stimulate further research to the fullest extent.

Besides quality, diversity is also an important consideration in all the volumes and in the series as a whole: diversity of theoretical and methodological approaches, diversity in the languages studied, diversity in the geographical and academic backgrounds of the contributors. After all, like the IASCL itself, the IASCL-TiLAR Series is there for child language researchers from all over the world.

The five previous TiLAR volumes were on (1) bilingual acquisition, (2) sign language acquisition, (3) language development beyond the early childhood years, (4) the link between child language disorders and developmental theory, and (5) neurological and behavioural approaches to the study of early language processing. We are delighted to present the current volume on the use of corpora in language acquisition research. We owe a lot of gratitude to the volume editor, Heike Behrens, for her willingness to take on the task of preparing this sixth TiLAR volume, especially since it coincided with taking up a new position.

The present volume is the last that we as General Editors will be presenting to the IASCL community. For us, the job has come full circle. This will be the last TiLAR volume we are responsible for. We find it particularly fitting, then, that this volume deals with a subject with a long history indeed, while at the same time, it is a subject that is of continued basic interest and importance in language acquisition studies: What are the types of data we need to advance our insights into the acquisition process? We are proud to have the latest thinking on this issue represented in the TiLAR series so that child language researchers from all different backgrounds worldwide have the opportunity to become acquainted with it or get to know it better.

Finally, we would like to take this opportunity to once again thank all the previous TiLAR volume editors for their invaluable work. Also, our thanks go to all the contributors to the series. We also thank the TiLAR Advisory Board consisting of IASCL past presidents Jean Berko Gleason, Ruth Berman, Philip Dale, Paul Fletcher and Brian MacWhinney for being our much appreciated 'sounding board'. Seline Benjamins and Kees Vaes of John Benjamins Publishing Company have given us their continued trust and support throughout. We appreciate this very much. Finally, we would like to particularly express our gratitude to past presidents Paul Fletcher and Brian MacWhinney: The former, for supporting our idea for the TiLAR series at the very start, and the latter, for helping to make it actually happen.

Antwerp, November 2007

Annick De Houwer and Steven Gillis
The General Editors

Corpora in language acquisition research

History, methods, perspectives

Heike Behrens

1. Introduction

Child language research is one of the first domains in which conversation data were systematically sampled, initially through diary studies and later by audio and video recordings. Despite rapid development in experimental and neurolinguistic techniques to investigate children's linguistic representations, corpora still form the backbone for a number of questions in the field, especially in studying new phenomena or new languages.

As a backdrop for the six following chapters that each demonstrate new and sophisticated uses of existing corpora, this chapter provides a brief history of corpus collection, transcription and annotation before elaborating on aspects of archiving and data mining. I will then turn to issues of quality control and conclude with some suggestions for future corpus research and discuss how the articles represented in this volume address some of these issues.

2. Building child language corpora: Sampling methods

Interest in children's language development led to the first systematic diary studies starting in the 19th century (Jäger 1985), a movement that lasted into the first decades of the 20th century. While the late 20th century was mainly concerned with obtaining corpora on a variety of languages, populations, and situations, aspects of quality control and automatic analysis have dominated the development of corpus studies in the early 21st century thanks to the public availability of large samples.

Ingram (1989: 7–31) provides a comprehensive survey of the history of child language studies up to the 1970s. He divided the history of language acquisition corpora into three phases: (1) diary studies (2) large sample studies and (3) longitudinal studies. However, since diary studies tend to be longitudinal, too, I will discuss the development of data recording in terms of longitudinal and cross-sectional studies and add some notes on more recent techniques of data collection. All of these sampling methods reflect both the technical and methodological resources at the time, and the research questions that seemed most imminent.

2.1 Longitudinal data

2.1.1 *Diaries*

Wright (1960) distinguishes two types of diary taking in developmental psychology: comprehensive diaries in which general aspects of child development and their interaction are observed, and topical diaries with a narrower focus. Historically, the earlier diary studies (up to 1950) tend to be comprehensive, whereas more modern ones tend to be topical diaries.

Comprehensive diaries in the 19th and early 20th Century

Although the supposedly first diary on language development was created in the 16th century by Jean (Jehan) Héroard (Foisil 1989, see http://childes.psy.cmu.edu/topics/louisXIII.html), the interest in children's development experienced a boom only in the late 19th century.

The early phase of diary studies is characterized by their comprehensiveness because in many cases the researchers did not limit their notes to language development alone. Several diaries provide a complete picture of children's cognitive, but also social and physical development (e.g., Darwin (1877, 1886) and Hall (1907) for English; Baudouin de Cortenay, unpublished, for Polish; Preyer (1882); Tiedemann (1787); Scupin and Scupin (1907, 1910); Stern and Stern (1907); for German. See Bar-Adon and Leopold (1971) for (translated) excerpts from several of these early studies).

The method of diary taking varied considerably: Preyer observed his son in a strict regime and took notes in the morning, at noon, and in the evening for the first three years of his life. Clara and William Stern took notes on the development of their three children over a period of 18 years, with a focus on the first child and the early phases of development. They emphasized the necessity of naturalistic observation which implies a strong role of the mother – note that this is one of the few if not the only early diary in which the mother took a central role in data collection and analysis. All through the day they wrote their observations on small pieces of paper that were available all over the house and then transferred their notes into a separate diary for each child. Their wide research focus was supposed to yield 6 monographs, only two of which materialized dealing with language development and the development of memory (Stern and Stern 1907, 1909). Additional material went into William Stern's (1921) monograph on the psychology of early childhood.

Probably the largest data collection using the diary method is that of Jan Baudouin de Cortenay on Polish child language (Smoczynska 2001). Between 1886 and 1903 he filled 473 notebooks (or 13000 pages) on the development of his 5 children, having developed a sophisticated recording scheme with several columns devoted to the external circumstances (date, time, location), the child's posture and behaviour, as well as the linguistic contexts in which an utterance was made, and the child utterance itself in semi-phonetic transcription as well as adult-like "translation". He also included special symbols to denote children's overgeneralizations and word creations. Unfortunately he never published anything based on the data, although the accuracy and sophistication of data recording show that he was an insightful and skilled linguist who drew on his general insights from his observations in some of his theoretical articles (Smoczynska 2001).

After the 1920s very few of this type of general diary study are evident. Leopold's study on his daughter Hildegard is the first published study of a bilingual child (Leopold 1939–1949), and one of the few case studies that appeared in the middle of the past century. These extensive diaries provided the material for 4 volumes that cover a wide range of linguistic topics.

Topical diaries

A new surge of interest in child language as well as new types of data collection began in the late 1950ies and 1960ies (see next section). Modern recording technology became available and allowed researchers to record larger samples and actual conversations with more precision than possibly subjective and imprecise diary taking. But diaries continued to be collected even after the advent of recording technology. The focus of data collection changed from comprehensive to so-called topical diaries (Wright 1960): diaries where just one or a few aspects of language development are observed. Examples of this kind are Melissa Bowerman's notes on her daughters' errors and overgeneralizations especially of argument structure alternations like the causative alternation (Bowerman 1974, 1982); Michael Tomasello's diary notes on his daughter's use of verbs (Tomasello 1992); or Susan Braunwald's collection of emergent or novel structures produced by her two daughters (Braunwald and Brislin 1979). Vear, Naigles, Hoff and Ramos (2002) carried out a parental report study of 8 children's first 10 uses of a list of 35 English verbs in order to test the degree of productivity of children's early verb use.

These modern diary studies show that this technique may still be relevant despite the possibility of recording very large datasets. Since each hour of recording involves at least 10–20 hours of transcription – depending on the degree of detail – plus time for annotation and coding, collecting large databases for studying low-frequency phenomena is a very costly and time-consuming endeavour. Such large datasets can at best be sampled for a small number of participants only. For such studies, topical diaries can be an alternative, because the relevant examples can be recorded with less effort, provided the data collectors (usually the parents) are trained properly to spot relevant structures in the child's language. In addition, it is possible to include a larger number of children in the study if their caregivers are trained properly. But since diary notes are taken "on the go" when the child is producing the structures under investigation, the concept of the study must be well designed because it is not possible to do a pilot study or revise the original plan with the same children. Also, the diary must contain all context data necessary for interpreting the children's utterances (cf. Braunwald and Brislin (1979) for a discussion of some of the methodological pitfalls of diary studies).

2.1.2 *Audio- and video-recorded longitudinal data*

Roger Brown's study on the language development of Adam, Eve and Sarah (Brown 1973; the data were recorded between 1962 and 1966) marks a turning point in acquisition research in many respects. The recording medium changed as well as the "origin" of the children. Regarding the medium, the tape recorder replaced the notepad, and this makes reliability checks of the transcript possible. Since tape recordings typically only last 30 minutes or half an hour, it became also possible to dissociate the role of recorder and recorded subject, i.e., it became more easily possible to record children from a variety of socioeconomic backgrounds – and this was one of the aims of Brown's project. Moreover, data collection and transcription is no longer a one- or two-person enterprise, but often a whole research team is engaged in data collection, transcription, and analysis.

On a theoretical level, the availability of qualitative and quantitative data from three children made it possible for new measures for assessing children's language to be developed such as Mean Length of Utterance (MLU) as a measure of linguistic complexity, or morpheme order that not only listed the appearance of morphemes but also assessed their productivity. For example, in his study on the emergence of 14 grammatical morphemes in English Brown (1973) set quite strict productivity criteria. In order to count as acquired, a morpheme had to be used in 90% of the obligatory contexts. Only quantitative data allow for setting such criteria because it would be impossible to track obligatory contexts in diaries.

On a methodological level, new problems arose in the process of developing appropriate transcription systems. Eleanor Ochs drew attention to the widespread lack of discussion of transcription conventions and criteria in many of the existing studies (Ochs 1979) and argued that the field needed a set of transcription conventions in order to deal with the verbal and non-verbal information in a standardized way. She points out, for example, that (a) transcripts usually depict the chronological order of utterances and (b) we are biased to read transcripts line by line and to assume that adjacent utterances are indeed turns in conversation. These two biases lead to the effect that the reader interprets any utterance as a direct reaction to the preceding one, when in fact it could have been a reaction to something said by a third party earlier on. Only standardized conventions for denoting turn-taking phenomena can prevent the researcher from misinterpreting the data.

In 1983, Catherine Snow and Brian MacWhinney started to discuss the possibility of creating an archive of child language data to allow researchers to share their transcripts. In order to do so, a uniform system of computerizing the data had to be developed. Many of Ochs' considerations are now implemented in the CHAT (Codes for Human Analysis of Transcripts) conventions that are the norm for the transcripts available in the CHILDES database (= CHIld Language Data Exchange System; MacWhinney

1987a, 2000). Early on, the CHAT transcription system provided a large toolbox from which researchers could – within limits – select those symbols and conventions that they needed for the purposes of their investigation. More recently, however, the transcription conventions have become tighter in order to allow for automated coding, parsing, and analysis of the data (see below and MacWhinney this volume).

The research interests of the researcher(s) collecting data also influence in many ways what is recorded and transcribed: researchers interested in children's morphology and syntax only may omit transcribing the input language, or stop transcription and/or analysis after 100 analyzable utterances (e.g., in the LARSP-procedure [= Language Assessment, Remediation and Screening Procedure] only a short recording is transcribed and analyzed according to its morphosyntactic properties to allow for a quick assessment of the child's developmental level; Crystal 1979).

Depending on the research question and the time and funds available, the size of longitudinal corpora varies considerable. A typical sampling regime used to be to collect 30 minutes or 1 hour samples every week, every second week or once a month. More recently, the Max-Planck-Institute for Evolutionary Anthropology has started to collect "dense databases" where children are recorded for 5 hours or even 10 hours a week (e.g., Lieven, Behrens, Speares and Tomasello 2003; Behrens 2006). These new corpora respond to the insight that the results to be obtained can depend on the sample size. If one is looking for a relatively rare phenomenon in a relatively small sample, there is a high likelihood that relevant examples are missing (see Tomasello and Stahl (2004) for statistical procedures that allow to predict how large a sample is needed to find a sufficient number of exemplars). But even with small datasets, statistical procedures can help to balance out such sampling effect. Regarding type-token ratio, there is a frequency effect since a large corpus will contain more low-frequency items. Malvern and Richards (1997) introduced a new statistical procedure for measuring lexical dispersion that controls for the effect of sample size (the program VOCD is part of the CHILDES software package CLAN; see also Malvern, Richards, Chipere and Purán (2004); for statistical procedures regarding morphosyntactic development see Rowland, Fletcher and Freudenthal this volume).

Finally, technological advances led to changes in the media represented in the transcripts. The original Brown (1973) tape recordings, for example, are not preserved because of the expense of the material and because the researchers did not think at the time that having access to the phonetic or discourse information was relevant for the planned study (Dan Slobin, personal communication). In the past years, the state of the art has become multimodal transcripts in which each utterance is linked to the respective segment of the audio or even video file. Having access to the original recordings in an easy fashion allows one not only to check existing transcriptions, but also to add information not transcribed originally. On the negative side, access to the source data raises new ethical problems regarding the privacy of the participants because it is extremely labour intensive and even counterproductive to make all data anonymous. For example, the main motivation for studying the original video-recordings would be to study people's behaviour in discourse. This would be impossible if the faces were blurred in order to guarantee anonymity. Here, giving access only to registered users is the only compromise between the participants' personal rights and the researcher's interest (cf. http://www.talkbank.org for a discussion of these issues).

2.1.3 *Cross-sectional studies*

Cross-sectional corpora usually contain a larger number of participants spread across different age ranges, languages, and/or socio-cultural variables within a given group, such as gender, ethnicity, diglossia or multilingualism. Recording methods include tape- or video-recordings of spontaneous interaction, questionnaires (parental reports), or elicited production data like narratives based on (wordless) picture books or films.

Ingram (1989: 11–18) describes large sample studies from the 1930s to the 1950s in which between 70 and 430 children were recorded for short sessions only. The data collected in each study varied from 50 sentences to 6-hour samples per child. These studies focussed on specific linguistic domains areas such as phonological development or the development of sentence length. Ingram notes that the results of these studies were fairly general and of limited interest to the next generation of child language studies that was interested in more complex linguistic phenomena, or in a more specific analysis of the phenomena than the limited samples allowed.

In a very general sense, the parental reports that form the basis of normed developmental score like the CDI can be considered topical diaries. The CDI (MacArthur-Bates Communicative Development Inventories; Fenson, Dale, Reznick, Bates, Thal and Pethick 1993) is one of the most widespread tests for early linguistic development. The CDI measures early lexical development as well as early combinatorial speech based on parental reports: Parents are given a questionnaire with common words and phrases and are instructed to check which of these items their child comprehends or produces. Full-fledged versions are available for English and Spanish, adaptations for 40 other languages from Austrian-German to Yiddish (http://sci.sdsu.edi/adaptations_ol.html). Although these data do not result in a corpus as such, they nevertheless provide information about children's lexical and early syntactic development.

Cross-sectional naturalistic interactions have also been collected keeping the type of interaction stable. For example, Pan, Perlman and Snow (2000) provide a survey of studies using recordings of dinner table conversations as a means for obtaining children's interaction in a family setting rather than just the dyadic interaction typical for other genres of data collection.

Another research domain in which cross-sectional rather than longitudinal data are common is the study of narratives (e.g., the *Frog Stories* collected in many languages and for many age ranges; cf. Berman and Slobin 1994). Typically, the participants are presented with a wordless picture book, cartoon, or film clip and are asked to tell the story to a researcher who has not seen the original. Such elicited production tasks typically generate a large amount of data that can be used for assessing children's language development both within a language and crosslinguistically. Since the elicitation tool and procedure are standardized, children's narratives provide a useful data source for the analysis of reference to space and time, sentence connectors, or information structure.

2.1.4 *Combination of sampling techniques*

Diaries can be combined with other forms of sampling like elicited production or audio- or video-recordings. In addition to taking diary notes, Clara and William Stern also asked their children to describe sets of pictures at different stages of their language development. These picture descriptions provided a controlled assessment of their language development in terms of sentence complexity, for example, or the amount of detail narrated.

The MPI for Evolutionary Anthropology combined dense sampling (five one-hour recordings per week) with parental diary notes on new and the most complex utterances of the day (e.g., Lieven *et al.* 2003). The diary notes were expected to capture the cutting-edge of development, and to make sure that no important steps would be missed. A combination of parental diaries with almost daily recordings enables researchers to trace children's progress on a day-to-day basis.

Of course, a combination of research methods need not be limited to corpus collection. Triangulation, i.e. addressing a particular problem with different methodologies, is a procedure not yet common in first language acquisition research. It is possible, for example, to systematically combine of observational and experimental data, production and comprehension data.

3. Data archiving and sharing

Once a corpus has been collected it needs to be stored and archived. When computers became available, digitizing handwritten or typed and mimeographed corpora was seen as a means for archiving the data and for sharing them more easily. And indeed, in the past 20 years we have seen a massive proliferation of publicly available corpora, and even more corpora reserved for the use of smaller research group, many of which will eventually become public as well. Downloading a corpus is now possible from virtually every computer in the world.

3.1 From diaries and mimeographs to machine-readable corpora

The earliest phase of records of child language development relied on hand-written notes taken by the parents. In most cases, these notes were transferred into notebooks in a more or less systematic fashion (see above), sometimes with the help of a typewriter. Of course, these early studies were unique, not only because they represent pioneering work, but also because they were literally the only exemplar of these data.

The majority of diary data is only accessible in a reduced and filtered way through the publications that were based (in part) on these data (e.g., Darwin 1877, 1886; Preyer 1882; Hall 1907; Leopold 1939–1949; Scupin and Scupin 1907, 1910; Stern and Stern 1907). In a few cases, historical diary data were re-entered into electronic databases. This includes the German data collected by William and Clara Stern at the Max-Planck-Institute for Psycholinguistics (Behrens and Deutsch 1991), as well as Baudouin de Courtenay's Polish data (Smoszynska, unpublished, cf. Smoszynska 2001).

Modern corpora (e.g., Bloom 1970; Brown 1973) first existed as typescript only, but were put in electronic format as soon as possible, first on punch cards (Brown data), then into CHILDES (Sokolov and Snow 1994).

3.2 From text-only to multimedia corpora

Writing out the information in a corpus is no longer the only way of archiving the data. It is now possible to have "talking transcripts" by linking each utterance to the corresponding segment of the speech file. Linked speech data can be stored on personal computers or be made available on the internet. Having access to the sound has several obvious advantages: the researcher has direct access to the interaction and can verify the transcription in case of uncertainty, and get a first hand impression of hard-to-transcribe phenomena like interjections or hesitation phenomena. Moreover, in CHILDES the data can be exported to speech analysis software (e.g., PRAAT, cf. Boersma and Weenink 2007) for acoustic analysis.

More recently tools have been developed that enable easy analysis of video recordings as well (e.g., ELAN at the Max-Planck-Institute for Psycholinguistics; http://www.lat-mpi.eu/tools/elan). In addition to providing very useful context information for transcribing speech, video information can be used for analyzing discourse interaction or gestural information in spoken as well as sign language communication.

3.3 Establishing databases

Apart from archiving and safe-keeping, another goal of machine-readable (re)transcription is data-sharing. Collecting spoken language data, especially longitudinal data, is a labour-intensive and time-consuming process, and the original research project typically investigates only a subset of all possible research questions a given corpus can be used for. Therefore, as early as in the 1980s, child language researchers began to pool their data and make them publicly available. Catherine Snow and Brian MacWhinney started the first initiative for what is now the CHILDES archive. To date, many, but by no means all, longitudinal corpora have been donated to the CHILDES database. The database includes longitudinal corpora from Celtic languages (Welsh, Irish), East Asian languages (Cantonese, Mandarin, Japanese, Thai), Germanic languages (Afrikaans, Danish, Dutch, English, German, Swedish), Romance (Catalan,

French, Italian, Portuguese, Spanish, Romanian), Slavic languages (Croatian, Polish, Russian), as well as Basque, Estonian, Farsi, Greek, Hebrew, Hungarian, Sesotho, Tamil, and Turkish. In addition, narratives from a number of the languages listed above, as well as Thai and Arabic are available. Thus, data from 26 languages are currently represented in the CHILDES database. With 45 million words of spoken language it is almost 5 times larger than the next biggest corpus of spoken language (MacWhinney this volume).

Most corpora study monolingual children, but some corpora are available for bilingual and second language acquisition as well. In addition to data from normally developing children, data from children with special conditions are available, e.g., children with cochlear implants, children who were exposed to substance abuse in utero, as well as children with language disorders.

The availability of CHILDES has made child language acquisition a very democratic field since researchers have free access to primary data covering many languages. Also, the child language community observes the request of many funding agencies that corpora collected with public money should be made publicly available.

However, just pooling data does not solve the labour bottleneck since using untagged data entails that the researcher become familiar with the particular ways each corpus is transcribed (it would be fatal, for example, to search for lexemes in standard orthography when the corpus followed alternative conventions in order to represent phonological variation or reduction of syllables or morphemes). Also, without standardized transcripts or morphosyntactic coding, analysing existing corpora requires considerable manual analysis: one must read through the entire corpus, perhaps with a very rough first search as a filter, to find relevant examples. Therefore, corpora not only need to be archived, but they also require maintenance.

3.4 Data maintenance

The dynamics of the development of information technology, as well as growing demands regarding the automatic analysis of corpora have had an unexpected consequence: corpora are now very dynamic entities – not the stable counterpart of a manuscript on paper.

While having data in machine readable format seemed to rescue them from the danger of becoming lost, this turned out to be far from true: operating systems and database programs as well as storage media changed more rapidly than anyone could have anticipated. Just a few years of lack of attention to electronic data could mean that they become inaccessible because of lack of proper backup in the case of data damage, or simply because storage media or (self-written) database programs could no longer be read by the next generation of computers. Thus, maintenance of data is a labour-intensive process that requires a good sense of direction as to where information technology was heading. It is only recently that unified standards regarding fonts and other issues of data storage have made data platform-independent. Previously, several versions of the same data had to be maintained (e.g., for Windows, Mac and Unix), and users had to make sure to have the correct fonts installed to read the data properly. Also, for a while, only standard ASCII-characters could be used without problems. This lead to special renditions of the phonetic alphabet in ASCII characters. With new options like UNICODE it is possible to view and transfer non-ASCII characters (e.g., diacritics in Roman fonts, other scripts like Cyrillic or IPA) to any (online) platform.

Another form of data maintenance is that of standardization. The public availability of data from allows for replication studies and other forms of quality control (see below). But in order to carry out meaningful analyses to over data from various sources, these data must adhere to the same transcription and annotation standards (unless one is prepared to manually analyze and tag the phenomena under investigation). To this purpose, several transcription standards were developed. SALT and CHILDES (CHAT) are the formats most relevant for acquisition research. SALT (Systematic Analysis of Language Transcripts) is a format widely used for research on and treatment of children with language disorders (cf. http://www.languageanalysislab.com/salt/). SALT is a software package with transcription guidelines and tools for automatic analyses. It mainly serves diagnostic purposes and does not include an archive for data.). The CHILDES initiative now hosts the largest child language database (data transcribed with SALT can be imported), and provides guidelines for transcriptions (CHAT: Codes for the Human Analysis of Transcripts) as well as the CLAN-software for data analysis specifically designed to work on data transcribed in CHAT (CLAN: Computerized Language ANalysis).

3.5 Annotation

The interpretability and retrievability of the information contained in a corpus critically depends on annotation of the data beyond the reproduction of the verbal signal and the identification of the speaker. Three levels of annotation can be distinguished: The annotation regarding the utterance or communicative act itself, the coding of linguistic and non-linguistic signals, and the addition of meta-data for archiving purposes.

Possible annotations regarding the utterance itself and its communicative context include speech processing phenomena like pauses, hesitations, self-corrections or retracings, and special utterance delimiters for interruptions or trailing offs. On the pragmatic and communicative level, identification of the addressee, gestures, gaze direction, etc. can provide information relevant to decode the intention and meaning of a particular utterance.

But also the structural and lexical level can be annotated, for example by adding speech act codes or by coding the morphosyntactic categories of the words and phrases in the corpus. The availability of large datasets entails that coding is not only helpful but also necessary because it is no longer realistic for researchers to analyze these datasets manually. Coding not only speeds up the search process, but also makes data retrieval more reliable than hand searching (see below for issues of quality control and benchmarking and MacWhinney (this volume) for a review of current morphological and syntactic coding possibilities and retrieval procedures).

On a more abstract level, so-called meta-data help researchers to find out which data are available. Meta-data include information about participants, setting, topics, and the languages involved. Meta-data conventions are now shared between a large number of research institutions involved in the storage of language data, without there being a single standard as yet (cf. http://www.mpi.nl/IMDI/ for various initiatives). But once all corpora are indexed with a set of conventionalized meta-data, researchers should be able to find out whether the corpora they need exist (e.g., corpora of 2-year-old Russian children at dinnertime conversation).

4. Information retrieval: From manual to automatic analyses

The overview of the history of sampling and archiving techniques shows that corpora these days are a much richer source of information than their counterparts on paper used to be. Each decision regarding transcription and annotation determines if and how we can search for relevant information. In addition to some general search programs using regular expressions, databases often come with their own software for information retrieval. Again, the CLAN manual and MacWhinney (this volume) provide a survey of what is possible with CHILDES data to date. Searches for errors, for example, used to be a very laborious process. Now that they have been annotated in the data (at least for the English corpora), they can be retrieved within a couple of minutes.

As mentioned earlier, corpora are regularly transformed to become usable with new operating systems and platforms. This only affects the nature of their storage while the original transcript remains the same. To allow for automated analysis, though, the nature of the transcripts changes as well: new coding or explanatory tiers can be added, and links to the original audio- and video-data can be established. Again, this need not affect the original transcription of the utterance, although semi-automatic coding requires that typographical errors and spelling inconsistencies within a given corpus be fixed. As we start to compile data from various sources, however, it becomes crucial that they adhere to the same standard. This can be obtained through re-transcription of the original data by similar standards, or by homogenizing data on the coding tiers. MacWhinney (this volume) explains how small divergences in transcription conventions can lead to massive differences in the outcome of the analyses. To name just a few examples: Whether we transcribe compounds or fixed phrases with hyphen or without affects the word count, and lack of systematicity within and between corpora has impact on the retrievability of such forms. Also, a lack of standardized conventions or annotations for non-standard vocabulary like baby talk words, communicators, and filler syllables makes their analysis and interpretation difficult, as it is hard if not impossible to guess from a written transcript what they stand for. Finally, errors can only be found by cumbersome manual searches if they have not been annotated and classified. Thus, as our tools for automatic analysis improve, so does the risk of error unless the data have been subjected to meticulous coding and reliability checks.

For the user this means that one has to be very careful when compiling search commands, because a simple typographical error or the omission of a search switch may affect the result dramatically. A good strategy for checking the goodness of a command is to analyse a few transcripts by hand and then check whether the command catches all the utterances in question. Also, it is advisable to first operate with more general commands and delete "false positives" by hand, then trying to narrow down the command such that all and only the utterances in questions are produced.

But these changes in the data set also affect the occasional and computationally less ambitious researcher: the corpus downloaded 5 years ago for another project will have changed – for the better! Spelling errors will have been corrected, and inconsistent or idiosyncratic transcription and annotation of particular morphosyntactic phenomena like compounding or errors will have been homogenized. Likewise, the structure of some commands may have changed as the command structure became more complex in order to accommodate new research needs. It is thus of utmost importance that researchers keep up with the latest version of the data and the tools for their analysis. Realistically, a researcher who has worked with a particular version of a corpus for years, often having added annotations for their own research purposes, is not very likely to give that up and switch to a newer version of the corpus. However, even for these colleagues a look at the new possibilities may be advantageous. First, it is possible to check the original findings against a less error-prone version of the data (or to improve the database by pointing out still existing errors to the database managers). Second, the original manual analyses can now very likely be conducted over a much larger dataset by making use of the morphological and syntactic annotation.

For some researchers the increasing complexity of the corpora and the tools for their exploitation may have become an obstacle for using publicly available databases. In addition, it is increasingly difficult to write manuals that allow self-teaching of the program, since not all researchers are lucky enough to have experts next door. Here, web forums and workshops may help to bridge the gap. But child language researchers intending to work with corpora will simply have to face the fact that the tools of the trade have become more difficult to use in order to become much more efficient.

This said, it must be pointed out that the child language community is in an extremely lucky position: thanks to the relentless effort of Brian MacWhinney and his team we can store half a century's worth of world-wide work on child language corpora free of charge on storage media half the size of a matchbox.

5. Quality control

5.1 Individual responsibilities

Even in an ideal world, each transcript is a reduction of the physical signal present in the actual communicative situation that it is trying to reproduce. Transcriptions vary widely in their degree of precision and in the amount of time and effort that is devoted to issues of checking intertranscriber reliability. In the real world, limited financial, temporal, and personal resources force us to make decisions that may not be optimal for all future purposes. But each decision regarding how to transcribe data has implications for the (automatic) analysability of these data, e.g., do we transcribe forms that are not yet fully adult like in an orthographic fashion according to adult standards, or do we render the perceived form (see Johnson (2000) for the implications of such decisions). The imperative that follows from this fact is that all researchers should familiarize themselves with the corpora they are analyzing in order to find out whether the research questions are fully compatible with the method of transcription (Johnson 2000). Providing access to the original audio- or video-recordings can help to remedy potential shortcomings as it is always possible to retranscribe data for different purposes. As new corpora are being collected and contributed to databases, it would be desirable that they not only include a description of the participants and the setting, but also of the measures that were taken for reliability control (e.g., how the transcribers were trained, how unclear cases were resolved, which areas proved to be notoriously difficult and which decisions were taken to reduce variation or ambiguity).

In addition, the possibility of combining orthographic and phonetic transcription has emerged: The CHAT transcription guidelines allow for various ways of transcribing the original utterance with a "translation" into the adult intended form (see MacWhinney (this volume) and the CHAT manual on the CHILDES website). This combination of information in the corpus guarantees increased authenticity of the data without being an impediment for the "mineability" of the data with automatic search programs and data analysis software.

5.2 Institutional responsibilities

Once data have entered larger databases, overarching measures must be taken to ensure that all data are of comparable standard. This concerns the level of the utterance as well as the coding annotation used. For testing the quality of coding, so-called benchmarking procedures are used. A representative part of the database is coded and double-checked and can then serve as a benchmark for testing the performance of automatic coding and disambiguation procedures. Assume that the checked corpus has a precision of 100% regarding the coding of morphology. An automatic tagger run over the same corpus may achieve 80% precision in the first run, and 95% precision after another round of disambiguation (see MacWhinney (this volume) for the techniques used in the CHILDES database). While 5% incorrect coding may seem high at first glance, one has to keep in mind that manual coding is not only much more time-consuming, but also error-prone (typos, intuitive changes in the coding conventions over time), and the errors may affect a number of phenomena, whereas the mismatches between benchmarked corpora and the newly coded corpus tend to reside in smaller, possibly well-defined areas.

In other fields like speech technology and its commercial applications, the validation of corpora has been outsourced to independent institutes (e.g., SPEX [= Speech Processing EXpertise Center]). Such validation procedures include analysing the completeness of documentation as well the quality and completeness of data collection and transcription.

But while homogenizing the format of data from various sources has great advantages for automated analyses, some of the old problems continue to exist. For example, where does one draw the boundary between "translating" children's idiosyncratic forms into their adult form for computational purposes? Second, what is the best way to deal with low frequency phenomena? Will they become negligible now that we can analyse thousands of utterances with just a few keystrokes and identify the major structures in a very short time? How can we use those programmes to identify uncommon or idiosyncratic features in order to find out about the range of children's generalizations and individual differences?

6. Open issues and future perspectives in the use of corpora

So far the discussion of the history and nature of modern corpora has focussed on the enormous richness of data available. New possibilities arise from the availability of multimodal corpora and/or sophisticated annotation and retrieval programs. In this section, I address some areas where new data and new technology can lead to new perspectives in child language research. In addition to research on new topics, these tools can also be used to solidify our existing knowledge through replication studies and research synthesis.

6.1 Phonetic and prosodic analyses

Corpora in which the transcript is linked to the speech file can form the basis for acoustic analysis, especially as CHILDES can export the data to the speech analysis software PRAAT. In many cases, though, the recordings made in the children's home environment may not have the quality needed for acoustic analyses. And, as Demuth (this volume) points out, phonetic and prosodic analyses can usually be done with a relatively small corpus. It is very possible, therefore, that researchers interested in the speech signal will work with small high quality recordings rather than with large databases (see, for example, the ChildPhon initiative by Yvan Rose, to be integrated as PhonBank into the CHILDES database; cf. Rose, MacWhinney, Byrne, Hedlund, Maddocks and O'Brien 2005).

6.2 Type and token frequency

Type and token frequency data, a major variable in psycholinguistic research, can be derived from corpora only. The CHILDES database now offers the largest corpus of spoken language in existence (see MacWhinney this volume), and future research will have to show if and in what way distribution found in other sources of adult data (spoken and written corpora) differ from the distributional patterns found in the spoken language addressed to children or used in the presence of children. Future research will also have to show whether all or some adults adjust the complexity of their language when speaking to children (Chouinard and Clark 2003; Snow 1986). This research requires annotation of communicative situations and coding of the addressees of each utterance (e.g., van de Weijer 1998).

For syntactically parsed corpora, type-token frequencies cannot only be computed for individual words (the lexicon), but also for part of speech categories and syntactic structures (see MacWhinney this volume).

6.3 Distributional analyses

Much of the current debate on children's linguistic representations is concerned with the question of whether they are item-specific or domain general. Children's production could be correct as well as abstract and show the same range of variation as found in adult speech. But production could also be correct but very skewed such that, for example, only a few auxiliary-pronoun combinations account for a large portion of the data (Lieven this volume). Such frequency biases can be characteristic for a particular period of language development, e.g., when young children's productions show less variability than those from older children or adults, or they could be structural in the sense that adult data show the same frequency biases.

Such issues have implications for linguistic theory on a more general level. For example, are frequency effects only relevant in language processing (because, for example, high frequency structures are activated faster), or does frequency also influence our competence (because, for example, in grammaticality judgement tasks high frequent structures are rated as being more acceptable) (cf. Bybee 2006; Fanselow 2004; Newmeyer 2003, for different opinions on this question)?

6.4 Studies on crosslinguistic and individual variation

Both Lieven and Ravid and colleagues (this volume) address the issue of variation: Lieven focuses on individual variation whereas Ravid *et al.* focus on crosslinguistic and cross-typological variation. Other types of variation seem to be less intensely debated in early first language acquisition, but could provide ideal testing grounds for the effect of frequency on language learning and categorization. For example, frequency differences between different groups within a language community can relate to socioecomic status: Hart and Risley (1995) studied 42 children from professional, working class and welfare families in the U.S., and found that the active vocabulary of the children correlated with their socioeconomic background and the interactive style used by the parent.

In addition, multilingual environments, a common rather than an exceptional case, provide a natural testing ground for the effect of frequency and quality of the input. For instance, many children grow up in linguistically rich multilingual environments but with only low frequency exposure to one of the target languages.

6.5 Bridging the age gap

Corpus-based first language acquisition research has a strong focus on the preschool years. Only a few corpora provide data from children aged four or older, and most longitudinal studies are biased towards the early stages of language development at age two. Older children's linguistic competence is assessed through experiments, cross-sectional sampling or standardized tests for language proficiency at kindergarten or school. Consequently we have only very little information about children's naturalistic linguistic interaction and production in the (pre-)school years.

6.6 Communicative processes

With the growth of corpora and computational tools for their exploitation, it is only natural that a lot of child language research these days focuses on quantitative analyses. At the same time, there is a growing body of evidence that children's ability to learn language is deeply rooted in human's social cognition, for example the ability to share joint attention and to read each other's intention (Tomasello 2003). The availability of video recorded corpora should be used to study the interactive processes that may aid language acquisition in greater detail, not only qualitatively but also quantitatively (cf. Allen, Skarabela and Hughes this volume; Chouinard and Clark 2003). In addition, such analyses allow us to assess the richness of information available in children's environment, and whether and how children make use of these cues.

6.7 Replication studies

Many results in child language research are still based on single studies with only a small number of participants, whereas other findings are based on an abundance of corpus and experimental studies (e.g., English transitive, English plural, past tense marking in English and German and Dutch). With the availability of annotated corpora it should be easily possible to check the former results against larger samples. Regarding the issue of variation, it is also possible to run the analyses over various subsets of a given database or set of databases in order to check whether results are stable for all individuals, and what causes the variation if they are not (see MacWhinney (this volume) for some suggestions).

6.8 Research synthesis and meta-analyses

Child language is a booming field these days. This shows in an ever-growing number of submissions to the relevant conferences: the number of submissions to the Boston University Conference on Language Development doubled between 2002 and 2007 (Shanley Allen, personal communication) as well as the establishment of new journals and book series. However, the wealth of new studies on child language development has not necessarily led to a clearer picture: different studies addressing the same or similar phenomena typically introduce new criteria or viewpoints such that the results are rarely directly compatible (see Allen, Skarabela and Hughes (this volume) for an illustration of the range of coding criteria used in various studies).

Research synthesis is an approach to take inventory of what is known in a particular field. The synthesis should be a systematic, exhausting, and trustworthy secondary review of the existing literature, and its results should be replicable. This is achieved, for example, by stating the criteria for selecting the studies to be reviewed, by establishing super-ordinate categories for comparison of different studies, and by focussing on the data presented rather than the interpretations given in the original papers. It is thus secondary research in the form of different types of reviews, e.g., a narrative review or a comprehensive bibliographical review (cf. Norris and Ortega 2006a: 5–8) for an elaboration of these criteria). Research synthesis methods can be applied to qualitative research including case studies, but research synthesis can also take the form of meta-analysis of quantitative data. Following Norris and Ortega (2000), several research syntheses have been conducted in L2 acquisition (see the summary and papers in Norris and Ortega 2006b).

In first language acquisition, this approach has not been applied with the same rigour, although there are several studies heading in that direction. Slobin's five volume set on the crosslinguistic study of first language acquisition (Slobin 1985a,b; 1992; 1997a,b) can be considered an example since he and the authors of the individual chapters agreed to a common framework for analysing the data available for a particular language and for summarizing or reinterpreting the data in published sources.

Regarding children's mastery of the English transitive construction, Tomasello (2000a) provides a survey of experimental studies and reanalyzes the existing data using the same criteria for productivity. Allen *et al.* (this volume) compare studies on argument realization and try to consolidate common results from studies using different types of data and coding criteria.

6.9 Method handbook for the study of child language

Last but not least, a handbook on methods in child language development is much needed. While there are dozens of such introductions for the social sciences, the respective information for acquisition is distributed over a large number of books and articles. The CHAT and the CLAN manuals of the CHILDES database provide a thorough discussion of the implication of certain transcribing or coding decisions, and the *info-childes* mailing list serves as a discussion forum for problems of transcription and analysis. But many of the possibilities and explanations are too complicated for the beginning user or student. Also, there is no comprehensive handbook on experimental methods in child language research. A tutorial-style handbook would allow interested researchers or students to become familiar with current techniques and technical developments.

7. About this volume

The chapters in this volume present state-of-the-art corpus-based research in child language development. Elena Lieven provides an in-depth analysis of six British children's development of the auxiliary system. She shows how they build up the auxiliary system in a step-wise fashion, and do not acquire the whole paradigm at once. Her analyses show how corpora can be analyzed using different criteria for establishing productivity, and she establishes the rank order of emergence on an individual and inter-individual basis, thus revealing the degree of individual variation. Rank order of emergence was first formalized in Brown's Morpheme Order Studies (Brown 1973), and is adapted to syntactic frames in Lieven's study.

A systematic account for crosslinguistic differences is the aim of the investigation of a multinational and multilingual research team consisting of Dorit Ravid, Wolfgang Dressler, Bracha Nir-Sagiv, Katharina Korecky-Kröll, Agnita Souman, Katja Rehfeldt, Sabine Laaha, Johannes Bertl, Hans Basbøll, and Steven Gillis. They investigate the acquisition of noun plurals in Dutch, German, Danish, and Hebrew, and provide a unified framework that predicts the various allomorphs in these languages by proposing that noun plural suffixes are a function of the gender of the noun and the noun's sonority. They further argue that child directed speech presents the child with *core morphology*, i.e., a reduced and simplified set of possibilities, and show that children's acquisition can indeed by predicted by the properties of the core morphology of a particular language. Their work shows how applying the same criteria to corpora from different languages can provide insights into general acquisition principles.

The predictive power of linguistic cues is also the topic of the chapters by Monaghan and Christiansen, and by Allen, Skarabela, and Hughes. Shanley Allen, Barbora Skarabela, and Mary Hughes look at accessibility features in discourse situations as cues to the acquisition of argument structure. Languages differ widely as to the degree to which they allow argument omission or call for argument realization. Despite these differences, some factors have a stronger effect for argument realization than others. E.g., contrast of referent is a very strong cue for two year olds. Allen *et al.* show not only the difference in predictive power of such discourse cues, but also how children have to observe and integrate several cues to acquire adult-like patterns of argument realization.

Padraic Monaghan and Morten Christiansen investigate multiple cue integration in natural and artificial learning. They review how both distributional analyses and Artificial Language Learning (ALL) can help to identify the cues that are available to the language-learning child. While single cues are normally not sufficient for the identification structural properties of language like word boundaries or part of speech categories, the combination of several cues from the same domain (e.g., phonological cues like onset and end of words, and prosodic cues like stress and syllable length) may help to identify nouns and verbs in language-specific ways. They conclude that future research will have to refine such computational models in order to simulate the developmental process of arriving at the end-state of development, with a particular focus on how the learning process is based on existing knowledge.

This chapter also connects with Allen *et al.*'s as well as Ravid *et al.*'s chapters on multiple cue integration. All three papers state that the predictive power of an individual cue like phonology or gender can be low in itself, but powerful if this cue is omnipresent like phonology. What learners have to exploit is the combination of cues. In addition, Ravid *et al.* have a look at the distributional properties of CDS and propose that certain aspects of the language found in particular in CDS may be more constrained and instrumental for acquisition than the features found in the adult language in general.

The remaining two chapters address methodological issues. Rowland, Fletcher and Freudenthal develop methods for improving the reliability of analyses when working with corpora of different size. They show how sample size affects the estimation of error rates or the assessment of the productivity of children's linguistic representations, and propose a number of techniques to maximize the reliability in corpus studies. For example, error rates can be computed over subsamples of a single corpus or by comparing data from different corpora, thus improving the estimation of error rates.

MacWhinney presents an overview of the latest developments in standardizing the transcripts available in the CHILDES database, and provides insights regarding the recent addition of morphological and syntactic coding tiers for the English data. The refined and standardized transcripts and the morphosyntactic annotation provide a reliable and quick access to common but also very intricate morphological or syntactic structures. This should make the database a valuable resource for researchers interested the formal properties of child language, but also the language used by adults, as the database is now the largest worldwide for spoken language. With these tools, the CHILDES database also becomes a resource for computational linguists.

The volume concludes with a discussion by Katherine Demuth. She emphasizes that for corpus research, a closer examination of the developmental processes rather than just the depiction of "snapshots" of children's development at different stages is one of the challenges of the future (see also Lieven this volume). Another understudied domain is that of relating children's language to the language actually present in their environment, rather than to an abstract idealization of adult language. Demuth also shows how corpus and experimental research can interact fruitfully, for example by deriving frequency information from a corpus for purposes of designing stimulus material in experiments.

Taken together, the studies presented in this volume show how corpora can be exploited for the study of fine-grained linguistic phenomena and the developmental processes necessary for their acquisition. New types of annotated corpora as well as new methods of data analysis can help to make these studies more reliable and replicable. A major emerging theme for the immediate future seems to be the study of multiple cue integration in connection with analyses that investigate which cues are actually present in the input that children hear. May these chapters also be a consolation for researchers who spent hours on end collecting, transcribing, coding, and checking data, because their corpora can serve as a fruitful research resource for years to come.

How big is big enough?

Assessing the reliability of data from naturalistic samples*

Caroline F. Rowland, Sarah L. Fletcher and Daniel Freudenthal

1. Introduction

Research on how children acquire their first language utilizes the full range of available investigatory techniques, including *act out* (Chomsky 1969), *grammaticality judgements* (DeVilliers and DeVilliers 1974), *brain imaging* (Holcomb, Coffey and Neville 1992), *parental report checklists* (Fenson, Dale, Reznick, Bates, Thal and Pethick 1994), *elicitation* (Akhtar 1999). However, perhaps one of the most influential methods has been the collection and analysis of spontaneous speech data. This type of naturalistic data analysis has a long history, dating back at least to Darwin, who kept a diary of his baby son's first expressions (Darwin 1877, 1886). Today, naturalistic data usually takes the form of transcripts made from audio or videotaped conversations between children and their caregivers, with some studies providing cross-sectional data for a large number of children at a particular point in development (e.g., Rispoli 1998) and others following a small number of children longitudinally through development (e.g., Brown 1973).

Modern technology has revolutionized the collection and analysis of naturalistic speech. Researchers are now able to audio or video-record conversations between children and caregivers in the home or another familiar environment, and transfer these digital recordings to a computer. Utterances can be transcribed directly from the waveform, and each transcribed utterance can be linked to the corresponding part of the waveform (MacWhinney 2000). Transcripts can then be searched efficiently for key utterances or words, and traditional measures of development such as Mean Length of Utterance (MLU) can be computed over a large number of transcripts virtually instantaneously.

* Thanks are due to Javier Aguado-Orea, Ben Ambridge, Heike Behrens, Elena Lieven, Brian MacWhinney and Julian Pine, who provided valuable comments on a previous draft. Much of the work reported here was supported by the Economic and Social Research Council, Grant No. RES000220241.

However, although new technology has improved the speed and efficiency with which spontaneous speech data can be analysed, data collection and transcription remain time-consuming activities; transcription alone can take between 6 and 20 hours for each hour of recorded speech. This inevitably restricts the amount of spontaneous data that can be collected and results in researchers relying on relatively small samples of data. The traditional sampling regime of recording between one and two hours of spontaneous speech per month captures only 1% to 2% of children's speech if we assume that the child is awake and talking for approximately 10 hours per day. Even dense databases (e.g., Lieven, Behrens, Speares and Tomasello 2003) capture only about 10% of children's overall productions.

In the field of animal behaviour, the study of the impact of sampling on the accuracy of observational data analysis has a long history (Altmann 1974; Lehner 1979; Martin and Bateson 1993). In the field of language acquisition, however, there have been very few attempts to evaluate the implications that sampling may have on our interpretation of children's productions (two notable exceptions are Malvern and Richards (1997), and Tomasello and Stahl (2004)). In research on language acquisition, as in research on animal behaviour, however, the sampling regime we choose and the analyses we apply to sampled data can affect our conclusions in a number of fundamental ways. At the very least, we may see contradictory conclusions arising from studies that have collected and analysed data using different methods. At worst, a failure to account for the impact of sampling may result in inaccurate characterizations of children's productions, with serious consequences for how we view the language acquisition process and for the accuracy of theory development. In this chapter we bring together work that demonstrates the effect that the sampling regime can have on our understanding of acquisition in two primary areas of research; first, on how we assess the amount and importance of error in children's speech, and second, on how we assess the degree of productivity of children's early utterances. For each area we illustrate the problems that are apparent in the literature before providing some solutions aimed at minimising the impact of sampling on our analyses.

2. Sampling and errors in children's early productions

Low error rates have traditionally been seen as the hallmark of rapid acquisition and are often used to support theories attributing children with innate or rapidly acquired, sophisticated, usually category-general, knowledge. The parade case of this argument is that presented by Chomsky (Piatelli-Palmerini 1980), who cited the absence of ungrammatical complex *yes/no*-questions in young children's speech (e.g., *is the boy who smoking is crazy?*), despite the rarity of correct models in the input, as definitive evidence that children are innately constrained to consider only structure-dependent rules when formulating a grammar. Since then, the rarity of many types of grammatical errors, especially in structures where the input seems to provide little guidance as to correct production, has been cited as decisive support for the existence of innate constraints on both syntactic and morphological acquisition (e.g., Hyams 1986; Marcus 1995; Marcus *et al.* 1992; Pinker 1984; Schütze and Wexler 1996; Stromswold 1990).

However, others have suggested that grammatical errors are often highly frequent in children's speech, and cite findings which, they suggest, point to much less sophisticated knowledge of grammatical structure in the child than has previously been assumed. They argue that the pattern of errors in children's speech reveals pockets of ignorance in children's grammatical knowledge that can provide useful evidence about the difference between the child and adult systems and the process of acquisition (e.g., DeVilliers 1991; Maratsos 2000; Maslen, Theakston, Lieven and Tomasello 2004; Pine, Rowland, Lieven and Theakston 2005; Rubino and Pine 1998; Santelmann, Berk, Austin, Somashekar and Lust 2002).

Confusingly, both sets of researchers often base their arguments on analyses of the same (or similar) spontaneous data sets and even on analyses of the same grammatical errors. Some even come to very different conclusions about the same errors produced by the same children (e.g., compare Pine *et al.*'s (2005) and Schütze and Wexler's (1996) analyses of the data from Nina). In our view, these apparent contradictions usually stem from the choice of analysis method. There are at least two ways in which the use of naturalistic sampled data can influence an analysis of error. The first is the impact of the size of the sample. In smaller samples, rare phenomena may be missed; so errors that are rare, or that tend to occur in sentence types that are themselves infrequent, may be missing completely from the corpus. Even when such errors are captured in a sample, the calculation of error rates on small amounts of data will often yield an unreliable estimate of the true rate of error. The second factor is the choice of analysis technique. The most popular method of reporting error rates is to count up the number of errors and divide these by the number of contexts in which the error could have occurred (see e.g., Stromswold's (1990) analysis of auxiliaries, Marcus *et al.*'s (1992) analysis of past tense errors). This method has the advantage of maximising the amount of data and thus increasing the reliability of the error rate calculation. However, it fails to distinguish between error rates in different parts of the system (e.g., does not tell us whether error rates are higher with some auxiliaries than others) and fails to consider that error rates may change over time. Another method is to analyse the subsystems of a structure separately, calculating error rates subsystem by subsystem (e.g., auxiliary by auxiliary). This has the advantage that it reflects individual error rates but, since these rates are likely to be calculated across smaller amounts of data, brings us back to the problems inherent in analysing small samples of data.

In summary, there are two constraints that have a fundamental impact on how the literature represents errors – the effect of sample size and the effect of the error rate calculation method. In the following sections we illustrate the broader implications of these constraints before providing some solutions to the analysis of error rates in naturalistic data analysis.

2.1 The effect of sample size on error estimates

2.1.1 *Small samples fail to capture infrequent errors*

The chance of capturing an error in any particular sample of speech relies crucially on both the frequency of the error and the density of the sampling regime. Traditional sampling densities are extremely unlikely to capture low or even medium frequency errors.

Tomasello and Stahl (2004) used simple mathematical models to estimate the probability that sampling densities of 0.5, 1, 5 and 10 hours per week would reliably capture target utterances that occurred seven, 14, 35 and 70 times a week (given a certain set of assumptions about children's speech[1]). They demonstrated that very large sampling densities are required to capture even medium frequency errors. For example, an error produced on average once per day (7 times a week) requires a 10 hour per week sampling regime to capture on average just one example per week (if 7 errors are produced in 70 hours, a one hour sample will capture only 0.1 errors; so 10 hours are required to capture 1 error). Even with a target that occurs relatively frequently (e.g., 10 times a day), we would need to record for one hour per week in order to capture, on average, just one example each week (10 times a day = 70 errors per 70 hours = 1 error produced on average every hour).

Even more worryingly, these calculations only give us the average chance of capturing an error. Given that errors are unlikely to be evenly distributed across the child's speech, an error that occurs, on average, once per hour may not occur at all in some hours, and may occur multiple times in another hour. Thus, whether we capture even one example of the error will depend on which hour we sample. In order to be certain of capturing the error in our sample, we would have to sample much more often than this (see section 2.3.1.1 below for details of how to calculate optimum sample size).

Of course, existing datasets tend to be longitudinal. Thus, even sampling densities of 1 hour per week in effect are composed of multiple samples collected over time; which should increase our chance of capturing a particular target error (assuming the error is produced throughout the time sampled). However, increasing sample size simply by collecting longitudinal data creates an additional problem – in small samples the distribution of errors across development will reflect chance variation not developmental changes. For example, let us assume a child produces an error once a day, every day for 100 weeks (approximately 2 years). Let's assume the child is awake and talking

1. These assumptions are that a) a normal child is awake and talking 10 hours/day (70 hours/week), b) that each sample is representative of the language use of the child, c) that any given target structure of interest occurs at random intervals in the child's speech, with each occurrence independent of the others. The final assumption is not wholly valid because factors such as discourse pressures mean that linguistic structures are likely to occur in "clumps in discourse" (Tomasello and Stahl 2004: 105). However, Tomasello and Stahl argue that they cannot take this into account since they have no information about how this interdependence manifests itself. A later analysis demonstrates that interdependence is likely to increase the size of the samples required, so the conclusions they report are likely to be conservative.

for 10 hours per day (which means for 70 hours per week or 7000 hours over the whole 100 weeks). This child will produce 7 errors per week – 700 errors in total throughout the 100 weeks. A sampling density of 1 hour per week (giving us a sample of 100 hours out of a possible 7000 hours) will capture only 10 of these errors on average (700 errors in 7000 hours = 0.1 error per hour; 0.1 x 100 hours sampled = 10 errors captured per year). More importantly, chance will determine how these ten errors are distributed across our 100 samples. At one extreme, all ten could appear in one sample by chance; leading researchers to the conclusion that the error was relatively frequent for a short time. At the other extreme, each error could appear in each of ten different samples randomly distributed across the year; leading researchers to conclude that the error was rare but long-lived.

2.1.2 *Small samples fail to capture short-lived errors or errors in low frequency structures*

The fact that analyses of small samples miss rare errors may not be too problematic – the conclusion would still be that such errors are rare, even with bigger samples. A more important problem is that small samples are unlikely to capture errors that are frequent but that only occur in low frequency constructions. This raises the more serious problem that errors that constitute a large proportion of a child's production of a particular structure or that occur for a brief period of time may be misidentified as rare or non-existent.

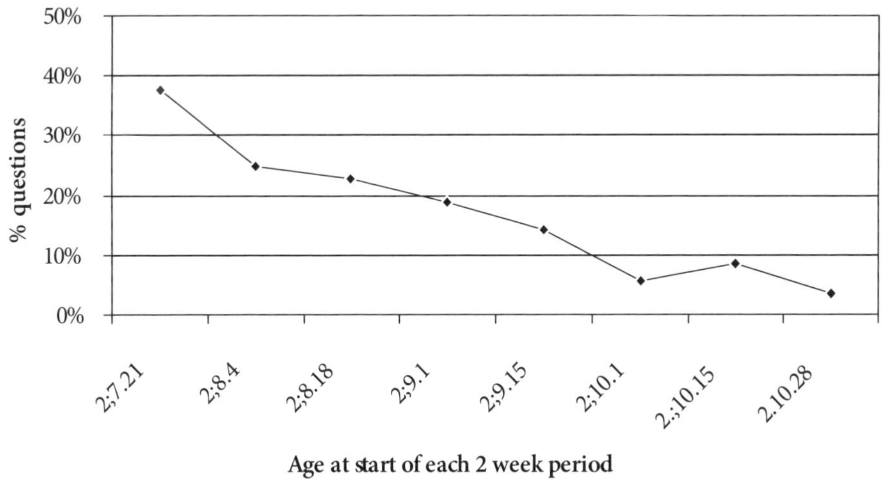

Figure 1. Percentage of Lara's *wh*-questions with forms of DO/modal auxiliaries that were errors of commission over Stage IV.[2]

2. Figure 1 is based on the data presented in Rowland *et al.* (2005).

The problem is illustrated in a study by Rowland, Pine, Lieven and Theakston (2005). As part of a larger study on *wh*-question acquisition, they calculated commission error rates for *wh*-questions containing a form of auxiliary DO or a modal auxiliary (e.g., errors such as *where he can go?, where did he went?*). For twelve of the children they studied (children from the Manchester corpus; Theakston, Lieven, Pine and Rowland 2001) the mean rate of commission error for these questions was never higher than 11% (across 4 developmental stages). However, for one of the children – Lara – commission errors accounted for over 37% of these questions for a two week period at the beginning of Brown's (1973) Stage IV (aged 2;7.21 to 2;8.3, see Figure 1 above). The error rate then decreased steadily over a period of several weeks.

Rowland *et al.* (2005) demonstrated that the discrepancy between the results from the Manchester corpus (no period of high error) and from Lara (short period of high error followed by a gradual decrease) was explained solely in terms of differences in the grain of analysis allowed by the data collection regime. Lara's data were collected intensively by caregivers who recorded every *wh*-question she produced in their hearing. The data represented approximately 80% of the questions she produced during the sampled period, capturing, on average, 18 questions with auxiliary DO/modals per week and allowing a fine-grained analysis of how Lara's question use changed every fortnight. For the Manchester corpus, only two hours of data were collected every three weeks per child, representing only 1% of the questions they produced, and capturing on average only 1.15 DO/modal questions per child per week. Thus, these children's data could only be analysed by summing over much longer periods of time. The combination of a low frequency structure (questions with DO/modals accounted for only 14% of questions) and a sparse sampling regime meant that the Manchester corpus data failed to capture the relatively short period of high error.

2.1.3 *Small corpora yield unreliable error rates, especially in low frequency structures*

The previous sections illustrated the problem of capturing rare errors in small samples. However, simply capturing errors is often not enough; we often want to calculate rates of error. Unfortunately, the smaller the sample, the less likely it is that we will be able to estimate error rates accurately. This is because with small samples, the chance presence or absence of only one or two tokens in a sample has a substantive effect on the error rate.

Rowland and Fletcher (2006) provided a demonstration of this problem using the intensive *wh*-question data collected from Lara (see section 2.1.2 for details). Their aim was to compare the efficiency of different sampling densities at capturing the rates of inversion error (e.g., errors such as *what he can do?, where he is going?*) in high frequency *wh*-question types (questions requiring copula BE forms) and low frequency *wh*-question types (questions requiring an auxiliary DO or modal form). First, they established a baseline error rate figure based on all the data available (613 object/adjunct *wh*-questions).[3] They found that the inversion error rate was low for questions with copula BE (1.45%) but high for questions with DO/modals (20%). Given the denseness of the data, these were taken as accurate approximations of the true error rates.

Rowland and Fletcher then used a randomising algorithm to extract questions from the intensive data (which contained 613 questions) to create three smaller sampling density regimes (equating to four hours, two hours and one hour's data collection per month).[4] For each sampling density, seven samples were created to provide a measure of variance, and each was comprised of a different set of utterances to ensure that the results could not be attributed to overlap between the samples. They then re-calculated error rates for questions with copula BE and auxiliary DO/modal forms in each sample. Table 1 demonstrates their results.

Table 1. Rates of inversion error in Lara's *wh*-questions calculated from samples of different sizes (% of questions).

	COPULA BE				DO MODALS			
Sample size	Mean across seven samples	Lowest error rate from individual samples	Highest error rate from individual samples	Sd	Mean across seven samples	Lowest error rate from individual samples	Highest error rate from individual samples	Sd
4-hour samples	1.91	0	7.14	2.74	25.90	12.50	57.14	14.60
2-hour samples	0.79	0	5.56	2.10	17.14	0	100	37.29
1-hour samples	1.30	0	9.09	3.44	26.19	0	100	38.32

The results showed that samples at all sampling densities were accurate at estimating the error rates for the frequently produced questions (the questions with copula BE, see Table 1). Estimates from individual samples ranged from only 0% to 9% even for the smallest samples, and the standard deviation (SD, which provides a measure of variance across samples) was small. However, for the rarer questions types (those requiring DO/modal auxiliaries), estimated error rates varied substantially across samples, especially for the smaller samples, and standard deviations were large. For both the two-hour/month and one-hour/month sampling density, error rates varied from 0% to 100% across the seven samples (SDs = 37.29% and 38.32% respectively). Even

3. The analysis used only data collected when Lara was 2;8 to control for developmental effects.

4. An eight-hour audio-recorded sample recorded when Lara was 2;8 captured 143 questions. Thus, the authors estimated that a sampling regime of four hours per month would capture approximately 72 questions, two hours per month would capture approximately 36 questions and one-hour per month would capture approximately 18 questions.

some of the four-hour/month samples yielded inaccurate estimates (range = 12.50% to 57%, SD = 14.60%).

Importantly, the variance across samples was caused only by chance variation in the number of correct questions and errors captured in any particular sample. In real terms, the only difference between the samples that showed no or low error rates and those that showed high error rates was the inclusion or exclusion of one or two inversion errors. However, this chance inclusion/exclusion had a large impact on error rates because so few questions overall were captured in each sample (on average, six questions with DO/modals in the four-hour samples, three in the two-hour samples, two in the one-hour samples). Rowland and Fletcher concluded that studies using small samples can substantially over or under-estimate error rates in utterance types that occur relatively infrequently, and thus that calculations of error rates based on small amounts of data are likely to be misleading.

2.2 The effect of calculating overall error rates

To sum up so far, small samples can lead to one missing rare phenomena, can fail to capture short lived errors or errors in low frequency structures, and can inaccurately estimate error rates. Given these facts, the temptation is to sacrifice a more fine-grained analysis of performance in different parts of the system in favour of an overall error rate in order to ensure enough data for reliable analysis. Thus, the most popular method of assessing the rate of error is to calculate the total number of errors as a proportion of all the possible contexts for error. For example, Stromswold (1990) reports the error rate of auxiliaries as:

$$\frac{\text{Number of auxiliary errors}}{\text{Total number of contexts that require an auxiliary (i.e. correct use + errors)}}$$

This method clearly maximizes the amount of data available in small samples. However, this method also leads to an under-estimation of the incidence of errors in certain cases, particularly errors in low frequency structures or short-lived errors. There are three main problems. First, overall error rates will be statistically dominated by high frequency items, and thus will tend to represent error rate in high, not low frequent items. Second, overall error rates fail to give a picture of how error rates change over time. Third, overall error rates can hide systematic patterns of error specific to certain subsystems.

2.2.1 *High frequency items dominate overall error rates*

High frequency items will statistically dominate overall error rates. This problem is outlined clearly by Maratsos (2000) in his criticism of the "massed-token pooling methods" (p.189) of error rate calculation used by Marcus *et al.* (1992). In this method, Marcus *et al.* calculated error rates by pooling together all tokens of irregular verbs (those that occur with correct irregular past tense forms and those with over-regularized pasts) and calculating the error rate as the proportion of all tokens of irregular pasts that contain over-regularized past tense forms. Although this method maximizes the sample size (and thus the reliability of the error rate), it gives much more weight to verbs with high token frequency, resulting in an error rate that disproportionately reflects how well children perform with these high frequency verbs. For example, verbs sampled over 100 times contributed 10 times as many responses as verbs sampled 10 times and "so have statistical weight equal to 10 such verbs in the overall rate" (Maratsos 2000 :189).

To illustrate his point, Maratsos analysed the past-tense data from three children (Abe, Adam and Sarah). Overall error rates were low as Marcus *et al.* (1992) also reported. However, Maratsos showed that overall rates were disproportionately affected by the low rates of errors for a very small number of high frequency verbs which each occurred over 50 times (just 6 verbs for Sarah, 17 for Adam, 11 for Abe). The verbs that occurred less than 10 times had a much smaller impact on the overall error rate simply because they occurred less often, despite their being more of them (40 different verbs for Abe, 22 for Adam, 33 for Sarah). However, it was these verbs that demonstrated high rates of error (58% for Abe, 54% for Adam, 29% for Sarah). Thus, Maratsos showed that overall error rates disproportionately reflect how well children perform with high frequency items and can hide error rates in low frequency parts of the system.

2.2.2 *Overall error rates collapse over time*

A second problem with using overall error rates is that they provide only a representation of average performance over time, taking no account of the fact that since children will produce fewer errors as they age, error rates are bound to decrease with time. This problem is intensified by the fact that since children talk more as they get older, overall error rates are likely to be statistically dominated by data from later, perhaps less error-prone, periods of acquisition. This is illustrated by Maslen, Theakston, Lieven and Tomasello's (2004) analysis of the past tense verb uses in the dense data of one child, Brian, who was recorded for five hours a week from age 2;0 to 3;2, then for four or five hours a month (all recorded during the same week) from 3;3 to 3;11. Because of the denseness of the data collection, Maslen *et al.* were able to chart the development of irregular past tense verb use over time, using weekly samples. They reported that, although the overall error rate was low (7.81%), error rates varied substantially over time, reaching a peak of 43.5% at 2;11 and gradually decreasing subsequently. They concluded that "viewed from a longitudinal perspective, … regularizations in Brian's speech are in fact more prevalent than overall calculations would suggest" (Maslen *et al.* 2004: 1323).

2.2.3 *Overall error rates collapse over subsystems*

Third, the use of overall error rates can hide systematic patterns of error specific to some of the sub-systems within the structure under consideration. Aguado-Orea and Pine's (2005, see also Aguado-Orea 2004) analysis of the development of subject-verb agreement in children learning Spanish demonstrates this problem. Aguado-Orea and Pine (2005) analysed dense data from two monolingual Spanish children (approximately aged 2 years). They reported that the overall rate of agreement error in present tense contexts over a six month period was 4% for both children (see Table 2), as had been systematically reported in the literature (Gathercole, Sebastián and Soto 1999; Hoekstra and Hyams 1998; Hyams 1986; Pizzuto and Caselli 1992).[5] Yet this figure overwhelmingly represented how good the children were at providing the correct inflections in 1st and 3rd person singular contexts, which made up over 85% of verb contexts. Error rates for the other, less frequent, inflections were much higher, especially when the rarer 3rd person plural inflections were required (which comprised only 8% of all verb contexts). For Juan, 31% of the verbs that required 3rd person plural inflections had inaccurate inflectional endings. For Lucia, this figure was 67%; in other words, agreement errors occurred in over two thirds of the verbs that required 3rd person plural inflections.[6]

Not only were rates of error higher for low frequency inflectional contexts, error rates for high frequency verbs were significantly lower than error rates for low frequency verbs even within the frequent 3rd person singular inflectional contexts. Thus, the conclusion of Aguado-Orea and Pine (2005) was not only that agreement error rates can be high in certain parts of the system, but that they are high in low frequency parts of the system – with a strong relation between the frequency of a verb form in the input and the accuracy with which a child can use that verb form in his/her own production. In other words, overall error rates – which are bound to disproportionately reflect the children's performance on high frequency structures – will inevitably under-estimate the true extent of errors in low frequency structures.

Table 2. Number of verb contexts requiring present tense inflection and percentage rate of agreement error.*

Child	**% Agreement error (no. of contexts)**						
	Total	Singular			Plural		
		1st person	2nd person	3rd person	1st person	2nd person	3rd person
Juan	4.5 (3151)	4.9 (693)	10.2 (147)	0.7 (1997)	0 (61)	33.3 (3)	31.5 (251)
Lucia	4.6 (1676)	3.0 (469)	22.9 (96)	0.5 (1018)	0 (14)	– (0)	66.7 (48)

* The table is based on data from Aguado-Orea (2004)

5. % agreement error = (Number of incorrect inflections/Number of incorrect + correct inflections) x 100

6. High rate of errors remained even the when verbs produced before the children attested knowledge of the correct inflections were removed.

2.3 Sampling and error rates: Some solutions

To recap, sample size can have a significant effect on the calculation of error rates. Small samples are unlikely to capture even one instance of a low frequency error. Even when errors are recorded, error rates based on small amounts of data are unreliable because the chance absence or presence of a few tokens can have a substantial effect on the calculation. Using overall error rates can help alleviate this problem (by maximising the amount of data included in the calculation) but can misrepresent error rates in low frequency subsections of the system. Thus, it is important to analyse different subsystems separately. However, analysing data at such a fine-grained level sometimes means that the amount of data on which error rates are based can be very small, even in substantial corpora. And this leads back to the original problem – when analysing small samples of data, we often fail to capture rare errors.

The most obvious solution is to collect a lot more data but this is not always practical or cost-effective. There are a number of alternate solutions, both for those recording new corpora and those using existing datasets.

2.3.1 *Techniques for maximising the effectiveness of new corpora*

2.3.1.1 *Statistical methods for assessing how much data is required*

The simplest way to calculate how much data is necessary for the study of a particular error is to estimate the number and proportion of errors we would expect to capture given the proportion of data that we are sampling (e.g., a one hour/week sampling density might capture one example of an error that occurs once an hour every week). However, this works only if the child regularly produces one error every hour, an improbable assumption. In reality, children's errors are likely to be more randomly distributed across their speech.

Given this fact, Tomasello and Stahl (2004) suggest calculating hit rates (or hit probabilities). A hit rate is the "probability of detecting at least one target during a sampling period" (p. 111), and supplies an estimate of the likelihood of capturing an error given a particular error rate and sampling density. Figure 2 reproduces Tomasello and Stahl's analysis, using the same method of calculation[7] and based on the same assumptions (see Footnote 1). The figure plots hit rate (y-axis) against sampling density (x-axis) for a number of rates of occurrence. This figure can then be used to work out

7. Hit rate is defined as the probability of detecting one (or more) Poisson distributed target event, which is equal to 1 minus the probability of no events occuring, and is thus calculated:

$$\text{Hit rate} = 1 - [p(k=0)]$$

where $p(k=0)$ is the probability that no Poisson distributed target will be captured and is calculated:

$$p(k=0) = e^{-\lambda}$$

where e is the base of the natural logarithm (e = 2.71828) and λ = (expected error rate * sampling rate)/waking hours.

how dense the sampling needs to be to capture errors of different frequency (an accompanying Excel file which can be downloaded and used to calculate the required sampling density for targets of any frequency is available at http://www.liv.ac.uk/psychology/clrc/clrg.html).

For example, let us assume that we want to be 95% certain that our sampling regime will capture at least one error (i.e. we set our criterion to p = 0.05), and that we estimate that an error occurs 70 times a week. Figure 2 shows that we need to sample for three hours a week to be 95% certain of capturing at least one error. If the error occurs only 35 times per week, we need to sample for six hours per week.

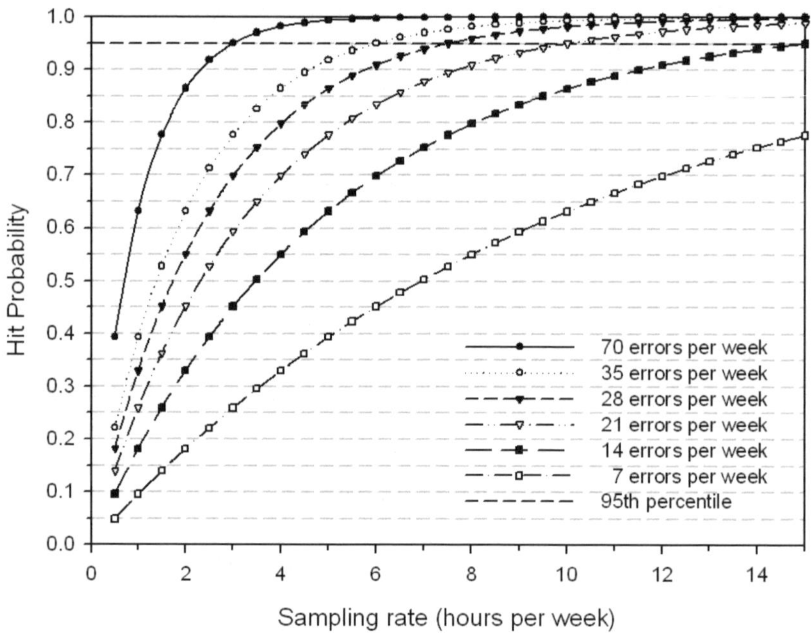

Figure 2. Probability of capturing at least one target during a one week period, given different sampling densities and target frequencies.

For more infrequent errors (those that occur only 14 or 7 times/week), the figure demonstrates that even intensive sampling regimes may not be enough. For errors that occur 14 times/week, we need 15 hours data collection per week to be 95% sure of capturing one or more errors. Even sampling for 15 hours per week, we would only be 78% certain of capturing at least one error at the 7 errors/week rate. More importantly, the figure only provides information about the sampling density required to capture at least one error in our sample. If we wish to capture more errors (which is necessary if, for example, we want to calculate an accurate error rate) we will need to sample even more intensively. Since this is unlikely to be cost-effective, for rare errors it is important to consider alternatives to simply increasing sampling density.

2.3.1.2 *Using different types of sampling regimes*

The most popular sampling regime in the child language literature is what we will call continuous sampling, where data is collected at regular intervals (e.g., every week, every fortnight) over a period of time. However, there are a number of alternatives that might be better suited to analyses of phenomena that occur with low frequency. One alternative is to sample densely for a short period of time, with long temporal gaps between samples (interval sampling). For example, we could sample 5 hours every week, but only for one week per month (Abbot-Smith and Behrens 2006; Maslen *et al.* 2004). This way we can be sure of gaining a detailed picture of the child's language at each time point. Another idea is to sample all utterances but only those of interest (targeted sampling; similar to sequence sampling in the animal behaviour literature). This is the technique used by Tomasello (1992) and Rowland (e.g., Rowland and Fletcher 2006, Rowland *et al.* 2005) and involves recording all (or nearly all) the productions of a particular structure (e.g., utterances with verbs, *wh*-questions). Alternatively we could sample only during situations likely to elicit the target structures (situational sampling; e.g., Rowland's Lara produced most of her *why* questions during car journeys). Finally, a more systematic investigation of a particular structure could be achieved by introducing elicitation games into the communicative context. For example, Kuczaj and Maratsos (1975) introduced elicited imitation games designed to encourage the production of low frequency auxiliaries into their longitudinal study of Abe's language. These games not only provided detailed information about Abe's auxiliary use, but also demonstrated where the naturalistic data failed to provide an accurate picture of development (e.g., Abe was able to produce non-negative modals correctly in elicited utterances even though he never produced them in spontaneous speech).

2.3.2 *Techniques for maximising the reliability of analyses on existing corpora*

For researchers using datasets that have already been collected (e.g., those available on CHILDES, MacWhinney 2000), it is important to use statistical procedures to assess the accuracy of error rates. Tomasello and Stahl's (2004) hit rate method (described above) can be used to calculate whether an existing sample is big enough to capture a target structure. However, there are also ways of maximising the use of datasets that, though too small for reliable analysis in isolation, can be combined with other datasets to provide accurate estimates of error rates.

2.3.2.1 *Statistical methods*

The simple fact that "a group of individual scores has more reliability than the individual scores" themselves (Maratsos 2000: 200) can be exploited to provide more accurate error estimates. In particular, mean error rates calculated either over a number of children or over a number of different sub-samples from the same child will provide a much more reliable estimate than each individual error rate, even in low frequency structures.

This fact is illustrated by the results of the sampling analysis conducted by Rowland and Fletcher (2006) on the Lara data and summarized above (see section 2.1.3). The analysis demonstrates that small samples of data are extremely inaccurate at estimating true error rates for infrequent structures – error rates for questions with DO/modal auxiliaries varied from 0% to 100% for the smallest sampling density (see Table 1). However, for each sampling density, the mean error rate calculated across seven samples was often quite accurate, despite the fact that the estimates from the individual samples contributing to these means varied widely (mean error rate: four-hour sample = 26%, two-hour sample = 17%, one-hour sample = 26%; compared to 20% for the intensive data). Thus, mean error rates calculated across a range of samples provide a more accurate method of error rate.

Maratsos (2000) has also used means across verb types to provide reliable figures for past tense over-regularization errors in low frequency verbs (verbs that occurred only between one and nine times in the samples). Maratsos calculated error rates for each individual verb type and then averaged across these error rates to provide a mean error rate. As well as controlling for small sample size by providing a more accurate measure of error rate, this method also ensured that each verb type contributed equally to the calculation (thus controlling for verb token frequency). The resulting figure gives, as Maratsos (2000: 200) says "an average rate more believable than each individual verb-rate that went into it".

The samples from which means are derived do not have to be multiple samples from the same participant. Means calculated across samples from a number of children will also provide more reliable measures of error rates. Of course, this approach does not record individual differences either across children or across items, nor does it tell us about the reliability of individual samples. However, information about the standard deviation and the range can be used to assess the reliability of each individual sample, and to identify outliers with extreme scores.

The range and standard deviation are two commonly used measures of statistical dispersion. The range of a group of samples is simply the spread between the largest and smallest estimate and is calculated by subtracting the smallest observation from the greatest. However, the range only provides information about the spread of the samples as a whole; it does not provide information about how the individual sample estimates pattern within this range. The standard deviation (SD) is a more sophisticated measure of statistical dispersion that provides information about how tightly all the estimates from all the samples are clustered around the mean.[8] A small standard deviation means that most (if not all) estimates are close to the mean. Since the mean of a number of samples is a reliable estimate of error rate, a small standard deviation indicates that the estimates from each individual sample are likely to be reliable. A large standard deviation means that many of the samples have yielded estimates that are substantially different (far) from the mean (and also from each other). This would indicate that estimates from individual samples are more likely to be inaccurate.

For example, returning to the data on questions from Lara (see section 2.1.3 and Table 1), we can see that the standard deviation derived from the seven one-hour samples was large for questions with DO/modal auxiliaries (38.32%). This indicates that each individual sample at this sampling density was likely to give an inaccurate estimate. However, for questions with copula BE, the standard deviation for the same sample density (1 hour/week) was much smaller (3.44%); indicating that each sample provided a relatively accurate estimate of error rate. Thus, standard deviations can be used to assess the reliability of a particular sampling density. A low standard deviation across samples at a particular sampling density indicates that each individual sample may be large enough to provide reliable error rate estimations on its own. These figures can then be used to assess optimum sampling density for new data collection studies.

2.3.2.2 *Combining different types of samples*

Although combining data from a number of samples may give us accurate error rates, sometimes we wish to assess the accuracy of an error rate from an individual sample or, more often, from an individual child. For example, we may have collected dense data from one child (which we assume give us accurate error rates) but want to check whether our results can be taken as indicative of language learning in the wider population (i.e. is the child representative or do the results simply reflect idiosyncrasies of this particular child?). The solution to this problem is to use statistical methods to compare the dense data with data from a larger number of children, albeit collected in smaller samples.

Rowland *et al.* (2005) performed such an analysis. They reported that one child – Lara – produced large numbers of inversion error in *wh*-questions with DO/modal auxiliaries for a short period of time at the beginning of Brown's (1973) Stage IV (see section 2.1.2) but that these high error rates were not reflected in the much less dense data collected from twelve other children (the Manchester corpus). Rowland *et al.* concluded that the Manchester corpus data was not dense enough to capture the very

8. Most statistics and spreadsheet packages will calculate standard deviations (SDs). The SD is the square root of the variance and is calculated using the formula below (where x is the individual score, $\bar{x}$ is the mean, and n is the total number of scores)

$$SD = \sqrt{\frac{\Sigma(x - \bar{x})^2}{n - 1}}$$

short period of high error, but recognized that the differences could be due to individual differences between Lara and the Manchester corpus children. To check, Rowland *et al.* compared Lara's data with the Manchester corpus in terms of the percentage of correct questions and errors produced at Stage IV overall, and the percentage of correct questions and errors produced with DO/modal auxiliaries at Stage IV overall. The data on which this analysis was based are reproduced in Table 3.

Using means, standard deviations and 95% confidence intervals they demonstrated that Lara was not an outlier on any of the comparison measures. For example, her rate of correct question production (67.02%) over the whole of Stage IV was very close to the mean rate demonstrated by the Manchester corpus children (68.43%) and was well within one standard deviation of the mean (68.43% +/- 25.73%). In other words, when we analyse Lara's data at the same grain size as the Manchester corpus, the high rate of error disappears. These comparisons indicated that Lara's data can be considered representative and that the difference between corpora was due to the fact that the Manchester corpus was not large enough to capture the short period of high error in the lower frequency structures.

Table 3. Comparison of Descriptive Statistics: Manchester Corpus Children and Lara

Question type	**Stage iv Manchester corpus data**			**Stage iv Lara data**
	Mean % of questions	Standard deviation	95% Confidence interval	% Of total questions
All *wh*-questions				
Correct	68.43	25.73	49 – 88	67.02
Omission error	24.13	28.45	4 – 48	23.84
Inversion error	1.39	1.84	0 – 3	2.35
Other commission error	4.40	3.45	2 – 7	5.29
Questions with do/ modal forms				
Correct	53.32	34.39	27 – 80	68.64
Inversion error	35.30	38.22	6 – 65	16.38
Inversion error	8.51	9.42	1 – 16	12.89
Other commission error	2.87	4.44	0 – 6	2.08

2.4 Summary

To conclude this section, estimates of error rates are dependent upon the size of the sample and the analysis methods used. In order to estimate error rates accurately, we need datasets big enough or statistical measures sensitive enough to capture examples of, and to estimate rates of, low frequency errors, short lived errors and errors in low frequency structures. However, even if we employ such methods, we should be especially cautious about drawing conclusions about how data support our hypothesis when we know that the methods we have used may bias the results in its favour. Those who hypothesize that error rates will be low for a certain structure (e.g., Hyams 1986) must recognize that overall error rates are likely to under-estimate rates of error in low frequency parts of the system. Those who argue for high error rates in low frequency structures (e.g., Maratsos 2000) cannot point to high error rates in individual samples or at particular points in time as support for their predictions, unless they have also demonstrated that such error rates cannot be attributed to chance variation.

3. Sampling and the investigation of productivity

A second issue at the heart of much recent work is the extent to which children have productive knowledge of syntax and morphology from a very early age. Many have claimed that children have innate knowledge of grammatical categories from the outset (e.g., Hyams 1986; Pinker 1984; Radford 1990; Valian 1986; Wexler 1998). In support is the fact that even children's very first multi-word utterances obey the distributional and semantic regularities governing the presence and positioning of grammatical categories.

However, others have claimed that children could demonstrate adult like levels of correct performance without access to adult like knowledge, simply by applying much narrower scope lexical and/or semantic patterns such as *agent + action* or even *ingester + ingest* or *eater + eat*. In support are studies on naturalistic data that suggest that children's performance, although accurate, may reflect an ability to produce certain high frequency examples of grammatical categories, rather than abstract knowledge of the category itself (e.g., Bowerman 1973; Braine 1976; Lieven, Pine and Baldwin 1997; Maratsos 1983). These studies suggest that we cannot attribute abstract categorical knowledge to children until we have first ruled out the possibility that their utterances could be produced with only partially productive lexically-specific knowledge.

This is clearly a valid argument. However, it is equally important that we do not assume that lexical specificity in children's productions equates simply and directly to partial productivity in their grammar. In fact, the apparent lexical specificity of children's speech may sometimes simply be an artefact of the fact that researchers are analysing samples of data. There are three potential problems. First, even in big samples, we capture only a proportion of the child's speech, which means children are unlikely to demonstrate their full range of productions. Second, the frequency statistics of the language itself may bias the analysis in favour of a few high frequency structures. Third, the productivity of the child's speech is limited by the range of lexical items they have in their vocabulary. These three problems are illustrated below.

3.1 The effect of sample size on measures of productivity

In small samples, the presence or absence of just one or two utterance types can have a large effect on the proportion of utterances that can be explained in terms of a small number of lexical frames. In particular, the chance capture of just one or two tokens of a high frequency utterance type can increase the proportion of data accounted for by this utterance type quite dramatically. Conversely, the chance capture of one or two tokens of a low frequency utterance type will decrease the amount of data accounted for by high frequency types. In other words, the smaller the sample, the greater the possibility that the analysis will either over- or under-estimate the degree of lexical specificity in the data.

Rowland and Fletcher (2006) tested the effect of sample size on estimates of lexical specificity in English *wh*-question acquisition directly. The idea that children's early *wh*-questions may be based on semi-formulaic question frames dates back over 20 years to Fletcher (1985), who argued that the earliest correct wh-questions produced by the child in his study could be explained in term of three formulaic patterns. Rowland and Fletcher used the intensive data from Lara at age 2;8 (described in section 2.1.2) to compare the lexical specificity of *wh*-question data in different sized samples. They extracted all correct object and adjunct *wh*-questions from the intensive sample, and then created three further smaller sample sizes out of these data using a randomizing algorithm. The smaller samples represented sampling densities of four hours per month, two hours per month and one hour per month. For each sample, they then calculated how many of the child's *wh*-questions could have been produced simply by the application of the three most frequent lexical frames. A frame was defined as a *wh*-word + auxiliary unit (a *pivot*; e.g., *what are, where have*), which combined with a number of lexical items *(variable)* to produce a *pivot* + *variable* pattern (e.g., *what are* + *X; where have* + *X*; see Rowland and Pine 2000).

Table 4 indicates the effect of sample size on estimates of lexical specificity, based on the same data that has been reported in Rowland and Fletcher (2006). The table demonstrates that a substantial number (76%) of the questions recorded in the intensive diary data could have been based on just three lexical frames. Some of the smaller samples yielded measures of lexical specificity very similar to those gathered from the

Table 4. Effect of sample size on estimates of lexical specificity in Lara's *wh*-questions

	% Questions accounted for by three most frequent lexical frames			
Smaller samples	Mean across seven samples (%)	Standard deviation (sd)	Lowest rate from any individual sample (%)	Highest rate from any individual sample (%)
4-Hour samples	78.00	5.77	70	86
2-Hour samples	78.29	8.90	68	92
1-Hour samples	76.19	14.77	50	92
Intensive Diary data		76%		

intensive data despite being based on much smaller numbers of utterances. However, many of the individual small samples yielded inaccurate estimations, which meant that the chances of any one sample grossly under- or over-estimating the rate of lexical specificity increased with reducing sample size. For example, the estimates based on the one-hour samples varied between 50% and 92%. Thus, if Lara's questions had been sampled for only one-hour per month, the data would be equally likely to over-estimate (92%) as under-estimate (50%) the lexical specificity of Lara's data. In other words, with a small sample, it would be chance that determined whether Lara's data supported or undermined the claim that lexical frames underlie children's early productions.

3.2 The effect of frequency statistics on measures of productivity

A second possible confound is the effect of the frequency statistics of the language being learned on estimates of lexical specificity/productivity. The traditional measure of lexical specificity is to calculate the proportion of children's utterances that could be produced using a small number of lexical frames (e.g., *a* + *X*; *the* + *Y*; Pine and Lieven 1997). However, even in adult speech, speakers tend to over-use a small number of words (e.g., the verbs *do* and *be*), and under-use a much larger number of words (e.g., *bounce, gobble*; see e.g., Cameron-Faulkner, Lieven, and Tomasello 2003). This means that a small number of items will tend to account for a large proportion of the observed occurrences of a grammatical category, even in speakers with abstract adult like knowledge of the category. Thus, analyses on naturalistic data samples are likely to under-estimate the variety and productivity of children's speech (Naigles 2002).

Similarly, correlations between frequency of use in caregiver's speech and order of acquisition in the child's speech have traditionally been seen as evidence that children are first acquiring knowledge of the most highly frequent lexical constructions that they are hearing, (e.g., Diessel and Tomasello 2001). However, the correlation could simply reflect the fact that the most frequently produced examples of a structure are those that are most likely to occur in the early samples. For example, suppose that, in order to investigate the order of acquisition of different verbs, we collect 100 utterances per week for five weeks. We are very likely to capture frequent verbs (e.g., verbs that occur at least once per 100 utterances) in our very first sample (after we have collected 100 utterances). However, verbs that occur less frequently are very unlikely to occur in our first sample. For example, it is only after 2 weeks (i.e. after we have collected 200 samples) that we are likely to capture at least one example of verbs that occur once every 200 utterances. It will take us five weeks (500 utterances) before we can be certain of capturing a verb that occurs once every 500 utterances. In other words, more frequent verbs are more likely to occur in earlier samples (and thus be identified as early acquired) than less frequent verbs, even if both verbs were acquired before the beginning of the sampling period.

3.3 The effect of vocabulary size on productivity measures

The third possible confound on estimates of productivity is the fact that children's vocabularies are smaller than those of adults. Since speakers can only produce utterances using vocabulary items they have already learned, children are less likely than adults to be capable of demonstrating productivity with a wide range of grammatical structures. For example, a child who knows only two determiners will have far less opportunity to demonstrate a sophisticated knowledge of the determiner category than a child who knows four, even if both children have equally abstract knowledge of the category (Pine and Lieven 1997). Thus, lexical specificity in the data could also be due to a limited knowledge of vocabulary, not to limited grammatical knowledge.

3.4 Assessing productivity: A solution

To recap, the accuracy with which any one sample assesses productivity is affected by sample size, by the frequency statistics of the language, and by the vocabulary size of the child. Importantly, even collecting much bigger samples will not overcome these problems. There will still be an impact of sample size and frequency statistics on measures of productivity, no matter how many utterances are collected. In addition, children's limited vocabulary knowledge will still affect the range and variability of the syntactic structures they produce. In order to attribute limited productivity to children reliably it is important to control for the effect of sample size and vocabulary, while taking into account the frequency statistics of the language. The best way to do this is to use a comparison measure based on a matched sample of adult data.

Aguado-Orea and Pine's (Aguado-Orea and Pine 2002; Aguado-Orea 2004) study on Spanish verb morphology provides such a comparison measure. They investigated the productivity of children's verb morphology in Spanish, controlling for a number of methodological factors that could explain limited flexibility in verb inflection use.

Using the dense data from the two children discussed in section 2.2.3 (Juan and Lucia, aged 2;0 to 2;6), they investigated the effects of (a) limited vocabulary, (b) limited sample size, and (c) limited knowledge of particular inflections, on estimates of productivity. They reasoned that if limited productivity in children's speech was due to these three methodological constraints, there should be no difference between estimates of productivity based on children's and adults' speech, if the samples were matched on vocabulary, sample size and knowledge of inflections. However, if the children's speech was significantly more limited than we would expect, given the size of their samples and their knowledge of verbs and inflections, we should find significant differences between estimates of productivity based on child and adult speech.

The study focused on present tense verb inflectional contexts and the measure of productivity used was the average number of inflections per verb (where one inflection per verb was the minimum level of productivity and four inflections per verb was the maximum).[9] The analyses compared the child's speech with that of his or her own primary caregivers (mothers and fathers).

The researchers controlled for knowledge of inflection by restricting the analysis to those transcripts recorded after the child had already produced the inflections in his or her speech. They controlled for vocabulary by restricting the analysis to verb stems that occurred in both the child's and the adult's speech. Finally, they controlled for sample size by excluding a random number of utterances from the larger of the two samples, so that both samples contained the same number of verb tokens. Table 5 provides a summary of results, based on data from Aguado-Orea (2004).

The results for the adults clearly demonstrated that restricting sample size, vocabulary and inflection knowledge had an impact on the extent to which the speakers were able to demonstrate productivity. Presumably all four adults had productive knowledge of all four inflections and how to apply them to all verbs, but they only produced between 2.48 and 2.17 inflections per verb in the samples. Similarly, neither Juan nor Lucia was able to show knowledge of more than 2.24 inflections per verb, even in the biggest samples. However, importantly, the children's use of verb inflection was always significantly less productive than that of their mothers and fathers, and improved over time to more adult like levels. Thus, although there was a substantial effect of limited lexical knowledge and of sample size, Aguado-Orea and Pine demonstrated that it is possible to find evidence for limited productivity in children by comparing adult and child data in order to control for these confounds.

9. The requirement to control for knowledge of inflection restricted the analysis to only four of the six present tense inflections because two were produced too late on in the collection process to yield enough data. The inflections finally included were 1st singular, 2nd singular, 3rd singular and 3rd plural inflections.

Table 5. Average number of inflections per verb in the data from Juan, Lucia and their parents.

Participant	No. of verb tokens	No. inflections per verb
Juan (sample equivalent to father)	2414	2.18
Juan's father	2414	2.44
Juan (sample equivalent to mother)	2058	2.24
Juan's mother	2058	2.35
Lucia (sample equivalent to father)	874	1.87
Lucia's father	874	2.48
Lucia (sample equivalent to mother)	809	1.90
Lucia's mother	809	2.17

To conclude this section, the effects of sample size, frequency statistics and vocabulary limitations on children's utterances are large. Adults are able to demonstrate a much greater degree of productivity in their speech than children, simply because they speak more – yielding bigger samples of speech for analysis – and because they possess a larger vocabulary – allowing them to demonstrate their grammatical knowledge with a wider range of words and a larger number of structures. When samples of adult speech are equated to samples of child speech on these measures, the apparent productivity of adult speech reduces substantially.

However, it remains possible to demonstrate lexical specificity in child's speech, even when the appropriate controls are applied. Aguado-Orea and Pine (2005) demonstrated that Spanish children produced significantly fewer inflections per verb than adults, even after the application of methodological controls. Pine and Martindale (1996), in a study of determiner acquisition, reported similar findings: applying controls for vocabulary and sample size reduced the difference between the productivity of child and adult speech, but, children's utterances remained significantly more lexically-specific than those of adults. Rowland and Fletcher (2006) showed that Lara's *wh*-question use was more restricted than a matched sample of maternal questions, once knowledge of *wh*-word and auxiliary and sample size was equated. However, the difference between the composition of adult and of child speech is likely to be less striking than has sometimes previously been claimed.

4. Conclusion

In the present chapter, we have demonstrated some of the possible consequences of taking sampled naturalistic data at face value. First, we have shown that estimates of error rates calculated using small samples of data may be misleading, either over- or under-estimating error rates quite substantially or even failing to capture rare errors altogether. Second, we have illustrated that analyses of error must incorporate the fact that error rates are likely to change over time and that errors may be more frequent in some parts of the system than in others. Analyses of overall error rates (collapsed across time or across sub-systems) will disproportionately reflect how well children perform with high frequency items or how well children are doing at the later stages of development (when children tend to produce more utterances). Since errors seem to be more frequent at earlier points of development and in low frequency structures, overall error rates are likely to under-estimate error rates in low frequency structures.

One solution to the sampling problem lies in suiting the sampling regime to the structure under investigation – whether by mathematical methods such as hit probability, or by using different sampling techniques. Another solution lies in calculating average error rates across a number of samples – whether across children or across different samples from the same child. Although averaging error rates across children will give no indication of the scale of the impact of individual differences or of different sampling densities, inspection of the range and standard deviation, as well as the mean error rate, will give researchers an indication of the heterogeneity of the samples and allow further investigation if there is evidence for substantial variation.

Second, we have demonstrated that estimates of productivity are affected by the sampling regime in three ways. First, in spoken languages, a small number of highly frequency words dominate utterances, so apparent limited productivity may simply reflect the frequency statistics of the language being spoken. Second, the greater the sample size, the more utterances will be collected and the more productive the speaker will appear. Since children tend to produce fewer utterances per minute than adults (at least early in the acquisition process), children's utterances are bound to seem less productive. Third, a child who knows only a small number of words will be unable to demonstrate the same level of productivity as an adult. We have shown that with small sample sizes, even adults can appear to demonstrate limited productivity, but that it is possible to investigate the development of productivity in child speech, while controlling for sampling and vocabulary constraints, by comparing matched samples of adult and child data.

Given the constraints imposed by sampling on naturalistic data analysis, one might argue that we should abandon the use of naturalistic data in favour of experimental techniques. We would argue that this is too extreme a reaction to the constraints. At the very least, the analysis of naturalistic data allows us to identify phenomena that we can then investigate further in an experimental context. However, we suggest that the analysis of naturalistic data can provide more than just the initial description of a phenomenon. Naturalistic data analysis avoids some of the pitfalls of experimental techniques (e.g., the Clever Hans effect) and can reveal levels of sophistication in children's behaviour that are simply not captured in an experimental situation (see, for example, Dunn's (1988) work on the development of social cognition). It is important, though, to apply controls, as we would to experimental techniques, and to take account of the confounds inherent in using naturalistic data to interpret and evaluate theories of language acquisition.

Appendix: The use of error codes with the CHAT transcription system and the CHILDES database

All the error rates analyses we have discussed in this paper rely on the accurate transcription and coding of error. Coding errors is extremely time-consuming when dealing with large datasets, so system of reliable, consistent retrieval codes for marking specific error types at the time of transcription is invaluable (see MacWhinney this volume). MacWhinney has recently provided such a method for marking morphological errors in datasets that are transcribed in CHAT format. The system allows researchers to search generally for a particular code (e.g., [* +ed]) to locate all errors of a certain type (past tense over-regularization errors). This is described in section 7.5 of the CHAT manual (available on the CHILDES website at http://childes.psy.cmu.edu) and is reproduced here. The system can be extended to provide further functionality. Examples of the use of the coding system can be seen in the Brown (1973) corpus and the Manchester corpus (Theakston *et al.* 2001), both of which are available to download on the CHILDES website.

System for coding morphological errors

Form	Function	Error	Correct
+ed	past overregularization	breaked	broke
+ed-sup	superfluous –ed	broked	broke
+ed-dup	duplicated –ed	breakeded	broke
virr	verb irregularization	bat	bit
+es	present overregularization	have	has
+est	superlative overmarking	most	mostest
+er	agentive overmarking	rubber	rubberer
+s	plural overregularization	childs	children
+s-sup	superfluous plural	childrens	children
+s-pos	plural for wrong part of speech	mines	mine
pos	general part of speech error	mine	my
sem	general semantic error		

Examples:

CHI: I goed [: went] [+ed] home.
*CHI: I bat [: bit] [* virr] the cake.

Core morphology in child directed speech

Crosslinguistic corpus analyses of noun plurals*

Dorit Ravid, Wolfgang U. Dressler, Bracha Nir-Sagiv, Katharina Korecky-Kröll, Agnita Souman, Katja Rehfeldt, Sabine Laaha, Johannes Bertl, Hans Basbøll and Steven Gillis

1. Introduction

Learning inflectional systems is a crucial task taken up early on by toddlers. From a *distributional* point of view, inflection is characterized by high token frequency, and general and obligatory applicability (Bybee 1985). From a *semantic* point of view, inflection exhibits transparency, regularity and predictability. These aspects of inflection render it highly salient for young children and facilitate the initial mapping of meaning or function onto inflectional segments. At the same time, many inflectional systems are also fraught with *morphological* and *morpho-phonological* complexity, opacity, inconsistency, irregularity, and unpredictability. These *structural* aspects of inflection constitute a serious challenge to the successful launching of this central function of human language.

Most studies of inflectional morphology start from an analysis of the adult system, and reason from that system the *when* and *how* of children's acquisition. However, the discrepancy between the complexity of the mature system, on the one hand, and the need to facilitate acquisition, on the other, has to be resolved. Child Directed Speech (CDS) – simply defined as input to children from caregivers and early peer-group – has been shown to account for emerging lexical and morphosyntactic features in child

* For German and Hebrew: An important part of this work has been funded by the mainly experimental project Nr. P17276 "Noun development in a cross-linguistic perspective" of the Austrian Science Fund (FWF). For Dutch: Preparation of this paper was supported by a grant from the FWO (Flemish Science Foundation), contract G.0216.05. For Danish: Part of the Danish work was funded by the Carlsberg Foundation. Invited by Heike Behrens to contribute to this volume on the importance of the input children receive, we limited ourselves to longitudinal data only.

language (Gallaway and Richards 1994; Ninio 1992; Ziesler and Demuth 1995).[1] The literature indicates that such linguistic input to young children consistently differs from speech among adults (Cameron-Faulkner, Lieven and Tomasello 2003; Gleitman, Gleitman, Landau and Wanner 1988; Morgan 1986; Snow 1995): it presents children with those aspects of the system which are particularly frequent, transparent, regular and consistent. These could make the child's job of understanding what the system is about and how it works much simpler.

We term these aspects of the adult inflectional system that are most easily transmitted to children *core morphology*. In the current study we consider core morphology within the domain of plural inflection in nouns. Specifically, we will show that across the languages we investigate here, the way the system is represented in CDS provides the child with clear and consistent information regarding its distributional aspects. This refers to the conditions for the distribution of types of plural suffixes as well as to the token-frequency of unproductive plural patterns. To the best of our knowledge, no crosslinguistic work has to date been carried out to document, define and analyze the nature and distribution of core morphology in child directed speech and / or in young children's output. In our view, such work requires a systematic longitudinal analysis of spontaneous speech data of the type presented here: a crosslinguistic comparison of noun plurals in the input to, and output of, young children learning German, Dutch, Danish, and Hebrew.

Our concept of *core morphology* is clearly different in nature, scope and function from Chomsky's (1980) notion of *core grammar* (Joseph 1992), which equals innate Universal Grammar (also called the *Narrow Language Faculty* – Chomsky 1995; Fitch, Hauser and Chomsky 2005). Core grammar is language-specific only insofar as universally open parameter values are fixed in one of the universally given options. While both core morphology and core grammar relate to acquisition and psycholinguistic modelling in general, we do not share Chomsky's concepts of luxurious grammatical innateness, of the logical problem of learnability, or of insufficient and erroneous input evidence (MacWhinney 2004).

An older concept, only partially comparable to ours, is the Prague School notion of the *centre* of a linguistic system, as opposed to its periphery (Daneš 1966; Popela 1966). The overlapping criteria for the appurtenance of a morphological construction to the centre of a language are its prototypicality, its high degree of integration into a (sub)system (cf. the notion of system adequacy in Natural Morphology, Kilani-Schoch and Dressler 2005), its high type and token frequency and productivity – understood as applicability of a pattern to any new word that fits the structural description of the

1. In a recent, pertinent discussion on InfoChildes (4.12.2006), Dan Slobin commented that he preferred the term "exposure language" to other terms such as "input" (which assumes the child takes everything in), "motherese" and "caregiver talk" (which exclude talk from non-parents and non-caregivers), and "child directed speech" (which excludes what children learn from overheard speech). However, given later commentaries on CDS as a register, he conceded that this is a compact and convenient term. All participants commented on the need to specify the linguistic characteristics of CDS.

pattern (or of the input of a morphological rule). In the later literature, productive patterns were regarded as the core of morphology (and the rest of the grammar) by Dressler (1989; 2003) and Bertinetto (2003: 191ff), that is, unproductive patterns were regarded as marginal, inactive lexically stored parts of grammar.

Age of acquisition plays a crucial role in our current conception of *core morphology*. As pioneered by Jakobson (1941) and empirically investigated in abundant psycholinguistic research, early-emerging linguistic patterns are better stored and faster accessed by adults than what is acquired later on (Bonin, Barry, Méot and Chalard 2004; Burani, Barca and Arduino 2001; Lewis, Gerhard and Ellis 2001; Zevin and Seidenberg 2002). Early acquired patterns evidently depend on more limited input than later acquisition, in two senses: Firstly, the *amount* of tokens instantiating a morphological category or system is smaller than their number in adult directed speech and speech addressed to older children; and secondly, their *variety* – that is, their different types and subtypes within and across categories – focuses on the most prototypical members of the category.[2]

1.1 Noun plurals in acquisition

Our window onto core morphology in this chapter is the path leading to the acquisition of *noun plurals* in three Germanic languages – Austrian German, Danish and Dutch – and one Semitic language, Hebrew. Plural formation is a basic category that emerges and develops early on in child language (Berman 1981; Ravid 1995; Stephany 2002). It has a large crosslinguistic distribution, including sign languages (Pfau and Steinbach 2006) and often exhibits much structural complexity (Corbett 2000). It plays a central role in the morphology of noun phrases and as the trigger of grammatical agreement. Plurals are signaled on nouns as the heads of noun phrases, if nouns carry any morphological marking in the respective language. Plural marking is the most basic morphological marker on nouns: if a language has a single category of morphological marking on the noun, it is grammatical number. Since singular marking is often zero, with duals having a much smaller distribution, plural is the central number marking in the world's languages. Accordingly, plural emerges as one of the earliest categories in child language development (Brown 1973; Slobin 1985c), and the path to its acquisition has been the topic of many studies and much controversy (Clahsen, Rothweiler, Woest and Marcus 1992; Marcus, Brinkmann, Clahsen, Wiese and Pinker 1995; Marcus, Pinker, Ullman, Hollander, Rosen and Xu 1992). The main concern in the current study is how children faced with complex and often inconsistent systems are able to 'break into the system' at the earliest stages of morphological acquisition.

2. By prototypicality *grosso modo* we mean here relatively high type frequency and/or token frequency, i.e. a medium amount of token frequency is necessary for allowing high type frequency to establish a prototype, but if there is only low type frequency, then high token frequency overrules it and establishes by itself a prototype.

1.1.1 *Dual-route accounts*

For the acquisition and representation of English plurals, it is relatively easy to argue for the adequacy of a dual-route model account to explain how plurals are acquired and represented. This view, as proposed by Pinker (1999), assumes that regular forms are computed in the grammar by combinatorial operations that assemble morphemes and simplex words into complex words and larger syntactic units (Clahsen 1999; Marcus 2000; Sahin, Pinker and Halgren 2006). An important feature of this view is the dissociation of singular stem (base) and suffix as distinct symbolic variables (Berent, Pinker and Shimron 2002; Pinker and Ullman 2002). Regular plurals are thus productively generated by a general operation of unification, concatenating plural *-s* with the symbol N and inflecting any word categorized as a noun.

Under this view, irregular forms behave like words in the lexicon, that is, they are acquired and stored like other words with the plural grammatical feature incorporated into their lexical entries. Learning irregular forms is governed by associative memory, which facilitates the acquisition of similar items and superimposes the properties of old items on new ones resembling them. A stored inflected form blocks the application of the rule to that form, but elsewhere the rule applies to any item appropriately marked. At some point in acquisition English-speaking children would extract from the input generalizations for the formation of the sibilant plurals, the only productive and *default* pattern. Plural minor patterns and exceptions are truly infrequent in English as both types and tokens: the very few cases of umlaut (e.g., *foot – feet*, *mouse – mice*) and *-en* plurals (*child – children*) relevant to children would be rote-learned and remain separately stored words with the feature [plural] incorporated into their lexical entries.

1.1.2 *Challenges to the dual-route*

Unfortunately, this dual-route account cannot be easily extended to accommodate all of the four languages analyzed in this contribution (nor to the noun and verb inflection systems of, say, Slavic languages). For example, the attribution of a dual-route model to *German* (notably by Bartke, Marcus and Clahsen 1995; Clahsen 1999) assumes *-s* plurals to be the default, rule-derived form. However, these studies have not come to grips with the fact that across the literature on German-learning children, and for all Austrian ones described so far, *-s* plurals are neither the first ones to emerge, nor are they the only ones to be overgeneralized. Acquiring German plurals is better accounted for by single-route models (including schema-based models), which are also compatible with a gradual continuum between fully productive and unproductive plurals (Laaha, Ravid, Korecky-Kröll, Laaha and Dressler 2006).

Dutch plurals are difficult (if not impossible) to account for in a dual-route model. First of all, the Dutch plural is incompatible with a single default, since it has two suffixes (*-en* and *-s*), which are considered to be in complementary distribution (Baayen, Schreuder, De Jong and Krott 2002; Booij 2001; De Haas and Trommelen 1993; van Wijk 2002; Zonneveld 2004; but see Bauer 2003). The distribution of the two suffixes is determined by the phonological structure of the singular, and more specifically, by the word-final segment as well as the word's stress pattern. In other words, a noun's regular plural suffix is determined on the basis of its phonological profile. Thus, both suffixes are productive in their respective phonological domain, which makes them both candidates for default application. Linguistic analysis reveals that, besides productivity, both suffixes have the characteristics of a default inflectional pattern (Baayen, Dijkstra and Schreuder 1997; Baayen *et al.* 2002; Zonneveld 2004).

Even staunch advocates of the dual-route model observe that there is no single default in this case: Pinker and Prince (1994) remark that "the two affixes have separate domains of productivity... but within those domains they are both demonstrably productive" and call it "an unsolved but tantalizing problem." Pinker (1999) writes: "Remarkably, Dutch has two plurals that pass our stringent tests for regularity, *-s* and *-en*... Within their fiefdoms each applies as the default." Thus, Dutch plurals appear to deviate from the dual-route account in at least two respects: (1) there are two defaults instead of one; and (2) plural formation cannot be seen as the 'blind' application of a symbolic rule to the category N, since phonological information is needed in order to decide on the choice of the affix (similar to what is well-known for inflection in Slavic languages). The latter is not an enigma: recently, Keuleers, Sandra, Daelemans, Gillis, Durieux and Martens (2007) have shown that Dutch-speaking adults also use orthographic information in order to decide about which suffix to use.

Finally, *Hebrew* plurals too pose a challenge to the dual-route model, from a different perspective. Two studies test and analyze plural formation in a small number of Hebrew noun categories (Berent, Pinker and Shimron 1999, 2002). The authors regard suffix regularity and base change as independent of each other, concluding that they represent two different mental computations: symbolic operations versus memorized idiosyncrasies. The problem is that the Berent *et al.*'s analysis hinges on viewing the base- and stress-preserving masculine plural as the default Hebrew plural – an assumption tested, as in German and English, on proper names homophonous with common nouns. Pluralization of proper names (e.g., *Dov)* would yield a form extremely 'faithful' to the singular base – no base change, no stress shift – with the masculine *-im* suffix. This is supposed to constitute the default Hebrew plural. Under the assumption that defaults constitute part of the plural system of a language, this test both overshoots and falls short of actually accounting for Hebrew plural formation (Ravid 2006), since it yields a non-Hebrew form. A critical factor is the fact that native Hebrew plurals – like all linear nominal suffixes[3] – always shift stress to the final syllable (e.g., *dov* – *dubím* 'bears'). Suffixation that fails to obey stress shift cannot be regarded as part of native Hebrew morphology, not to mention being considered a default plural. Moreover, the sensitivity of Hebrew suffix type to base-final phonology would lead to completely

3. Failure to move stress to the final syllable ("preserve stem faithfulness") in non-native words is not plural-specific and is a general feature of Hebrew nominal morphology: Compare foreign-based denominal adjectives *normáli* 'normal' or *fatáli* 'fatal' with native ultimate stressed *tsiburí* 'public'.

un-Hebrew forms under the proper name test. Thus for example *-it* final proper names such as *Maskít* would completely preserve base form and take masculine *-im* to yield *Maskítim* instead of undergoing *t*-deletion and stress shift and taking feminine *-ot* to yield *maskiyót* (Ravid 1995). *Maskítim* constitutes a plural form completely incompatible with native Hebrew morphology beyond toddlerhood (Berman 1985; Levy 1980). In general, plural formation of proper nouns is marginal both in plural use and in regard to morphological grammar in general. Thus, what is a default in plural formation (and inflection in general) should not be judged by what occurs in proper names.

Against this background, we now examine how single-route models handle plural formation (e.g., Daugherty and Seidenberg 1994; Plunkett and Marchman 1991; Rumelhart and McClelland 1986). Under this view, the learning network improves performance over many learning trials, resulting in a gradual developmental process where overgeneralization is conditioned by linguistic experience coupled with the similarity of the exemplar being learned to others already stored, its consistency and salience, as well as by frequency. Such single-route mechanisms can predict how grammatical representations are acquired. This cannot be said for dual-route models, which assume that children (like adults) eventually use a default rule and an associative memory system – but do not explain which mechanism accounts for how the default rule is acquired. Given these varied challenges to the dual route model, we adopt a single-route approach to plural acquisition.

We now turn to the problem of complexity in the plural systems under investigation, in order to assess the challenges faced by young learners.

1.2 Complexity in the formation of noun plurals

Plural formation takes on different degrees of complexity in the world's languages. For example, Turkish plural formation is most simple and homogeneous, involving just one, biunique suffix and almost no change in the nominal base; concomitantly plural emerges and consolidates early on in Turkish (Stephany 2002, with references). English plural formation is also relatively morphologically homogeneous, insofar as sibilant plurals represent the clear default and the only productive plural formation type with overwhelming type frequency. The three allomorphs in English *(-z, -s, -Iz)* can be accounted for in a purely phonological way. However, plural formation of many other languages, including those represented in the current study, is much more complex, but to date, no overall measures of classifying degree of complexity have been proposed.

Two important facets of plural systems which contribute to their complexity and which children eventually have to learn are (1) plural suffix application and (2) subsequent changes to the base. For example, Hebrew singular masculine *iš* 'man' takes the plural suffix *-im*, and consequently changes the base to *anaš-*, yielding plural *anaš-ím*. However, the scope of this chapter restricts us to focusing on plural suffix application in acquisition. This chapter thus presents a method of assessing complexity of *plural suffixation* in the four languages under investigation, to be used in the analyses of CDS and children's output.

Our comparative framework starts from the assumption that two recurrent factors are the most important ones for predicting the application of suffixation in our languages: *sonority* and *gender*. Phonological conditions have always been considered important for predicting suffixation patterns in many languages, but often not in any way that respects phonology systematically (a notable exception is palatality in Slavic languages). We propose the *sonority scale* (Goldsmith 1995) as one organizing phonological principle playing an important morphological role in all of the languages of this study. The sonority scale is a predictor of the order of segments within the syllable: the prototypical peak, i.e. the centre of the syllable, is (phonetically) a vowel, and among the consonants, obstruents (with noise, such as /p/ or /s/) are furthest away from the centre, whereas sonorants (noise-free, such as /l/, /m/) are closer to the centre. Our tables with sonority illustrate where on the sonority slope (from the peak rightwards) the final segment of the base is situated. This mirror-image of sonority in the syllable, with a peak in the middle and slopes to each side, is combined with inherent sonority (which does not predict order of segments in the syllable): stressed, low and full vowels are inherently more sonorous than unstressed, high and reduced vowels, respectively. Only the distinct position of Hebrew /t/ and /n/ cannot be derived from the sonority scale.

A second factor, shared by three of our four languages (German, Danish and Hebrew) is *gender* of the singular noun, a factor well-known for many Indo-European languages but often underrated for Germanic languages (Harbert 2006: 93, 96), with the exception of German (Köpcke 1993; Wegener 1999). We restrict our current analysis to these two factors since they allow us to put the four languages into the same perspective.

To illustrate how gender and degree of sonority of the base-final phoneme interact in determining the application of suffixation, Table 1 presents a fragment of German, consisting of four possible intersections of gender and sonority:

Table 1. A fragment of the interaction between gender and sonority in Austrian German

Sonority / **Gender**	**Obstruents**	**Schwa**
Feminine	Subregular: -*(e)n*, -*s*	Regular: -*n*
	Irregular: -*e*	Irregular: ø
Masculine	Subregular: -*e*, -*(e)n*, -s	Subregular: ø, -*n*

The four cells in Table 1 present the notion of regularity of suffixation as defined in the present context: the conditions under which rules (as formal expression of inflectional patterns) apply. Thus, the degree of regularity of suffixation is in fact the degree of predictability of the application of a specific suffixation rule in a given cell resulting from the interaction of sonority and gender (cf. Monaghan and Christiansen this volume, for further discussion of multiple cue integration). If there is a clear default for one productive suffixation to apply, we have regularity. For example, consider the suffixation of *-n* after feminine nouns ending in schwa in Table 1, as in *Orange-n* 'orange-s'. If any other rule applies in the same sonority-gender cell, we have irregularity, for example, feminine nouns ending in schwa with a zero suffix (e.g., *Mütter* 'mother-s'). But if two or more suffixation rules apply productively in the same cell (applying either optionally or alternatively to the same words or in complementary lexical distribution) we have subregularity. Thus both plural *-e* and *-s* may apply to the masculine noun *Park*, Pl. *Park-e, Park-s* 'park-s', and in other words *-en*, as in *Prinz-en* 'prince-s'.

Thus, based on Laaha *et al.* (2006: 280), we first distinguish between plural suffixations which freely apply, under a specific combination of gender and word-final phonology, to new words and are thus *productive*, and those which do not, and are thus *unproductive* – which we classify as *irregular*. Second, we distinguish between cells where just one productive plural suffixation pattern occurs (irrespective of whether there are some irregular exceptions) and those where two (or more) productive patterns compete. In the first case, we have a regular pattern (which is *fully predictable*, with possible irregular exceptions which have to be memorized according to all linguistic and psycholinguistic models); in the second case we identify two (or more) *subregular* patterns whose selection is only unpredictable.

Our approach to the puzzle of noun plural learning thus starts out from this rich and complex view of gender x sonority in mature systems as the target of children's acquisition in the four study languages. The aim of this chapter is to establish empirically in what way exactly core morphology facilitates acquisition by identifying the domain of core morphology within mature noun plurals systems; that is, to determine to what extent and in what ways plural input to young children is restricted.

2. Language systems

This section describes the application of plural suffixation as a function of gender and sonority in the four languages under investigation. While the general scale of base-final sonority guides us across the board in the four languages, the actual set of categories and segments manifesting the sonority scale and appearing in the top row of Tables 2–5 below are each dictated by plural formation in the specific language under consideration. In the same way, gender, the other axis creating the grid for plural formation (if the language has it), is also presented from a language-specific perspective.

The analysis of the Danish language system is original in its account for morphology departing exclusively from sound structure, and not via the written language, and in its use of base-final sonority (systematically) and in the application of our common gender and base-final sonority framework. The analysis of the German plural system is new in its classification of *regular, subregular* and *irregular* suffixations, in its extension of phonological conditioning from word-final vowels to consonants, and in the introduction of the sonority hierarchy. The analysis of the Hebrew system is completely new in the distinction it makes between regular and irregular plural suffixation, on the one hand, and gender-specific subregular patterning, as well as in the application of the sonority hierarchy to Hebrew plurals. The analysis of plural formation in Dutch provided here is fully in agreement with the linguistic descriptive tradition, in which two factors are considered to determine the choice of the plural suffix, viz. the final segment of the singular and the word's rhythm. This analysis dates back to Van Haeringen (1947), and since then analyses of plural formation have always stressed the importance of these two factors to different degrees (see De Haas and Trommelen 1993; Haeseryn, Romijn, Geerts, de Rooij and van den Toorn 1997 among others). Recently Van Wijk (2002) analyzed a corpus of written Dutch in order to establish where the balance lies between the rhythmic and the segmental factors.

2.1 Dutch plural formation

Plural formation of Dutch nouns consists in adding a suffix to the singular. There are two productive suffixes: *-en* /ə(n)/ and *-s* /s/, which are (largely) in complementary distribution.[4] Table 2 shows the distribution of the plural suffix according to the sonority scale only, since gender does not play a role in plural formation in Dutch. However there is an interesting interplay between the final segment(s) and the stress pattern of the word, and hence, for most types of words there is only subregularity (De Haas and Trommelen 1993; Van Wijk 2002).

Table 2. Sonority in Dutch

Obstruent	Sonorant	Schwa	Full Vowel
Subregular: *-en, -s*	Subregular: *-en, -s*	Regular: *-s*	Subregular: *-en, -s*
Irregular: *-en, -s*	Irregular: *-en, -s*	Irregular: *-en*	Irregular: *-en, -s*

Words ending in an obstruent take *-en* as their plural suffix if stress is on the final syllable, and *-s* if stress is on a pre-final syllable, so that the resulting plural form is a trochee. Thus, these patterns define the subregularity. But as Van Wijk (2002) points out in her corpus study: neither subregularity is exceptionless, which entails that both suffixes are also irregular. That is, *-s* is irregular for words with final stress and *-en* for words with prefinal stress.

Words ending in a sonorant tend to take the *-en* suffix when preceded by a full vowel and *-s* when preceded by a schwa. The latter regularity is very strong, though some of these words can take both suffixes (without an apparent meaning difference),

4. A third suffix, viz. *-eren*, is not productive any more and only 12 nouns are pluralized with *-eren*. In addition, there are non-Germanic plural markers as in *colleg<u>a</u>* – *colleg<u>ae</u>* ('colleague'), *music<u>us</u>* – *music<u>i</u>* ('musician'). These are all not productive and are often replaced by a plural *-s/-en*: *colleg<u>a</u>* – *colleg<u>ae</u>* – *colleg<u>as</u>*.

such as *appel – appel-s / appel-en* 'apple-s'. Thus, words ending in a schwa show a very straightforward picture: they take *-s* as a rule, though quite a few of these words can take the *-(e)n* plural as well: *syllabe – syllabe-s – syllabe-n* 'syllable-s'. The former has many exceptions, some of which can be explained by the metrical regularity that plurals are expected to end in a trochee, but still others are plain exceptions: *oom – oom-s* 'uncle-s', *roman – roman-s* 'novel-s'. Finally, diphthong-final words predominantly prefer the *-en* suffix (irrespective of the stress pattern of the word, e.g., *aardbei – aardbei-en* 'strawberrie-s' ['artbEi], *bij – bij-en* 'bee-s' ['bEi]), while words ending in a full vowel take *-s* (e.g., *positie – positie-s* 'position-s' [pozisi]). Again there are many exceptions, such as *zee – zee-en* 'sea-s', *koe* [ku:] – *koe-en* 'cow-s'.

2.2 German plural formation

The system of noun pluralization in German consists of more phonologically unrelated plural allomorphs than in Dutch, also with no single clearly dominant form. German noun plurals are formed by the four different suffixes *-s, -(e)n, -e, -er* or by zero. The three latter ones may combine with umlaut (base vowel change), disregarded here since this chapter is not concerned with base changes.

Table 3. Interaction of gender and sonority in Austrian German[5]

Sonority / Gender	**Obstruent**	**Sonorant**	**Schwa**	**Full Vowel**
Feminine	Subregular: *-(e)n, -s* Irregular: *-e*	Subregular: *-(e)n, -s* Irregular: *-e*	Regular: *-n* Irregular: ø	Subregular: *-s, -(e)n*
Masculine	Subregular: *-e, -(e)n, -s* Irregular: *-er*	Subregular: *-e, -(e)n, -s*, ø Irregular: *-er*	Subregular: ø, *-n*	Subregular: *-s, -e* Irregular: *-er, -er*, ø
Neuter	Subregular: *-e, -(e)n, -s* Irregular: *-er*	Subregular: *-e, -(e)n, -s*, ø Irregular: *-er*	Regular: ø Irregular: *-n*	Regular: *-s* Irregular: *-er, -e*, ø

5. In order to achieve sufficient numbers in each cell, the following simplifications have been made: base-final (fricative and affricate) sibilants have been put together with the other final obstruents, although *-s* suffixation is excluded after sibilants. Word-final central [ə] (= written *-e*) and lower [ɐ] (= written *-er*) of spoken Austrian German have been put together as schwa, and diphthongs have been united with vowels, in both cases despite minor differences in following plural suffixes. Among sonorant-final masculines and neuters zero occurs only if the sonorant is preceded by [ə] (when the [ə] is deleted, the sonorant is syllabic).

According to the system of plural suffixation (plus zero) of Table 3, there is no difference in the distribution after final obstruents and sonorants, except for the cases of sibilants and [ə] followed by sonorant (as mentioned in Footnote 5). Starting with feminine nouns, we find, among the productive suffixes, competition between *-en* and much less frequent *-s*, as in *Farm-en* = *Farm-s* 'farm-s' (the reverse distribution after full vowels), whereas *-e* suffixation is irregular, for example, *Braut*, Pl. *Bräut-e* 'bride-s'. After final schwa, only *-n* is regular, zero occurs unproductively after [ɐ], for example, *Vase-n* 'vase-s', *Mutter-n* 'female screw-s' vs. *Mütter* 'mother-s'.

Masculines and neuters differ only after final schwa: zero is the only regular plural type of neuters, as in *Gebirge* 'mountain range(-s)', whereas *-n* is irregular (only *Auge-n* 'eye-s'). With masculines, productive zero competes with productive *-n* (e.g., *Hase-n* 'hare-s'). Examples for the position after obstruents are the productive masculine types *Quiz-e, Prinz-en, Spot-s* 'quiz-es, prince-s, spot-s' and the unproductive *Wäld-er* 'woods'.[6]

2.3 Danish plural formation

The Danish system of nominal pluralization consists of a number of plural allomorphs, namely the suffixes *a*-schwa, *e*-schwa[7], zero, *-s*, *-a* and *-i*.[8] Among adult plural suffixes (Allan, Holmes and Lundskær-Nielsen 1995: 21–38), the learned suffixes *-a, -i* are irrelevant for our corpus and left out here, and plurals in *-s* occur only marginally in our corpus, for example in *Teletubbies* (in addition to the native form *Teletubbier*). Apart from such English loans, this leaves us with the plural suffixes zero and the two overt suffixes *a*-schwa and *e*-schwa, that is, the two neutral vowels in Danish.[9]

6. What is special for the system of oral (Eastern, thus also Viennese) Austrian German is that unstressed word-final orthographic *-er* is always realized as [ɐ] and thus falls into the cell of word-final schwa and not sonorant. Moreover, in contrast to other types of German, *-n* plurals are productive with masculines and neuters ending in *–l*. Finally, where *-s* plurals compete with other plural patterns, they are less frequent than in Northern Germany.

7. *e*-schwa is a highly assimilable central mid neutral vowel: [ə] (Basbøll 2005: 52–57) and *a*-schwa is a central retracted neutral vowel (a syllabic pharyngeal glide): [ɐ] (Basbøll 2005: 58).

8. Similar to German, the *a*-schwa plural suffix may combine with *Umlaut*, and *Umlaut* can also be the only plural marker (i.e. "combine with zero"). Although the syllable prosody *stød* plays a key role as a cue to morphological structure in Danish (cf. Basbøll 2005: 432–442), in lexical and grammatical respects parallel to tonal word accents in Swedish and Norwegian, it is disregarded in this chapter where only suffixes, not alternations of the base, are considered.

9. There exists a large discrepancy and mismatch between speech and writing in Danish, and there is scarcely any tradition for morphological analysis departing from sound (as against orthography), with the exception of the pronunciation dictionary by Brink, Lund, Heger and Jørgensen 1991: 1632-1659, noun plurals are treated on p. 1641–1645). Our morphological analysis, which departs from phonemes rather than letters, results in a completely different system from that found in the standard descriptions.

Danish has two genders, utrum (common) and neuter. The distribution of plural suffixes according to gender and sonority of the base-final phoneme is illustrated in Table 4,[10] where the native overt plural suffixes and zero are categorized according to regularity[11] in each of its eight cells (*e*-schwa does not apply to recent loans and thus does not qualify as subregular).

Table 4. Interaction of gender and sonority in Danish[12]

Sonority / Gender	Obstruent	Sonorant	Schwa	Full vowel
Neuter	Subregular: *-a-schwa, ø*	Subregular: *-a-schwa, ø*	Regular: *-a-schwa*	Subregular: *-a-schwa, ø*
	Irregular: *-e-schwa*	Irregular: *-e-schwa*	Irregular: ø	
Utrum	Subregular: *-a-schwa, ø*	Subregular: *-a-schwa, ø*	Regular: *-a-schwa*	Subregular: *-a-schwa, ø*
	Irregular: *-e-schwa*	Irregular: *-e-schwa*	Irregular: ø	

The fully mature plural system displayed in Table 4 shows no differences between the two genders in the distribution of plural suffixes according to regularity. However, it is well known from language history that zero plurals are found (relatively) more often in neuters than non-neuters in native simplex words. There are numerous unambiguous cues for the gender of the singular form of Danish nouns in the linguistic context. A number of such cues within the noun phrase are gender-specific indefinite and definite articles, definite inflectional suffixes of the noun, indefinite inflectional suffixes

10. The columns for base-final sonority of Table 4 make a distinction between glides and vowels, in agreement with the principles of Danish phonology: diphthongs are in all phonological respects VC-sequences (Basbøll 2005: 65–69), as against diphthongs in German, for example. Therefore sonorant consonants and glides are here taken together as constituting the natural sonority class of Sonorant Non-Vowels (cf. Basbøll 2005: 173–201). In relation to choice of plural suffix, *e*-schwa and *a*-schwa are so similar that they are here considered one sonority class of neutral vowels, called Schwa.

11. In addition to productivity, the distribution of plural suffixes in the lexicon has been included in our considerations, but not data from child language acquisition.

12. We gratefully acknowledge the valuable participation of Claus Lambertsen and Laila Kjærbæk Hansen in the work with the tables and on the computational tools used (the OLAM-system), and thank the latter for giving us access to her term paper *Dansk Nominalmorfologi - en empirisk undersøgelse af distributionen af pluralissufikser klassificeret ud fra et lydligt perspektiv i Child Directed Speech og skreven tekst* (University of Southern Denmark, 2006).

(including zero) of the adjective, and certain pronouns. The question is whether the child can combine information on gender (from singular forms only) with the distribution of plural suffixes, in particular zero.

Radical, partly optional, processes of sound reduction in Danish (Rischel 2003) in many cases obscure the distinction between an overt suffix and zero: for example, plural *bagere* (singular *bager* 'baker') in distinct pronunciation has a (lexicalized) agentive suffix *a*-schwa followed by a plural suffix *a*-schwa, but the difference between one *a*-schwa (in the singular) and two (in the plural) is not at all stable. Thus in reduced speech, there can be complete merger of the singular and plural form, that is, strictly speaking a "zero-plural" rather than the plural suffix *a*-schwa which is found in distinct speech.

A plural suffix in Danish may be followed by an inflectional suffix signalling definiteness and furthermore by a possessive ending (analysed as either a clitic (Herslund 2001, 2002) or an inflectional suffix), for example, *dreng, dreng-e, dreng-e-s, dreng-e-ne-s* (singular indefinite non-possessive, plural indefinite non-possessive, plural indefinite possessive, plural definite possessive of 'boy'). The fact that the plural suffix in such cases is not word-final would make it more opaque for the language acquiring child than suffixes which always occur at the end of the word (as is the case for overt plural suffixes in the other Germanic languages of this study, definite inflection being a typological characteristic of North Germanic). In the tables on Danish, all noun plurals are analysed together, whether followed by a definite and/or possessive suffix or not.

2.4 Hebrew plural formation

Hebrew is the only Semitic language to participate in this study, and thus its plural system is distinct from the other three languages under investigation here. Hebrew nouns come in two genders – masculine, taking the plural suffix *-im*, and feminine, taking the plural suffix *-ot*. All native Hebrew plurals are formed by suffixation to the final base consonant, with concurrent stress shift to the suffix,[13] for example, *tik* - *tik-ím* 'bag-s'. Singular masculine nouns are the unmarked form, ending with either a consonant or with the stressed vowel *-e* (e.g., *moré* 'teacher'). Singular feminine nouns end either with the stressed vowel *-a* (e.g., *sirá* 'boat') or with a variety of suffixes all ending with *-t*[14] (*-it* as in *sakít* 'bag'; *-ut* as in *xanút* 'shop'; *-éCet* as in *rakévet* 'train'[15]; *-ot* as in *axót* 'sister'). Nouns ending in a consonant (masculine) attach the plural suffix to the final base consonant (*xatúl* - *xatul-ím* 'cat-s'). Plural suffixation on nouns ending in stressed *-e* or *-a* replace them with the plural suffix (*moré* - *mor-ím* 'teacher-s', *sirá-sir-ót* 'boat-s'). Feminine nouns ending in *-t* delete it, attaching plural *-ot* to a *y*-final base (*sakít* – *sakiy-ót* 'bag-s').

13. Foreign stems do not undergo stress shift.

14. Spelled ת rather than ט.

15. With other allomorphic variations, such as *-áCat* (*caláxat* 'plate').

Table 5. Interaction of gender and sonority in Hebrew

Gender / Sonoriy	Masculine	Feminine
Obstruent -*t*	Subregular: -*im*, -*ot*	Regular: -*(y)ot* Irregular: -*im*
Obstruents other than -*t* and sonorants excluding -*n*	Regular: -*im* Irregular: -*ot*	Subregular: -*im*, -*ot*
Sonorant -*n*	Subregular: -*im*, -*ot*	Regular: -*im*
Unstressed -*a*	Subregular: -*im*, -*ot*	Subregular: -*im*, -*ot*
Stressed -*e*	Regular: -*im* Irregular: -*ot*	
Stressed -*a*		Regular: -*ot* Irregular: -*im*

The Hebrew-specific manifestation of the sonority scale expresses suffix regularity by the interaction of base-final segments and gender, as shown in Table 5. Masculine stems ending with non-suffixal non-deleting -*t* result in subregular patterns (*sharvit-ím* 'scepter-s', *ot-ót* 'signal-s'); while feminine stems delete suffixal -*t* yielding regular plurals (either replaced by -*y* as in *paxít* - *paxiy-ót* 'can-s'; or else, like all other plurals, directly attaching the suffix to the final consonant of the base, as in *rakévet* – *rakav-ót* 'train-s'). These are followed by masculine stems ending with all other obstruents and sonorants (excluding -*n*), yielding both regular (*pil-ím* 'elephant-s') and irregular suffixes (*kir-ót* 'wall-s'), while such feminine stems yield subregular patterns (*kos-ót* 'glass-es', *cipor-ím* 'bird-s'). Masculine stems ending in -*n* (typically -*an* and -*on*) result in subregular patterns (*xalon-ót* 'window-s', *balon-ím* 'baloon-s'), while such feminine stems (which are very scarce) yield regular -*ím* suffixation (*éven-avan-ím* 'rock-s'). Stems of both genders ending with an unstressed -*a* (e.g., masculine *c a'acúa* - *ca'acu'-ím* 'toy-s', feminine *cfardéa* - *cfarde-ím* 'frog-s') – the latter always actually ending with an underlying "guttural" or pharyngeal – also yield subregular patterns. Finally, stressed -*e* and -*a* yield both regular (masculine *moré* - *mor-ím* 'teacher-s', feminine *sirá* - *sir-ót*) and irregular patterns (masculine *mar'é* - *mar'-ót* 'sight-s' and feminine *nemalá* - *nemal-ím* 'ant-s').

3. Databases

The analyses presented here are all based on longitudinal recordings of spontaneous samples of speech input to young children and of corresponding children's output in the four languages under investigation. Below, we provide short descriptions of the four language corpora.

3.1 Dutch

The input data reported in this paper are from the Dutch corpora in the CHILDES (MacWhinney 2000) database (http://www.cnts.ua.ac.be/childes/data/Germanic/Dutch/), more specifically the input data to the children Abel, Daan, Iris, Josse, Laura, Matthijs, Niek, Peter, Sarah and Tom, providing information on speech directed to children from the age of 1;05 – 5;06.[16] The exact details concerning data collection, and transcription can be found in the CHILDES database manuals (http://www.cnts.ua.ac.be/childes/manuals/). The children's output data stem from the CHILDES' Dutch triplets corpora (Gijs, Joost, Katelijne and Arnold, Diederik, Maria) and from the unpublished Jolien corpus (Gillis 1997).

3.2 German

The German corpus consists of 137 recordings of two Austrian children aged 1;3 – 6;0 (Jan) and 1;6 – 3;0 (Katharina), audio-recorded at their homes in spontaneous interaction with their mothers. Recording intervals vary from one week (boy Jan from 1;8 – 2;11) to one month in later periods. The data were transcribed, coded and analyzed according to the CHILDES system.

3.3 Danish

The Danish corpus is a small sample of recordings from two Danish twin families, from the Odense Twin Corpus. The two pairs of twins were recorded in their homes in interaction (eating- or playing situation) with their parents or caretaker and the 28 sessions were recorded with intervals of approximately 1 month, when the children

16. Children's age ranges: Abel: 1;10 – 3;4; Daan: 1;8 – 2;3; Iris: 2;1 – 3;6; Josse: 2;0 – 3;4; Laura: 1;9 – 5;6; Matthijs: 1;10 – 3;7; Niek: 2;7 -3;1; Peter: 1;5 – 2;8; Sarah: 1;6 – 5;2; Tomas: 1;7 – 3;1.

were from age 1;1 to 2;5. The data were transcribed according to the CHILDES system and coded in the OLAM system.[17]

3.4 Hebrew

The study is based on the Berman Longitudinal Corpus, 268 audio-recordings containing naturalistic longitudinal speech samples of four Hebrew-speaking children between the ages 1;4 – 3;3.[18] Data consist of spontaneous interactions between the children and their parents. Recording took place in the children's homes, at intervals of approximately 10 days between sessions. Data were transcribed, coded, and analyzed using CHILDES (MacWhinney 2000).

3.5 General frequencies across the four data-sets

Table 6 presents the information on our four databases. Data are presented in wordforms and tokens, rather than in lemmas, since for this age group, lemmas are too few to really draw conclusions from, while wordforms indicate both lexical and inflectional growth. Also, wordforms cover singulars versus plurals, which is what we are interested in.

Table 6. General word frequencies in types and tokens across the four data-sets

Languages / Frequencies	Dutch up to 5;6	Austrian German up to 2;6	Danish up to 2;5	Hebrew up to 3;5
Number of word forms in CDS	49,554	6,382	4,384	8,275
Number of word forms in CS	11,868	2,730	1,129	4,142
Number of word tokens in CDS	1,217,341	134,629	117,617	245,384
Number of word tokens in CS	350,543	26,759	13,473	103,226

Our method will consist of identifying noun plurals and characterizing the distribution of noun plural categories in CDS directed to young children learning the four study languages, comparing these data with a similar analysis of the output of those children. We expect to find similar distributional patterns of restrictions in CDS and CS in all

17. The Olam system (developed by Claus Lambertsen, Berlin, and Hans Basbøll and Thomas O. Madsen, Odense) is partly a semi-automatic coding system, which, word by word, can supply texts in Danish orthography with phonological-/ phonetic-, morphological and segmental information; partly a system, OLAM-search, which can be used for linguistic search purposes, in particular involving phonology, morphology and their interaction.

18. Children's age ranges: Hagar (girl): 1;7–3;3; Lior (girl): 1;5–3;1; Leor (boy): 1;9–3;0; Smadar (girl): 1;4–2;4.

four languages, mediated by the typological differences between Germanic and Semitic languages, on the one hand, and by language-specific differences, on the other.

4. Plurals in child directed speech and child speech

For each language sample, we now present the following data: (i) the number of noun types and tokens in both input and output; (ii) the number of noun plurals in each of these samples, and (iii) their proportion out of all noun types and tokens. Note that we count *types* as *form types* (word forms) rather than word types (lemmas), as more appropriate for the evaluation of early lexical and grammatical development. Thus, Hebrew *tapuz* 'orange' and *tapuzim* 'oranges' would be counted as two types. Proper nouns (=names) were excluded from corpora. Table 7 presents noun and noun plural frequencies in speech directed to young children in various age ranges, up to age 6, with numbers representing the pooled data over all time points and children investigated in each language. These corpora will enable us to trace the changes in noun plural input to older preschoolers, reflecting fine-tuning patterns in parental input to children (Snow 1995).

Across our four languages, between 20% to 24% of the noun types young children are exposed to are noun plural types, while noun plural tokens constitute only between 10% to 15% of the noun tokens they hear. These crosslinguistic data indicate that young children start the route to learning about noun plurals from a small set of noun types and tokens constituting a scant percentage of the nouns they hear.

Table 7. Raw frequencies and percentages of nouns and noun plurals in CDS

Languages / **Frequencies**	**Dutch up to 5;6**	**Austrian German up to 6**	**Danish up to 2;5**	**Hebrew[19] up to 3;5**
Number of noun (form) types	8,812	4,009	1,886	2,136
Number of noun tokens	112,732	26,667	9,490	34,671
Number of noun plural (form) types	2,120	871	460	440
Percentage of plural noun (form) types (out of total noun forms)	**24**	**22**	**24**	**21**
Number of noun plural tokens	16,549	3,600	1,521	3,369
Percentage of plural noun tokens (out of total noun tokens)	**15**	**14**	**15**	**10**

19. The numbers for Hebrew plural nouns exclude dual nouns, compound nouns (*status constructus*) in the plural, and Pluralia Tantum.

Table 8. Raw frequencies and percentages of nouns and noun plurals in CS

Frequencies \ Languages	Dutch up to 3;1	Austrian German up to 2;6	Danish up to 2;5	Hebrew up to 3;5
Number of noun (form) types	2,459	916	439	1,224
Number of noun tokens	14,226	7,007	2,156	21,141
Number of noun plural (form) types	396	142	84	256
Percentage of plural noun (form) types (out of total noun forms)	**16**	**16**	**19**	**21**
Number of noun plural tokens	940	549	366	1,635
Percentage of plural noun tokens (out of total noun tokens)	7	8	17	8

Table 8 tells another interesting story, which echoes what we have just seen in the general CDS table: Young children's production of noun plurals in most cases lags somewhat behind that of the input they are exposed to. Thus, in two of our four languages (Dutch and Austrian German), children's noun plural types constitute about 16% of the total noun types, between 5–8% (one third) less than what they hear. Danish and Hebrew-speaking children produce more noun types (around 20%). While the gap between input and output observed for Dutch and German is maintained for Danish (about 5%), the Hebrew data shows no difference in the relative amount of noun plural types. One reason might be the fact that the Hebrew database comes up to age 3;5. Another might be typological – the rich morphological structures of Hebrew may entail earlier learning of morphological types. Regarding noun plural tokens, again three of our four languages show similar patterns of distribution, with about 7% plural tokens in children's output. Here, the Danish data are exceptional, with more than twice as many noun plural tokens.

4.1 Distribution of plural categories in CDS

Having outlined the kind of plural input children hear in Dutch, Austrian German, Danish, and Hebrew, and the kind of plural output they produce in these four languages, we are now ready to proceed to compare the complexity of the mature system with that of CDS and CS. Thus, we next present the distribution of suffixation categories in the speech input to children in each of the languages of our study, by sonority and gender (if the language has gender difference relevant for plural formation).

4.1.1 *Dutch*

Tables 9 and 10 present the analysis of suffix predictability in Dutch CDS. The figures for noun types are presented in Table 9 and those for tokens in Table 10. In each table the two productive suffixes (*-en*, *-s*) are represented, and the results are displayed as absolute figures and as percentages. The tables are further organized as follows: separate calculations were carried out for types and tokens regarding what proportion of the words take *-en* respectively *-s* as plural suffix. Thus, for words ending in an obstruent, there were 604 types with *-en* plural and 15 with *-s* plural, and out of 619 word types ending in an obstruent, 97.6% take *-en* as plural suffix, and only 2.4% take *-s*.

Table 9. Suffix distribution on the basis of word-final phonology: types in Dutch CDS

Sonority / Suffix	Consonant						Vowel					
	Obstruent		Sonorant				Schwa		Full vowel			
			Full vowel + sonorant		Schwa + sonorant				Final stress		Prefinal stress	
	#	%	#	%	#	%	#	%	#	%	#	%
-en	604	98	366	89	13	6	25	3	19	79	5	6
-s	15	2	44	11	209	94	730	97	5	21	72	94
N	619		410		222		755		24		77	

Table 10. Suffix distribution on the basis of word-final phonology: tokens in Dutch CDS

Sonority / Suffix	Consonant						Vowel					
	Obstruent		Sonorant				Schwa		Full vowel			
			Full vowel + sonorant		Schwa + sonorant				Final stress		Prefinal stress	
	#	%	#	%	#	%	#	%	#	%	#	%
-en	4,827	99.5	3,005	91	68	6	65	1	274	94	25	4
-s	24	0.5	296	9	1,147	94	5,862	99	18	6	668	96
N	4,851		3,301		1,215		5,927		292		693	

On the whole, the results show that the predictability of the plural suffix in CDS is very high: The token counts all reach a level of more than 90%, and also the type counts indicate predictability of more than 90% (except for one cell: words ending in a full vowel, with final stress). The most straightforward categories are words ending in an obstruent and words ending in a schwa: only the final segment determines the selection of the suffix. Especially for obstruent-final words this comes as a surprise since according to the analysis of the mature system (see section 2), the words' stress pattern plays a role: obstruent-final words with final stress take *-en* and those with penultimate stress take *-s*. However the generalization from CDS is that obstruent-final words take *-en*. Hence only one subregularity from Table 2 is actually represented in CDS. Informal observation shows that children overgeneralize the use of *-en*: *kok* 'cook' and *jeep* 'jeep' are often pluralized as *kok-en* and *jeep-en* instead of *kok-s* and *jeep-s*.

The choice of the plural suffix in sonorant-final words is also sensitive to the word's stress pattern in the adult system, according to Van Wijk (2002) 87.1% of word tokens with final stress take *-en*, and only 18.0% of word tokens with prefinal stress take *-en*). However in CDS the generalization is somewhat different: if the sonorant is preceded by a full vowel, *-en* is preferred in a majority of cases (tokens: 91%, types: 89%) and when a schwa precedes the sonorant *-s* is predominantly chosen (tokens: 94.4%, types: 94.1%).

The only category in which stress pattern appears to play a role (as in the mature system), are the words ending in a full vowel: when there is final stress, *-en* is the preferred suffix (tokens: 93.8%, types: 79.2%) and words with prefinal stress prefer *-s* (tokens: 96.4%, types: 93.5%).

4.1.2 *German*

The following tables present the analysis of suffix predictability in German CDS in terms of types (Table 11) and tokens (Table 12) up to 2;6.[20]

Table 11. Suffix distribution on the basis of item gender and word-final phonology: types in German CDS

Suffix	Gender \ Sonority	Obstruent		Sonorant		Schwa		Full vowel	
		#	%	#	%	#	%	#	%
-s	Feminine			1	4.55			3	50.00
	Masculine	3	4.92	3	5.08			8	61.54
	Neuter							11	57.89
-(e)n	Feminine	5	33.33	20	90.91	100	99.01	2	33.33
	Masculine	7	11.48	7	11.86	3	8.57		
	Neuter	4	7.84	17	26.56	2	22.22		
-e	Feminine	10	66.67	1	4.55			1	16.67
	Masculine	47	77.05	13	22.03			4	30.77
	Neuter	17	33.33	15	23.44				
-er	Feminine								
	Masculine	1	1.64	2	3.39				
	Neuter	29	56.86	4	6.25			4	21.05
zero	Feminine					1	0.99		
	Masculine	3	4.92	34	57.63	32	91.43	1	7.69
	Neuter	1	1.96	28	43.75	7	77.78	4	21.05
N		127		145		145		38	

20. The absolute numbers (both types and tokens) for plurals of nouns ending in obstruents, sonorants and schwa are very similar, which allows to roughly compare percentages in horizontal rows. This is also a reason why we did not introduce word-final sibilants (which block *-s* plural formation) as a separate category: cells for this category would contain rather small numbers but diminish the numbers of word-final obstruent cells, i.e. the numbers of obstruent-final and sonorant-final cells would differ much more.

Table 12. Suffix distribution on the basis of item gender and word-final phonology: tokens in German CDS

Suffix	Gender \ Sonority	Obstruent		Sonorant		Schwa		Full vowel	
		#	%	#	%	#	%	#	%
-s	Feminine			1	1.52			4	36.36
	Masculine	4	1.67	9	3.21			83	82.18
	Neuter							130	86.67
-(e)n	Feminine	5	10.20	64	96.97	331	99.70	5	45.45
	Masculine	32	13.39	20	7.14	15	11.63		
	Neuter	6	2.16	58	23.87	19	44.19		
-e	Feminine	44	89.80	1	1.52			2	18.18
	Masculine	194	81.17	87	31.07			17	16.83
	Neuter	43	15.47	121	49.79				
-er	Feminine								
	Masculine	1	0.42	11	3.93				
	Neuter	225	80.94	5	2.06			15	10.00
zero	Feminine					1	0.30		
	Masculine	8	3.35	153	54.64	114	88.37	1	0.99
	Neuter	4	1.44	59	24.28	24	55.81	5	3.33
N		566		589		504		262	

As in Dutch above, these percentages (calculated in the same way as in the Dutch Tables 9, 10) show clear divergences from what can be found in the German grammars and in the literature on ADS (see Köpcke 1993; Wegener 1999 with references): the plural suffix *-s* does not represent the default (as used in the respective claims by Clahsen (1999) and others cited there), because the *-s* plural is highly predictive only for masculine and neuter nouns that end in a full vowel, and its distribution depends clearly on word-final phonology (hardly discussed in the literature, except for vowels (Köpcke 1993: 128–33) and sibilants). Plurals with *-en* are much more of a default for feminines than often assumed in the literature (e.g., Clahsen 1999), not only in the sense of distributional asymmetry, but also in the sense of overall productivity, and there are clear frequency differences between masculines and neuters. The same holds for *-e* plurals, for which also dependency on word-final consonants (obstruents vs. sonorants) is a novel finding. Gender dependency of the distribution of unproductive *-er* plural formation is impressive in its novelty (more than what appears in Köpcke 1993: 39–43, 109–10) as well as the relevance of word-final consonant phonology in neuters.

The various differences between masculine and neuter gender are unexpected, because neuter and masculine inflection are generally considered to belong to the same inflectional classes (Wegener 1999). And in language usage, CDS clearly differs from the mature system in allowing much more predictability. This may also explain why children appear to acquire neuter and masculine gender inflection (Mills 1986) with no greater difficulty than feminine gender (except over-extension of the most frequent definite article form *die* 'Nom. & Acc. Sg. Fm. or Pl.'): they are confronted with much less ambiguous signals in CDS than what has been assumed so far.

The only sizable difference between types and tokens is in the much higher token frequency of *-s* plurals after full vowels of neuters. This is due to the frequent use of words like neuter *Auto-s* 'car-s' in CDS to the car-loving boy Jan and to the frequent neuter diminutives in *-i*, Pl. *-i-s*, such as *Has-i-s*, diminutive of *Hase* 'hare', a diminutive type that is restricted to CDS and early CS.

While only 3 of 12 cells in the fully mature system contain regular suffixation (Table 3), that is a clear default suffix, the table of CDS types contains a greater degree of predictability: 6 cells indicate more than 66.6% predictability of the occurrence of a suffix in a given combination of gender and phonological context, and the occurrence or non-occurrence of a given suffix or zero is highly predictable in at least 40 of 60 cells. The distribution of plural suffixation in CDS can thus be considered to represent the core of plural inflection.

If we compare the distributions in Tables 11 and 12 with the later input (of Jan up to 6;0, of Katharina up to 3;0) then we find little differences: They consist mainly in the filling of some empty slots of the earlier input, but always with very small numbers, so that predictability of non-occurrence decreases only very slightly. Furthermore, sometimes differences in percentages between competing suffixes (in terms of frequency) also decrease, which diminishes the predictability of the dominant competitor.

4.1.3 *Danish*

Table 13. Suffix distribution on the basis of item gender and word-final phonology: types in Danish CDS

Suffix	Sonority / Gender	Obstruent		Sonorant		Schwa		Full vowel	
		#	%	#	%	#	%	#	%
a-schwa	Neutrum	4	25	9	20	13	76	7	44
	Utrum	48	62	72	64	127	98	11	52
e-schwa	Neutrum	3	19	2	4	2	12	0	0
	Utrum	18	23	31	28	0	0	0	0
Zero	Neutrum	9	56	35	76	2	12	9	56
	Utrum	11	14	9	8	2	2	10	48
N		93		158		146		37	

Table 13 shows that in five out of the eight gender x sonority combinations there is relatively high predictability, more than 60%, for the occurrence of one native plural suffix[21] (either *a*-schwa or zero) – a finding which does not follow from the fully mature system displayed in Table 4. In addition, one marker (zero) in the sixth gender x sonority combination (neuters ending in an obstruent) is clearly dominant. For stems ending in a full vowel, *a*-schwa and zero are equally distributed. Only *e*-schwa (which is irregular in the system, see Table 4) is, expectedly, not dominant in any cell. For stems ending in a full vowel or schwa the degree of predictability agrees with the system. But for stems ending in an obstruent, and even more so for stems ending in a sonorant non-vowel, the predictability is clearly higher in CDS than in the system: for neuter nouns zero plurals are dominant whereas for utrum nouns *a*-schwa is dominant. This asymmetrical distribution of *a*-schwa and zero, which adds to the predictability of one suffix in a particular cell, is more clearly seen in the table of tokens, also for bases ending in a full vowel (Table 14).

Table 14. Suffix distribution on the basis of item gender and word-final phonology: tokens in Danish CDS

Suffix	Sonority / Gender	Obstruent		Sonorant		Schwa		Full vowel	
		#	%	#	%	#	%	#	%
a-schwa	Neutrum	18	25	18	11	51	61	8	13
	Utrum	134	60	208	56	370	99	65	57
e-schwa	Neutrum	3	4	4	2	20	24	0	0
	Utrum	44	20	110	29	0	0	0	0
Zero	Neutrum	50	71	140	86	13	15	53	87
	Utrum	45	20	56	15	3	1	50	43
N		294		536		457		176	

21. In our CDS corpus the plural suffix *-s* is marginally represented: In addition to the lexical exception *høns* 'hens' (cf. *høner*, '(female) hens', not in our corpus), we have *flutes* (from French *flûtes*, in Danish sometimes, like here in our corpus, pronounced with [s], unlike in French) and *Teletubbies* together with the parallel form *Teletubbier* (plural definite *Teletubbiesene* together with *Teletubbierne*, both in our corpus, cf. 2.3). Opaque plural definite forms like *indianerne* 'the Indians' (cf. 2.3) are represented, but only rarely.

4.1.4 *Hebrew*

Table 15. Suffix distribution on the basis of item gender and word-final phonology: types in Hebrew CDS

Suffix	Gender \ Sonority	Obstruent *-t*		Obstruents other than *-t* and sonorants [excluding *-n*]		Sonorant *-n*		Unstressed *-a*		Stressed *-e*		Stressed *-a*	
		#	%	#	%	#	%	#	%	#	%	#	%
-im	Masculine	4	80	208	92	13	52	12	80	4	80	–	
	Feminine	0	0	5	71	1	100	1	17	–		6	5
-ot	Masculine	1	20	18	8	12	48	3	20	1	20	–	
	Feminine	35	100	2	29	–		5	83	–		105	95
N		40		233		26		21		5		111	

In terms of gender, our CDS-sample has 271 masculine, but only 160 feminine noun types – reflecting the historical primacy of masculine *-im* suffixation in Hebrew (Schwarzwald 1983). The largest group of plural types contains nouns on the lower end of the sonority scale, ending with obstruents other than *-t* and sonorants other than *-n* (233 types in total), to which the suffix is directly attached. Table 15 reveals that, within this category, the most frequent noun plurals are masculine nouns, but also that the most frequent type of suffixation is through the application of the *-im* suffix (for both masculine and feminine nouns). In other words, the bulk of noun plurals with an obstruent or a sonorant (excluding /n/) in CDS are inflections of nouns ending with an obstruent, and under both gender conditions, it is highly predictable that such nouns will receive the suffix that is associated with masculine gender – whether such suffixation is regular or subregular in the system. That is, predictability of suffixation is a function of *base-final phonology*. Note, however, that predictability is lower for feminine nouns, in line with their subregular status. In general, these results may explain children's tendency to overgeneralize using the *-im* suffix (Berman 1981; Levy 1980, 1988).

The picture is quite different for the second largest group of noun plurals, 142 noun types ending with the most sonorous vowels as well as the sonorant /n/: For nouns ending with stressed vowels (either *-e* or *-a*), nouns marked for feminine gender consistently take the *-ot* suffix, and nouns marked for masculine gender take *-im* suffixation. And in the case of nouns ending with the sonorant /n/ (typically considered a marker of masculine gender), *-im* suffixation is somewhat more predictable, even though their status in the system is subregular. That is, when base-final phonology clearly marks gender, predictability of suffixation not only coincides but is also affected by system regularity.

The third and smallest group (61 types) is nouns ending with *-t* and unstressed *-a*, that is, nouns ending in the obstruent /t/ and in the least sonorous vowel on our scale. Here, it seems that suffixation is crucially dependent on *inherent gender*. Thus, *-im* suffixation is most predictable for masculine nouns ending with the obstruent /t/, while the *-ot* suffixation is most predictable for their counterpart feminine nouns: indeed, the overwhelming majority of nouns ending with the obstruent /t/ are feminine, as clearly shown by the higher number of types in this cell (35). Similarly, predictability of suffixation for nouns ending with an unstressed *a* vowel is also determined by gender – with an 80% chance of *-im* plurals being masculine nouns and 83% chance of *-ot* plurals being feminine nouns.

These results are not only strikingly similar but even more pronounced when considering noun plural tokens. Thus, for example, 81% of all feminine noun tokens ending with obstruents other than *-t* and sonorants other than *n* receive the *-im* suffix (as compared to 71% of the same nouns in terms of types); 96% of all nouns ending with stressed *-e* take *-im* suffixation (as compared to 80% in terms of types); predictability of *-im* suffixation for nouns ending with the sonorant /n/ is much higher (79% of all tokens as compared to 52% of all types); and for nouns ending with an unstressed *a* vowel, there's a 95% (as compared to 80%) chance of *-im* plurals being masculine nouns.

Table 16. Suffix distribution on the basis of item gender and word-final phonology: tokens in Hebrew CDS

Suffix	Gender \ Sonority	Obstruent *-t*		Obstruents other than *-t* and sonorants [excluding *-n*]		Sonorant *-n*		Unstressed *-a*		Stressed *-e*		Stressed *-a*	
		#	%	#	%	#	%	#	%	#	%	#	%
-im	Masculine	10	91	1604	92	113	79	255	95	21	96	–	
	Feminine	–		65	81	6	100	4	14	–		9	1
-ot	Masculine	1	9	150	8	30	21	13	5	1	4	–	
	Feminine	180	100	15	19	–		25	86	–		775	99
N	3278	191		1834		150		297		22		784	

Our application of the novel gender x sonority interaction to Hebrew plural suffixation has yielded two interesting insights. Firstly, it enabled us to uncover the core of the noun plural system as it is presented to children in CDS, which looks very different from the mature system: Masculine nouns have a much larger representation than do feminine nouns, and most nouns, whether masculine or feminine, take regular suffixation. Subregularities are almost absent from CDS plurals. These characteristics of the core plural system of Hebrew have never been outlined before. Secondly, our analysis also reveals that the distribution in the core system directs Hebrew-speaking children to adhere to two cues – suffixation following base-final phonology on the one hand, and suffixation following inherent gender on the other. These cues will enable them later on to untangle subregularities when the core system is extended to its more complex, mature version.

4.2 Distribution of plural categories in CS

To consider the relationship between noun plurals in the input to and output of young children, we now present the same information as in section 4 above in children's output, by sonority and gender: here we are restricted to three languages – German, Danish, and Hebrew.

4.2.1 *German*

Clear similarities and differences emerge in the comparison of the output and input in German plural marking: the *-s* plural tokens are much higher in the output, again due to Jan's predilection of *Auto-s*, *-en* plurals are more frequent in the output, reflecting their typical role in early overgeneralization (Klampfer and Korecky-Kröll 2002; Sedlak, Klampfer, Müller and Dressler 1998; Vollmann, Sedlak, Müller and Vassilakou 1997). Zero plurals are less frequent in the output: one possible reason is children's preference for iconic suffixation over non-iconic zero marking (Korecky-Kröll and Dressler in preparation). A second reason might be under-representation of zero plurals in children's output where, due to rigorous exclusion of ambiguous forms, some zero plurals may have been counted as singulars.

Table 17. Suffix distribution on the basis of item gender and word-final phonology: types in German CS up to 2;6

Suffix	Gender \ Sonority	Obstruent		Sonorant		Schwa		Full vowel	
		#	%	#	%	#	%	#	%
-s	Feminine								
	Masculine							1	25.00
	Neuter					1	25.00	7	63.64
-(e)n	Feminine			7	87.50	31	100.00		
	Masculine	6	35.29	4	19.05	2	25.00	1	25.00
	Neuter	1	6.67	5	31.25	1	25.00		
-e	Feminine	6	85.71	1	12.50				
	Masculine	10	58.82	7	33.33			1	25.00
	Neuter	6	40.00	7	43.75			1	9.09
-er	Feminine								
	Masculine			4	19.05				
	Neuter	8	53.33					2	18.18
zero	Feminine								
	Masculine	1	5.88	5	23.81	6	75.00	1	25.00
	Neuter			4	25.00	2	50.00	1	9.09
*-en+U	Feminine	1	14.29						
	Masculine			1	4.76				
	Neuter								
N		39		45		43		15	

Here, there are more empty cells in the output than in the input, which we interpret as children ignoring infrequent plural types in the input. Cases in point are *-s* plurals except after word-final full vowels and *-en* plurals after feminine nouns ending in obstruents. The greatest differences are in the distributions after word-final consonants: the children produce illegal umlauted *-en* plurals instead of feminine unproductive umlauted *-e* plurals (which are productive with masculines and neuters) or productive non-umlauted *-en* plurals. Thus they do not seem to grasp, at first, the mutual relevance of word-final phonology and gender in these distributions. After 2;6, Jan and Katharina cease to produce illegal umlauted *-en* plurals, whereas they continue to produce potential but non-existing umlauted *-e* plurals. We interpret this change as indicating that by then they have grasped an important property of core morphology.

Table 18. Suffix distribution on the basis of item gender and word-final phonology: tokens in German CS up to 2;6

Suffix	Gender \ Sonority	Obstruent		Sonorant		Schwa		Full vowel	
		#	%	#	%	#	%	#	%
-s	Feminine								
	Masculine							47	81.03
	Neuter					1	3.85	84	84.85
-(e)n	Feminine			15	93.75	91	100		
	Masculine	6	18.18	6	10.34	3	16.67	1	1.72
	Neuter	1	1.69	30	47.62	22	84.62		
-e	Feminine	25	89.29	1	6.25				
	Masculine	26	78.79	28	48.28			8	13.79
	Neuter	10	16.95	24	38.10			1	1.01
-er	Feminine								
	Masculine			8	13.79				
	Neuter	48	81.36					13	13.13
zero	Feminine								
	Masculine	1	3.03	14	24.14	15	83.33	2	3.45
	Neuter			9	14.29	3	11.54	1	1.01
*-en+U	Feminine	3	10.71						
	Masculine			2	3.45				
	Neuter								
N		120		137		135		157	

4.2.2 *Danish*

Comparing the output and the input tables we see a similar pattern in general with a distributional asymmetry after consonants between *a*-schwa and zero, depending on gender. Moreover, for nouns ending in a full vowel, zero plurals are strongly represented even in utrum nouns, in particular in token frequency (more so than in CDS).

Table 19. Suffix distribution on the basis of item gender and word-final phonology: types in Danish CS

Suffix	Gender \ Sonority	Obstruent		Sonorant		Schwa		Full vowel	
		#	%	#	%	#	%	#	%
a-schwa	Neutrum	1	33	1	17	2	67	1	33
	Utrum	7	50	11	53	24	100	4	57
e-schwa	Neutrum	0	0	0	0	1	33	0	0
	Utrum	5	36	10	48	0	0	0	0
Zero	Neutrum	2	67	5	83	0	0	2	67
	Utrum	2	14	0	0	0	0	3	43
N		17		27		27		10	

Table 20. Suffix distribution on the basis of item gender and word-final phonology: tokens in Danish CS

Suffix	Gender \ Sonority	Obstruent		Sonorant		Schwa		Full vowel	
		#	%	#	%	#	%	#	%
a-schwa	Neutrum	1	25	2	12	14	93	4	29
	Utrum	68	78	20	54	120	100	11	28
e-schwa	Neutrum	0	0	0	0	1	7	0	0
	Utrum	15	17	17	46	0	0	0	0
Zero	Neutrum	3	75	15	88	0	0	10	71
	Utrum	4	5	0	0	0	0	29	73
N		91		54		135		54	

To illustrate the pattern of productivity of the endings, we found, in a particular subcorpus[22], only one instance of an overgeneralization of the plural suffix *e*-schwa (**fiske* for the zero plural *fisk* 'fish'). In all other cases either *a*-schwa or zero were overgeneralized (e.g., **abekatter* for *abekatte* 'monkies' and **gulerød* for *gulerødder* 'carrots', respectively).

22. The subcorpus consists of one of the twin pairs in our main corpus, ages 2;6-5;8, only common nouns (1226 tokens) and proper nouns (233 tokens) are transcribed and analysed.

4.2.3 *Hebrew*

Hebrew child speech closely reproduces the system as it is presented to children in CDS. All of the phenomena described above characterize plurals produced by children: most noun plurals are masculine and take the suffix *-im*, followed by a much smaller group of feminine nouns marked by *-a* and *-t*, taking the regular feminine suffix *-ot*. Children are thus shown to faithfully adhere to the strongly predictable and regular characteristics of the Hebrew core plural system.

Table 21. Suffix distribution on the basis of item gender and word-final phonology: types in Hebrew CS

Suffix	Sonority / Gender	Obstruent *-t*		Obstruents other than *-t* and sonorants [excluding *-n*]		Sonorant *-n*		Unstressed *-a*		Stressed *-e*		Stressed *-a*	
		#	%	#	%	#	%	#	%	#	%	#	%
-im	Masculine	2	100	117	92	12	71	3	50	1	50	–	
	Feminine	1	6	5	83	1	100	1	25	–		7	11
-ot	Masculine	–		10	8	5	29	3	50	1	50	–	
	Feminine	16	95	1	17	–		3	75	–		60	89
N	249	19		133		18		10		2		67	

Table 22. Suffix distribution on the basis of item gender and word-final phonology: tokens in Hebrew CS

Suffix	Sonority / Gender	Obstruent *-t*		Obstruents other than *-t* and sonorants [excluding *-n*]		Sonorant *-n*		Unstressed *-a*		Stressed *-e*		Stressed *-a*	
		#	%	#	%	#	%	#	%	#	%	#	%
-im	Masculine	5	100	783	92	79	87	77	92	1	50	–	
	Feminine	1	1	48	98	7	100	2	23	–		16	4
-ot	Masculine	–		72	8	12	13	7	8	1	50	–	
	Feminine	69	99	1	2	–		7	77	–		349	96
N	1267	75		904		98		93		2		95	

5. General discussion

Our study has focused on noun plural formation, a central area of inflectional morphology, as transmitted by care-takers to young children from birth to the middle of their third year of life. For each of the four languages we investigate – Dutch, Austrian German, Danish, and Hebrew – we have shown two important and novel findings. First, we have shown that quantitatively, children's plural output is closely paced by the input they receive. The amount of noun plurals in speech addressed to children is rather low – about 20% of all noun types and 10% of noun tokens are plural (increasing to about 23% and 14% respectively in CDS of the two Austrian children of this study); and this ratio is closely echoed by the ratio of noun plurals in the output of those very children exposed to the speech we analyzed: about 16% plural types and 7% plural tokens, rising to 17,5% (types) and 11,8% (tokens) of the Austrian children in the period 2;7 – 3;0. This is the first time such a close quantitative relationship has been shown to exist between input and output of plurals.

A second major finding of this paper is qualitative, and provides a first window on what we term *core morphology*. Section 1 discussed the complex interface of gender and sonority in determining suffix predictability, while in section 2 we demonstrated specifically how this interface generates the complex plural systems of the three Germanic languages and the Semitic language under consideration. Examining the distribution of noun plurals in the longitudinal data of children and their caregivers, our second novel finding is to what extent the complex full adult plural systems described in section 2 above differs from the systems presented to children in the distribution of nouns in the cells created by the intersection of sonority and gender. In all four languages, our analyses reveal surprising distributions when compared to the fully mature systems. We have found, for all four languages, that plural suffixes directed to children are much more predictable and regular than in the fully mature systems, while regularities are given salient, prominent proportions and therefore support children's first forays into the system.

The Dutch analysis thus shows that plural suffixes in CDS are very highly predictable, and that final segments determine suffix selection much more than does the stress pattern. Only one subregularity (out of three) is represented as default/clearly dominant for Dutch in each phonological environment. In the same way, the German analysis resulted in novel findings regarding each of the plural suffixes, showing that *-en* or *-e* plurals rather than *-s* plurals are the default whenever there is a clear dominance of one suffix, links with word-final phonology in *-e* plurals, and interesting interactions with gender. Again, as in Dutch, suffix predictability pervades the child directed system. In Danish, zero plurals and *a*-schwa plurals after consonants seem to have a more complementary distribution, dependent on gender, and thus a higher predictability, in CDS than in the adult mature system. The complex Hebrew plural system is reduced in CDS mostly to masculine nouns predictably taking the masculine *-im* plural suffix, with regular suffixation of both masculine and feminine nouns. All of these qualitative patterns are echoed in children's output as analyzed in our work.

5.1 CDS compared with adult directed speech (ADS)

While the difference between the plural systems described in section 2 and CDS is eminently clear, it does not represent a difference between the speech directed to children versus the speech directed to adults. In order to gain an insight into the regularities of plural formation in adult directed speech (as opposed to child directed speech), and more specifically in order to compute the predictability of the plural suffixes in ADS, we needed to consult a database of spoken adult usage. Of the four languages under investigation, only Dutch has such an appropriate corpus. The Spoken Dutch Corpus[23] was consulted. This corpus of approximately 10 million words of contemporary spoken Dutch, collected around the turn of the 21st century, consists of a variety of discourse types (spontaneous conversations, face-to-face as well as over the telephone, lectures, radio and television broadcasts, etc.), which is stratified socially as well as geographically. Due to legal restrictions, the participants were all at least 18 years of age. Hence, this corpus is a genuine sample of adult directed spoken language.

The corpus is completely part of speech tagged and thus represents a rich source of data. 998,046 tokens of nominals were identified (excluding proper nouns), representing a rough 10% of the entire corpus, of which 213,699 (21.4%) nominal plural tokens (23,319 plural types). The distribution of the suffixes is as follows: 59.6% of all types take *-en*, 38.8% take *-s*, 0.4% take *-eren* and 1.2% take another suffix. And for tokens: 71.6% *-en*, 25.3% *-s*, 2.3% *-eren*, and 0.7% another suffix. The latter two categories will not be considered in what follows.

When we compute the distribution of the plural suffixes according to the phonological form of the singular, similar to Tables 9 and 10 for CDS, it appears that plural formation is highly predictable in ADS. Figures 1 (types) and 2 (tokens) compare the predictability of the plural suffix *-en* in Dutch ADS and CDS according to the form of the final rhyme.

23. http://www.tst.inl.nl/cgndocs/doc_English/start.htm

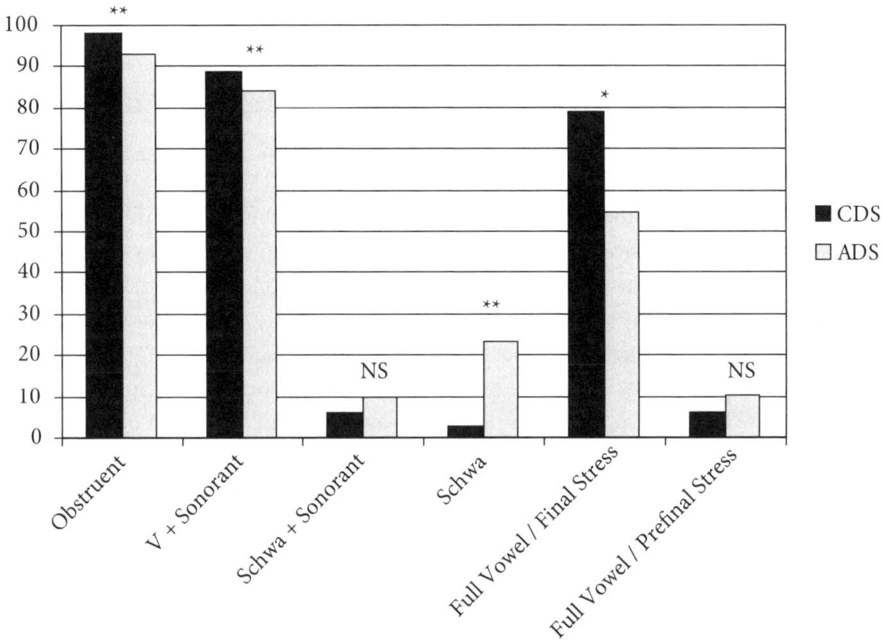

Figure 1. Predictability of the plural suffix *-en* in Dutch ADS and CDS according to the form of the final rhyme (word types)

Figure 1 clearly shows that in ADS the suffix *-en* (and consequently also the suffix *-s*) is indeed highly predictable, yet is slightly less predictable than in CDS. For instance, word types ending in an obstruent take *-en* as a suffix in 97.6% of the cases in CDS, while in only 93.0% of the cases in ADS (the levels of statistical significance are indicated in Figure 1: ** = $p<0.01$, * = $p<0.05$, NS = $p>0.05$). It appears that except for two categories of words for which the difference is only marginally significant, plural formation in ADS is significantly less predictable than in CDS. In other words, while predictability of the suffix is high in adult speech, it is even higher in CDS.

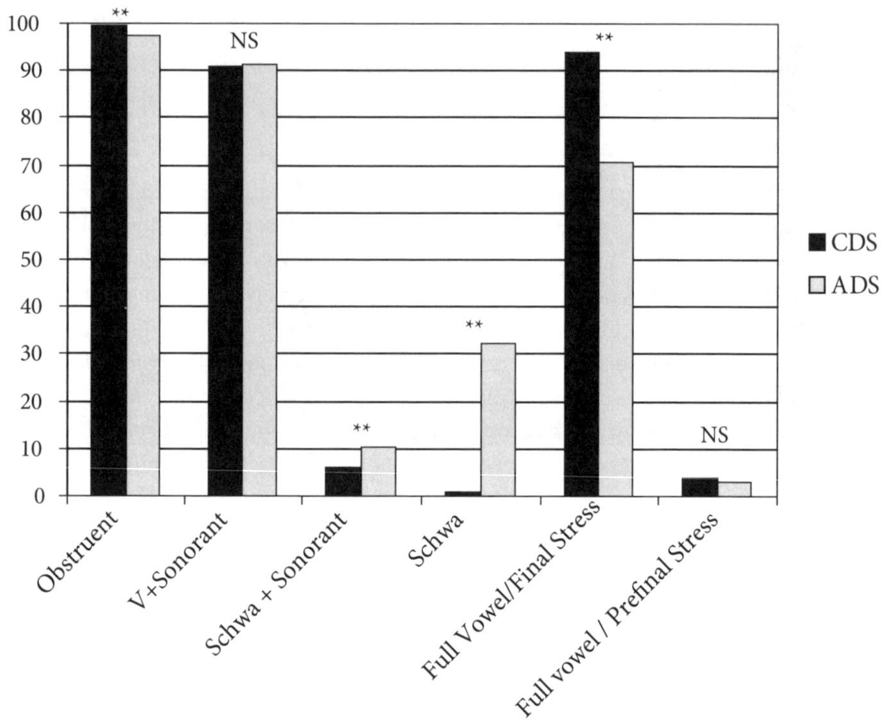

Figure 2. Predictability of the plural suffix *-en* in Dutch ADS and CDS according to the form of the final rhyme (word tokens)

In terms of word tokens, Figure 2 shows, again, that the predictability of the plural suffix is particularly high for all kinds of words. And yet again, CDS is even more predictable than ADS, except for two classes of words, viz. words ending in a full vowel plus a sonorant, and words ending in a full vowel that have prefinal stress. But the difference in predictability between CDS and ADS is not statistically significant for those categories.

Note that the major differences in predictability are to be found in words ending in a schwa and words ending in a full vowel with final stress. The latter category is not surprising: Dutch words ending in a full vowel are typically loans from Romance origin, which are not part of the CDS register. Words ending in a schwa are typically part of CDS, however, while a great majority of these words are diminutivized nouns in CDS (Gillis 1997), the proportion of diminutives is much lower in ADS: in our corpus of ADS only 5% of all nouns are diminutivized, and only 1% of all nouns are pluralized diminutives.

We have thus shown that under the same circumstances of production (speech), CDS has enhanced predictability compared with ADS. While this has been shown so far only for Dutch, we expect future analyses of spoken corpora in other languages to reveal the same results.

5.2 Typological perspectives

As expected from our previous work (Stephany 2002; Laaha and Gillis 2007), morphological language typology has an impact on the acquisition of core morphology via input to young children. Thus greater morphological richness has been found to stimulate children to acquire inflectional morphology more rapidly than a poorer morphological input system. As Gillis and Ravid (2006) demonstrate, children growing up in a language with a rich morphology carry over such morphologically based strategies even to written language.

If neither gender nor word-final phonology conditions the choice of plural suffixation, as is the case in Turkish, or when word-final phonology predicts plural allomorphy in a purely phonological way, as in English, we do not expect any morphological difference between CDS and ADS. When word-final phonology but not gender conditions the selection of plural suffixes in a phonologically arbitrary way, as in Dutch, then core morphology has been found to be more predictive than the adult system, due to more and stronger asymmetries in the distribution of plural suffixes. When, in addition to word-final phonology, overt gender differences are relevant for the selection of plural suffixes, then CDS also contrasts genders in a more predictive way, as in Danish and in Hebrew with its richer morphology. When even three genders are distinguished, as in German, then CDS even differentiates masculine and neuter gender in its impact on plural suffixation beyond the adult system. We would expect similar phenomena in Slavic languages, where the inflectional morphology of neuters and masculines is very similar as well. In Laaha and Gillis (2007) we established that the richer adult morphology, the speedier children tend to acquire it. A related effect has been found in this study, namely that Hebrew, with the richest morphology of our languages, appears to stimulate children to produce the highest percentage of plural types.

6. Conclusions

Input plurals, as identified and analyzed in this work, have been found to be simpler, more predictable and thus easier to acquire than the adult systems of plural formation as described in grammars. Plural formation in CDS is generally simpler than in the adult system in avoiding learned plurals and alternative plural variants of the same lexical entry or with the same base phonology. Third and most important, the dependence of the distribution of plural suffixation on gender and on the phonology of the right edge of lexical bases is much more predictable in CDS than follows from adult grammar.

Where do these differences come from? What is the source of the discrepancy between the full adult systems characterized with much irregularity and unpredictability, on the one hand, and the simpler, more regular and more predictable plurals addressed to children, on the other? More data and more analyses are needed to answer this question following the novel findings revealed in this crosslinguistic study. However, we can already point at some directions. It makes sense that singular and plural nouns occurring in the speech directed to children mostly refer to those concrete objects in the child's vicinity which are perceptually salient. Finally, the plurals used in CDS might reveal strong statistical tendencies inherent in each of the languages under investigation, in a sense, the core of each system, which is expanded and elaborated in later language development. Thus in the future, it remains to be investigated to what extent the pragmatic and semantic character of plural nouns addressed to children is related to their formal inflectional features.

Learning the English auxiliary

A usage-based approach*

Elena Lieven

1. Introduction

In general, English-speaking children start to produce utterances with auxiliaries and other complement-taking verbs around the beginning of their third year of life. However productive flexibility with a range of auxiliaries takes well over a year and production of the full range of modals, *wh*-questions and complements usually only occurs during the fourth year. Command of auxiliary syntax is often seen as reflecting relatively mature grammatical development. Compared to the learning of NP and verb argument structures, auxiliaries are, on the one hand, often thought of as relatively semantically 'empty' but on the other, they are centrally involved in the operations of negation (*I saw him, I didn't* [*=did not*] *see him*), modality (*I saw him, I might have seen him*), inversion (*You can see him, Can you see him*), tense (*I saw him, I have seen him*) and agreement (*I am going, You are going*). There are two groups: main auxiliaries: BE[1], HAVE and DO and modal auxiliaries e.g., CAN, WILL, MIGHT. In some contexts the auxiliaries can be cliticized: e.g., *I've seen him, I'll do it and* negation can be contracted: *We aren't going to school, I can't see him.* Other multi-verb constructions contain 'semi-auxiliaries', e.g., *want to (wanna), got to (gotta), have to (hafta).*

* Many thanks to Shanley Allen, Heike Behrens, Caroline Rowland, Anna Theakston and Michael Tomasello for their comments on an earlier draft of the paper. I am also very grateful to Helen Dresner-Barnes and Graeme Hutcheson who, with me, collected the data for the main study and to Silke Brandt and Roger Mundry for their help with some of the data analysis, and to Henriette Zeidler for help with formatting, layout and so much else. My intellectual debt for the ideas underlying this project is so great and reaches over so many years that I will confine myself to thanking Michael Tomasello in Leipzig and my colleagues on the 'Manchester' corpus: Julian Pine, Caroline Rowland and Anna Theakston. Finally, the biggest debt of gratitude goes to the children and their families who allowed us into their homes, all for at least a year. Data collection was funded by a University of Manchester research support grant and, for the Manchester corpus, by ESRC grants: R000236393 and R000237911.

1. Verb and auxiliary lemmas are in CAPS.

There is a long history in linguistic theory of attempts to capture the facts of English auxiliary syntax (Akmajian, Steele and Wasow 1979; Chomsky 1957; Gazdar, Pullum and Sag 1982; Huddleston 1980; Warner 1993). This is not an easy task since each auxiliary and its subforms patterns somewhat differently. In turn this makes the learning of the auxiliary system particularly interesting since children must learn the particular forms lexically, but they also clearly must and do, make generalizations across them. Most research on the development of the auxiliary system has focussed on the later stages when these generalizations start to occur and are applied to more complex constructions. In this paper, however, I examine the early stages of auxiliary learning using longitudinal corpora from children between 2;0 and 3;2 with a view to investigating the precursors to these later stages. The major issue in all studies of language development, whether experimental or corpus-based, is when and how children become productive with a structure. As we shall see, assessing productivity and its scope is central to this chapter as it is to this whole volume, and, of course, interacts crucially with the question of sampling.

1.1 The early stages of English auxiliary development

There is considerable agreement in the literature on the overall characteristics of auxiliary learning (Bloom, Lightbown and Hood 1975; Klima and Bellugi 1966; Pinker 1984; Richards 1990; Valian 1991):

- Early multiword speech contains no overt auxiliaries though main verbs are present.
- The earliest auxiliaries are likely to be unanalysed (e.g., *can't* and *don't*), both in the sense that they may only appear with one main verb (e.g., *(I) can't do it, (I) don't want it)* and in the sense that children do not have any other forms of these auxiliaries.
- Once children start producing utterances containing auxiliaries, there is a long period in which the auxiliary forms that the child can produce are also frequently omitted.
- There are relatively few errors of commission.
- When errors do occur they mainly involve the more complex processes of *do*-support, inversion and the coordination of tags.

1.2 Generativist accounts of auxiliary development[2]

From a linguistic point of view, the important characteristic of auxiliaries is that they act as a landing site for tense and agreement and interact with negation. The generativist assumption is that children possess the relevant linguistic abstractions from which

2. I use 'generativist' to cover theories that argue that sentences are generated by algorithmic operations on highly abstract symbols.

they can work out how the language they are learning does this (Hyams 1994). On this account, the difficulties that English-speaking children have are with the specific features of English. Thus Santelmann, Berk, Austin, Sosmashekar and Lust (2002) suggest that children should have no problem with auxiliaries in declaratives or with structures that are clearly inverted; only the workings of DO-support should cause errors. The assumption that children have the relevant linguistic abstractions from the outset has given rise to research suggesting that children make linguistically important distinctions relating to auxiliaries as a class from very early on. For instance, Stromswold (1990) argues that children distinguish between BE as a main verb and BE as an auxiliary from the outset and Valian (1991) suggests a very early general category of modals. These authors point to the lack of errors of commission as evidence for the abstract nature of children's early linguistic knowledge.

In the most detailed attempt to work out a generativist account that incorporates language-specific learning, Pinker (1984) analyses auxiliaries as complement-taking verbs with defective paradigms. He suggests that children probabilistically categorize an element as expressing the substantive universal, +AUX, when they identify it as showing a set of properties of which containing elements expressing tense and/or modality and consisting of a small, fixed non-productive set are two. Once an item is recognized as an auxiliary by virtue of these and other universal properties, the child actively searches for other forms. "All verbs including auxiliary verbs enter into paradigms with a dimension differentiating infinitival, participial and finite forms crossed with a dimension differentiating neutral, inverted, negated and emphatic sentence modalities" (Pinker 1984: 285). According to Pinker, the child bootstraps into these paradigms through semantic and pragmatic sensitivity and knowledge. Thus the child notices that temporal reference is undefined on the complement verb form and marks it as non-finite, yielding co-occurrence restrictions for the associated auxiliary. In addition, since children can already determine the illocutionary force of an utterance, they can discover that this is coded on the auxiliary and in its placement.

While there are a number of problematic features of this theory – in particular the precise ways in which innate predispositions, semantic bootstrapping and performance constraints are invoked to deal with particular issues, the idea that children come to treat auxiliaries as complement-taking verbs and that they learn the co-occurrence restrictions with different forms of the complement and, later, with other auxiliaries, in part through using prior semantic-pragmatic knowledge of sentence modality, makes a lot of sense. My reservations relate to precisely what has to be postulated as both innate and specifically syntactic. The main difference between this and the usage-based, constructivist approach taken by myself and my colleagues is that we see this knowledge as arrived at by abstraction from the actual use of language, rather than as pregiven (Lieven, Behrens, Speares and Tomasello 2003; Rowland and Pine 2000; Theakston, Lieven, Pine and Rowland 2002; Tomasello 2003).

1.3 Usage-based approaches

In usage-based theory, utterances are strings of speech for getting things said and understood. From these usage events, children build up an inventory of utterance-level constructions and sub-utterance constructions (for instance, the 'noun phrase' and morphological constructions). Each identified construction has a meaning or function which can change over development. Constructions can range from being item-specific to fully schematic and this is also true of the adult construction inventory. The difference between young children's inventories and those of adults is one of degree: many more, initially all, of children's constructions are either fully item-specific or contain relatively low scope slots, for instance for a category of referents. As well as being less schematic than many adult constructions, they are also simpler with fewer parts. And, finally, children's constructions exist in a less dense network – they are more 'island-like'.

A crucial distinction, developed by Bybee (1995) in the context of accounting for diachronic changes in inflectional morphology, is between token and type frequency. Token frequency entrenches the comprehension and use of concrete pieces of language – items and phrases (collocations). For instance, many children learning English often produce *What's that?* very early, presumably because adults use it to them with high frequency. But children will certainly not have mastery of the internal structure of this utterance nor, necessarily, of the full adult meaning – they have learned the utterance as a whole as a result of its salience and frequency and use it for their own communicative ends. Type frequency, on the other hand, promotes generalization by demonstrating to the learner that within the context of 'the same' construction, different concrete items may serve the same function (at the level of either the whole construction or some of its constituents). Thus, another very early *wh*-question produced by children is **Where's X gone?** [3] where *X* is substitutable by a range of referents – for some children, only animate, for others, also including object referents. This is also a highly frequent question in the input but adults use a wide variety of referring expressions with it. As a result, while some children may start with a fully item-specific construction, for example, *Where's Daddy gone?*, almost all children so far studied rapidly produce the construction with a slot for referents (Dąbrowska and Lieven 2005). So the difference between token and type frequency is between entrenching specific words or phrases and creating slots in which a range of words or phrases can occur.

As children's grammar develops, they add constructions to their inventory that are increasingly complex (with more parts) and increasingly abstract (in the scope of the slots) (Dąbrowska 2000; Tomasello 2003). It is important to note that children are capable of abstraction from the beginning of language. From the moment that a child is able to name a set of non-identical objects using the same label, they are already making an abstraction. What changes over development is the scope of the abstraction. Equally, as soon as a child uses a construction with a slot, they are being productive

3. Frames are in bold with X for the slot. Utterances are italicized.

– and many of these early constructions can be highly productive. Some constructions rapidly develop slots into which a range of items can be placed – these constructions are then partially schematic with fixed lexical material as well as slots (e.g., **I wanna** X). If the child can insert a novel item into the slot, this is evidence that a form-function abstraction has been made and schematization has occurred. While schematization may be confined initially to one construction, it may also generalize to others: the early development of a relatively abstract 'noun' category is an example of this (Tomasello, Akhtar, Dodson and Rekau 1997). In time, the child will learn to express communicative functions (e.g., reference, foregrounding and backgrounding) in increasingly complex ways.

A central feature of this account is that a child may go through a stage of partial representations. Partial representations occur when the child regularly produces a correct form for some items but not for others which are probably closely related in adult grammars. This can be caused either by the fact that the correct constructions are still of rather low scope and/or because they are competing with other, earlier learned constructions which are incorrect (for instance **I X-ing** vs. **I'm X-ing**). Verb and pronoun-island phenomena are examples (McClure, Pine and Lieven 2006; Tomasello and Abbot-Smith 2002). Another example is a study of children's omission of auxiliary HAVE and BE. Theakston and colleagues showed that rates of provision of these auxiliaries varied for different subject-auxiliary combinations (Theakston and Lieven 2005; Theakston, Lieven, Pine and Rowland 2005). Thus the children did not, as yet, show system-wide knowledge of the auxiliary as a 'landing site' for tense and agreement. As children's item-based strings become more schematic, the degree of schematicity of parts of constructions can also vary between constructions and between children. Thus one child might have a **It's V-ing** construction while another has a more schematic slot for subjects: **NP's V-ing.**[4]

Two crucial aspects of the usage-based approach are demonstrated by the Theakston *et al.* study (2005). First is the importance of analysing the precise nature of the relationship between what children produce and what they hear. When measured at the level of lexical form, in terms of particular more or less lexically-specific subject-auxiliary combinations (e.g., *he's, they've, proper name's*) there is a statistically close relationship between children's rate of provision of these combinations and their relative frequency in the input. Secondly, while, in the usage-based approach, the particular characteristics of the input are crucial to learning, they interact with other factors including the child's current system, the salience of the form in the input and children's own communicative interests. In this study these close relationships to the input did not apply to all constructions: in particular children showed some independence of input frequencies which could be related to either the phonological salience of the auxiliary form or the semantics of the frame – the children were more interested in

4. NP = noun V = verb

talking about themselves than others – and this affected the rate of provision for constructions with *I* and *you*.

1.4 Different approaches to accounting for children's auxiliary errors

Let me exemplify some of the differences between these two approaches by briefly considering accounts of auxiliary omission and of errors in children's production of auxiliaries. Of course, all researchers agree that it is important to establish that a child has learned the particular form and can produce it. The difference comes in what this means about the place of that form in a more abstract underlying representation. In UG accounts, all or most of the linguistic abstraction is present innately. One approach, therefore, is to treat the presence of a form as evidence of the underlying abstract category. Thus Valian cites the lack of distributional errors other than omission as evidence of the 'genuine' status of the modal category in very young children (1;10 – 2;8) and argues that 'any present criterion beyond initial correct use appears arbitrary' (Valian 1991: 10). For her, errors of omission are the result of performance limitations (for instance on the length of utterances).

An alternative way of accounting for errors of omission is in terms of maturation. The various proposals of Wexler's theories (the Optional-Infinitive Stage, the Agreement-Tense Omission Model, the Unique Checking Constraint: Schütze and Wexler (1996); Wexler (1998); Wexler, Schütze and Rice (1998)) also postulate that children know about abstract tense and agreement innately. However omission is not seen as a performance error but as a systematic reflection of a lack of maturation in the underlying system: the failure to realize that tense and agreement are both obligatory.

Finally a third, and not mutually exclusive, way of dealing with errors, both of commission and omission, is to suggest that children have difficulties with adapting UG to the specificities of the language that they are learning. An example comes from the well-attested errors of commission that English-speaking children make with interrogative syntax. A number of theories predict differences in error rates as a function of particular linguistic structures: for instance copula BE and sentences involving DO-support in *yes/no*-questions (Santelmann *et al.* 2002); or adjunct as opposed to argument questions (DeVilliers 1991; Valian, Lasser and Mandelbaum 1992) for example.

While UG theories do not explicitly rule out the possibility that provision might be different for different auxiliaries or different forms of the same auxiliary (Rice, Wexler and Hershberger 1998), the fact that this is the case (Ambridge, Rowland, Theakston and Tomasello 2006; Kuczaj and Brannick 1979; Pine, Conti-Ramsden, Joseph, Lieven and Serratrice 2008; Rowland, Pine, Lieven and Theakston 2005) requires add-on assumptions about performance which are usually not specified, making it difficult to test the proposals. In fact, most UG approaches do not distinguish between different forms of the same auxiliary, treating them as lemmas in their analyses (e.g., BE, CAN). By contrast, usage-based approaches start from the actual form and attempt to relate this to what the child is hearing. More schematic and abstract categories are only postulated when there is evidence for them.

An example comes from a study that investigated auxiliary BE omission in declaratives which were elicited following either a question or a declarative model (Theakston and Lieven 2008). This showed that, when producing declaratives, children exposed to questions tend to omit forms of auxiliary BE more often than those exposed to declaratives. Thus low rates of auxiliary provision may arise in part from the very high number of questions addressed to children, in which the subject is followed by a non-finite verb. Here, then, the learning of a high-frequency string may lead to errors of omission.

Another example comes from the well-attested errors of commission that English-speaking children make with question syntax. Although these have frequently been explained, as noted above, in terms of relatively abstract structures, children are significantly less likely to make errors with question frames that are frequent strings in the input (Rowland 2007; Rowland and Pine 2000). Thus the learning of high frequency strings can also protect the child from error in parts of the system. The important point is to start from the lexical form: treating different lexical forms in terms of adult grammatical categories can disguise major differences in the rates of error found with different forms (Aguado-Orea 2004; Aguado-Orea and Pine 2005; Pine, Rowland, Lieven and Theakston 2005).

1.5 Productivity

At the heart of the difference between these two approaches is the degree of abstraction in the child's grammar and whether this is present *ab initio* or develops. The issue of how to measure productivity and its scope is therefore crucial. In experimental studies, this can be done by asking children to generalize from one form to another, related form. However experiments have their limitations, especially when they involve production with very young children. There are also major interpretative problems when considering the results of preferential looking studies and their relationship to how best to characterize the representations that children have available. Thus there is a long tradition of corpus-based longitudinal research, particularly between the ages of 1;6 to 4;0, the period of early language acquisition during which auxiliaries start to be produced and the system becomes established.

Most researchers working with corpus data have always been aware of the problem of assessing productivity (see, for instance, Allen and Crago 1996; Brown 1973; Kuczaj and Maratsos 1983). It is clear that whether a particular criterion for productivity can, in principle, be achieved depends on the frequency with which the child's utterances are sampled (Tomasello and Stahl 2004; Rowland, Fletcher and Freudenthal this volume). How do the issues of sampling and productivity interact with previous research on auxiliary development?

In many linguistically-based studies, productivity is seen as an all-or-none matter: utterances are either rote-learned and, therefore, irrelevant to the development of the auxiliary as a grammatical category, or fully productive. From a UG perspective it is therefore crucial to exclude these unproductive forms. However, how they are treated varies between studies. Different researchers include or exclude particular forms in their analyses, often without objective criteria for doing so. Thus both Bellugi (1967) and Hyams (1986) treat *can't* and *don't* as unanalysed while Stromswold (1990) and Pinker (1984) include these forms in their analyses but exclude all contracted auxiliaries (e.g., *I'm*, *it's*). On the other hand, Valian (1991), as noted above, while recognising that forms may be rote-learned, decides that it is not possible to tell, so treats initial correct use of modals as an indication of abstract knowledge.

Many researchers with more empirically based approaches (e.g., Bloom *et al.* 1975; Kuczaj and Maratsos 1983) also noted that early auxiliaries may be unanalysed and have attempted to develop criteria for assessing productivity. This has usually involved either the number of different verbs occurring with a particular auxiliary lemma and/or the number of different forms of a particular auxiliary that a child uses.

The most systematic attempt to develop criteria for establishing the presence of an abstract auxiliary class is that of Richards (1990). He followed 7 children for about nine months, recording for 45 minutes every 3 weeks from a point where auxiliaries only occurred very rarely "in a few stereotyped phrases" (Richards 1990: 30) In his conclusions, Richards identified considerable problems with each of the criteria normally used to assess the presence of an auxiliary system (see also Jones (1996) for a comparison of different methods of defining productivity).

- A count of the number of different auxiliary forms can easily under- or over-estimate the child's knowledge, unless information about the sequence of development of these forms and the range of contexts in which they are used is also considered.
- The frequency of auxiliary use also runs the danger of failing to discriminate between stereotyped and genuinely diverse usage.
- A measure of the cumulative range of forms has the same problem.
- Presence in obligatory contexts runs the danger of under-estimating the child's knowledge since 'optionality' or 'omission' of auxiliaries continues for a very long period.
- Correct use of tags matched with a matrix clause is more than sufficient to identify the presence of an auxiliary class but Richards also points out the danger of over-estimating the child's knowledge (if children have a small repertoire of not fully productive tags) or of under-estimating it, since fully productive tags are a very late development for many children.

An important point to note is that all of these possible criteria interact with the level of sampling. Highly frequent forms will be picked up more often and one may have to sample for longer to pick up the less frequent forms. Thus it is possible that what looks like an order of emergence actually reflects frequency sampling (Palmer 1965; Tomasello and Stahl 2004). We will return to this issue in the discussion however the main conclusions of Richards' study were that, after nine months, less than half the children had produced tokens of all 4 of the NICE properties associated with the central class of auxiliaries (N=negation I=inversion C=code (ellipsis) E=emphasis).[5] Richards found that rapid development in one part of the system contrasted with piecemeal development in other parts. While the auxiliary seemed to be well established in declarative utterances by the time recordings ceased after 9 months, it was much less clearly part of a wider syntactic system and the children manifested considerable variation in the range of forms that they used and in the overlap between the verbs used with these different forms. Richards concluded that children develop a particular class of operators for each of the NICE functions rather than for the auxiliary class as a whole. While this detailed study made it clear that auxiliary development was piecemeal, slow to achieve any generality across the auxiliary system and, to some extent, differed between children, it was not set within a theoretical context that allowed these results to be easily interpreted.

From a usage-based perspective, however, productivity is a continuum from fully item-specific constructions through to fully abstract constructions and these latter depend on the former. It is therefore important to adopt an analysis that allows us to track the development of productivity from full lexical-specificity, through partial productivity to full schematicity. While auxiliaries are complex syntactically, many constructions in which they occur are semantically and pragmatically important to children and they start producing some forms relatively early in multi-word speech (e.g., *I don't know, I can't do it*). I am therefore interested in tracing whether, how and when these early, and almost certainly lexically-specific constructions become (a) more schematic and (b) part of a wider group of interconnecting constructions.

2. The present study

To investigate this I define frames around the lexical forms of different auxiliaries and trace their development in terms of the schematicity of the subject and verb slots with which they occur. The build-up of frames is measured cumulatively across recording sessions. While each instance of an utterance with a particular auxiliary form could have been learned as a whole, how frequently a particular auxiliary is used with the same or another verb will be a function of a wide range of factors. In a usage-based approach, utterances with the same forms are likely to be more closely associated than utterances with different forms, and this will lead over time to the development of a

5. This terminology was, I think, initiated by Palmer (1965). Negation and Interrogation are transparent terms in this context. Code refers to the role of the auxiliary in main verb ellipsis and Emphasis to the role of the stressed auxiliary for contradiction or contrastive emphasis.

schematic slot for the verb. Thus there seems no particularly good reason, in this approach, to limit the identification of a frame to within a recording session. Below I outline a number of measures used to explore the reality of these constructions in the child's grammar and to address the question of how they develop and become part of a more interconnected system. I take up the issue of their psychological reality again in the Discussion.

The study is of 6 children's auxiliary development between 2;0 – 3;0. For the reasons outlined below comparisons of maternal speech could not be made across mother-child dyads but I do use another sample of CDS to children from the same locality to draw some tentative conclusions about the relationship between the relative frequency of auxiliary constructions in the input and children's own production of auxiliaries.

2.1 Method

2.1.1 *Participants*

These are six of the twelve children whose language development was reported in Lieven, Pine and Dresner Barnes (1992). The other six children did not produce enough utterances with auxiliaries to make the analysis possible. The children were aged 1;0 at the start of the original study, although none of them produced utterances containing auxiliaries or semi-auxiliaries until they were just about 2;0. The study was completed as they reached 3;0. Three were boys (Charles, Ivan and Les) and three girls (April, Kathy and Mavis). The original aim of the study was to investigate individual differences between the children. To this end, we made an effort to recruit families who came from a wider range of backgrounds than has been typical in most longitudinal studies of language development. These have tended to collect data from very middle-class households and often only from first-born children (thus avoiding the problem of recording with a second child around). By contrast half the children in our study were not first-born and, with one exception, their families ranged from working class to lower middle class as defined by the Registrar-General's classification (Office of Population Censuses and Surveys 1970). As a result, and particularly with some of the mothers, the investigators talked more to the children than is usual in these studies and there were very varying amounts of maternal speech to the children in the recordings.

2.1.2 *Data collection*

Visits to the families took place approximately every three weeks depending on the child's level of language development. By the time the children were 1;6, audio tape-recordings were made on each visit. During these sessions the researchers behaved as participant observers while attempting to 'leave the floor' to the child as much as possible. In order not to make the situation feel uncomfortable, we did not insist that mothers stayed in the room with the child during the whole recording session. While some did, others relatively frequently availed themselves of the opportunity of the investigator's presence to leave the room and to carry on with household tasks.

In what follows each session has been assigned to a month dated from the child's birth date for ease of comparison across children. Sessions occurring in the first 15 days of the month were assigned to the current month and those occurring in the last 15 days to the next month. Occasionally this resulted in two sessions falling into one month.

2.2 Utterances and frames

Each transcript was searched for every utterance containing a multiple verb structure excluding immediate imitations of another speaker that were either exact or reduced, and immediate self-repetitions that were either exact or reduced. Only utterances that had an expressed auxiliary were counted. Copulas were excluded from quantitative analyses as were ellipted utterances and/or tags without auxiliaries in the matrix, though these two latter categories will be considered below. Table 1 presents summary data for the 6 children.

Table 1. Number of multi-verb utterances

Child	N multiverb utterances	N with auxiliaries*
April	378	292
Charles	657	500
Ivan	249	213
Kathy	295	246
Les	576	432
Mavis	833	744

* includes combinations of auxiliaries and semi-auxiliaries

The number of utterances with auxiliaries ranged from 213 (Ivan) to 744 (Mavis). In part these differences are due to talkativeness but Mavis was also the child who produced auxiliary utterances and frames earliest and Ivan was the last to start.

The build-up of a frame was measured cumulatively across sessions. Starting with each auxiliary form, frames were defined in terms of the numbers of verbs with which they occurred and the flexibility of their subject NPs. 1-verb frames were fully lexically specific and were defined if three examples of the same auxiliary-verb combination occurred without any variation in the verb with which the auxiliary form was combined for the whole period of the study (e.g., **(I) haven't got NP** (Ivan), **Do you want NP?** (April) or **Wouldn't go** (Charles)). 2-verb frames contained the same auxiliary form and only occurred with two different verbs during the study. The main analyses are conducted on the children's 3-verb frames. A 3-verb frame was defined as existing when a particular auxiliary form occurred with three different main verbs (e.g., if the child says: *Don't want*, *Don't know* and *Don't like*, s/he is defined as having an auxiliary frame of the form **Don't + VP**, where VP = minimally, a main verb). The number of further instances of each 3-verb frame with a new verb was noted as was any change to the frame (e.g., when the child showed variation in pronominal subjects (Pn), the inclusion of full nouns (N) or NP Subjects (NP), the addition of '*not*' to the frame).

Example 1: Examples of 3-verb frames[6]
Don't know, Don't want juice, Don't like it ⇒ **(I) don't VP**
He's falling, He's going up, It's singing ⇒ **Pn's VP-ing**
I can't see, Mummy can't do it, He can't have one ⇒ **N/Pn can't VP**

Errors were not excluded from the establishment of a frame: for instance Charles said first, *Father Xmas haven't got a key** [7] and then, *Haven't read it before** (with *read in* the present tense pronunciation) and *Them haven't made a big one**. Despite the fact that all these utterances contain errors, they establish the frame **N/Pn haven't VP.** For the frame analysis, partial imitations were not counted if the imitation was of the subject-auxiliary combination in the imitated utterance, but if the main verb was imitated by the child in combination with a different subject and auxiliary, the utterance was included in the analysis.

2.3 Analyses

Using these criteria I conducted the following analyses:

1. The proportion of utterances containing auxiliaries that could be accounted for by frames. If this proportion is high it suggests that an account at this level may capture the nature of the child's grammar
2. The rank order in which frames appeared for each child in order to assess the degree of commonality and difference across the children.
3. An error analysis to see whether errors can be related to particular frames. One would not expect to find errors with frames acquired early, since they will be likely to be close to the models in the input from which they are being learned. However as frames start to be interconnected and slots become schematic, the prediction is that errors will be more likely to occur.
4. An analysis of when each of the NICE operations emerges and how this can be related to the development of a more auxiliary-wide syntax
5. A correlation between the order of emergence of these frames and their frequency in the CDS of a different group of mothers, drawn from the same locality. In principle, a high and significant correlation would suggest that while it may not be the only factor, frequency in the input is closely implicated in the order of development of these frames. However it is important to note that since the data come

6. () = absent; I/() = form sometimes absent; Pn= Pronoun; N= Noun; VP = Verb Phrase, NP=Noun Phrase

7. * indicates a grammatical error in the subject-aux-verb group.

from different samples the conclusions from this part of the analysis can only be highly tentative.[8]

I will return, in the Discussion, to how the conclusions that can be drawn from these measures interact with issues of sampling.

2.4 Results

2.4.1 *Age and MLU*

Five of the six children had MLUs (measured in words) of between 1.89 and 2.26 and were aged between 2;2 and 2;4 when their first 3-verb frame was recorded.

Table 2. Age and MLU in words at the start and end of the study

	Emergence of first frame		End of study	
	Age	MLUw	Age	MLUw
April	2;3	1.89	3;0	2.86
Charles	2;2	2.26	3;0	3.40
Ivan	2;8	2.64	3;0	2.97
Kathy	2;4	1.96	2;11	3.24
Les	2;2	1.90	3;0	3.18
Mavis	2;2	2.19	3;0	3.58

Ivan is a clear exception: his first frame was recorded when he was 2;8 and had an MLUw of 2.64. Comparison with the figures in Miller and Chapman (1981)[9] indicates that all children were at the predicted age for their MLU and, with the exception of Ivan, were in Brown's late Stage 1 or Stage 2 as revised by DeVilliers and DeVilliers (1973). Ivan, on the other hand, would be assigned to late Stage III on the basis of his MLU. As we shall see in what follows, Ivan is interesting in a number of ways. The study ended when the children were 3;0 (or 2;11 in Kathy's case) with a MLUw of between 2.86 (April) and 3.58 (Mavis). Comparison with the figures in Miller and Chapman (1981) puts the children in early or late Stage IV, with April at exactly the predicted age for her MLU and the other five children being 1–5 months more advanced.

8. Though it may to some extent compensate for the fact that children are being spoken to by a number of people and not just their mothers.

9. The comparisons with Miller and Chapman (1981) were made using MLU calculated in morphemes. However MLU has been given throughout in words since I consider this gives a better comparison between English-speaking children at the early stages of language development. MLUw and MLUm are very highly correlated (see, for instance, Parker and Brorson, 2005).

Frame development

The cumulative development of 3-verb frames over the third year is shown in Figure 1 for each child. All the children except Ivan started producing frames in the first four months of their third year. Ivan and Kathy started producing frames later than the other children but, by 3;0, had caught up with April who added frames slowly over the whole year. Mavis, April and Charles added new frames at a relatively steady rate over the year while Ivan, Kathy and Les showed a steeper rise for part of the year (at about 2;6 for Kathy and Les and 2;8 for Ivan).

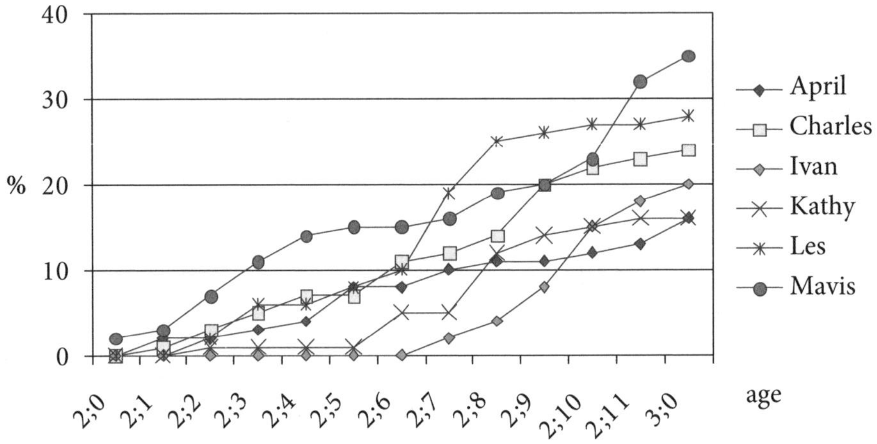

Figure 1. Cumulative 3-verb frames

Table 3. Number of frames and the percentage of utterances accounted for by frames

	3-Verb frames	2-Verb frames	1-Verb frames	Total no of utterances with auxiliaries	% Utterances accounted for by 3-verb frames	% Utterances accounted for by all frames
April	11	3	2	292	91	95
Charles	19	5	5	500	92	96
Ivan	17	2	4	213	75	91
Kathy	13	5	1	246	88	94
Les	25	10	3	432	88	94
Mavis	25	18	2	744	88	97
MEANS	18.3	6.7	2.8	404.5	87	94.5

Table 3 shows the proportion of the children's auxiliary utterances that are accounted for by the frame analysis and the number of utterances that cannot be accounted for. The number of 3-verb frames ranges from 11–25, with a mean of 18.3. A mean of 94.5% of the children's utterances are accounted for by all frames. Thus rather few utterances for each child lie outside these frames. Further, a large proportion of the children's utterances occur in 3-verb frames (a mean of 87%).

2.4.2 *Order of emergence of frames*

The rank order of emergence of the 3-verb frames is given in Tables 4 and 5 which together list all 3-verb frames produced by each child and their mean rank order of emergence across the group. The first frame to be produced would be given a rank of 1, the highest rank. Table 4 lists frames that at least 5 of the children produced and Table 5, all the other frames (i.e. those produced by 4 or fewer children). For each frame and each child the nature of the subject slot in the first three utterances to form the frame is shown.

There are a number of marked differences between the results presented in Table 4 and those in Table 5. First, there is little overlap between the two tables in the mean rank order of emergence of each frame, with the exception of 2 frames, each produced only by one child, Les (**X been –ing** and **X might – ing**) and of **Are X –ing?** which is in Table 5 but has a slightly higher rank than **X've** – in Table 4. Thus there is a core group of frames that come in earlier in development and are almost all produced by all the children. This is also largely true for the ranking of frames produced by the individual children. While there is some overlap in the order of emergence of frames for individual children between the two tables, this results from the following: (a) Les's two very early frames, mentioned above, which no other child produced (b) two frames each said by 4 of the children (**Will X -?** and **Shall X-?**) and (c) the fact that Ivan developed late and fast and so had closely overlapping ranks.

Table 4. Frames produced by at least 5 children and rank order of emergence

Frames	April	Charles	Ivan	Kathy	Les	Mavis	Mean rank
X 'is – ing	3	6.5		2	18.5	8	7.6
I'm – ing	9	6.5	16	5.5	1	2.5	6.75
X 'has -	6	17*	10	5.5	6	8	8.75
X've -	10.5		10	13	3	12	9.7
Don't – [IMP]	1	3.5	4	10.5	18.5	2.5	6.67
X don't -	6	1.5	4	1	3	2.5	3
X can't –	2	1.5	1.5*	5.5	9.5	2.5	3.75
X can –	6	6.5	10	5.5	9.5	10.5	8
Can X –?	10.5	11.5	1.5	5.5	9.5	8	7.75
X'll –	6	3.5		5.5	9.5	10.5	7
X won't -/will-'nt	6	9	16	10.5		5.5	9.4

* = errors

Table 5. Frames produced by fewer than 5 children and order of emergence

Frames	April	Charles	Ivan	Kathy	Les	Mavis	Mean rank
X're – ing	13	17*			9.5		13.17
Are X – ing?			4*		9.5*	14.5	9.33
What's X – ing?				13			13
X been – ing					3		3
X was – ing		11.5*				20	15.75
X is – ing		11.5*				20	15.75
Is X – ing?		19			14.5*	20	17.83
What are X – ing?					23.5	27.5	25.5
Have X –?			16*		23.5*	20*	19.83
X haven't -		14.5*			14.5	20	16.33
Has X –?						27.5	27.5
X hasn't –						27.5	27.5
Who's -?				13			13
X did –	13*					20	16.5
X doesn't -	13	17*				27.5	19.17
X didn't -			10		23.5*		16.75
Did X –?			10*		21*		15.5
Do X –?			10*		14.5	20*	14.83
Does X –?			10*		18.5	20*	16.17
How do X –?					23.5		23.5
What did X –?						27.5	27.5
X do –						27.5*	27.5
X will -		11.5	10			20	13.83
Will X –?		14.5	10		14.5	14.5	13.37
Shall X –?		6.5		9	18.5	13	11.75
X might					5	5.5	5.25
X might be						27.5	27.5

With the exception of two CAN frames, all the auxiliary frames in Table 4 involve either cliticized or contracted forms while only 12% of the frames in Table 5 involve these structures. This provides support for those researchers who have claimed that these structures are of low scope and not part of a wider knowledge of auxiliary syntax. This suggests that the frames in Table 4 form a group of low-scope constructions lexically-based on the particular auxiliary form with productive slots for the verb. In some cases, there are also productive slots for the subject but in others, the subject and auxiliary may have been learned together as a whole, particularly in the case of the clitics. It is possible that **Shall X -?** in Table 5 should be added to this group since it was said by 4 of the children and its mean rank is very close to the lowest rank in Table 4. Note that there are no tensed auxiliaries or *wh*-frames in Table 4.

The one child who shows some clear variation from this overall pattern is Ivan. In addition to producing almost all the frames in Table 4, he also has high ranks for 8 of the structures in Table 5. Six of these 8 frames are *yes/no*-questions and the high rank for Ivan's **Are you –ing?** explains why its mean rank for the group of children is so high. Of course, this is partly because he started so late that there were fewer sessions before the end of the study that could acquire lower ranks but it is also because he showed both rapid development overall and a unique development of *yes/no*-questions at the same time that he was developing the same group of frames as the other children.

For some children and some auxiliaries, a range of frames sharing a particular auxiliary also share the same rank (i.e. become productive in the same month). This is the case, for instance, for the 3 CAN frames for Kathy and Les. However if we look at the ranks within the 5 auxiliary groups for each of the 6 children, we can see that this is only the case for 6 out of the 30 possibilities, again suggesting that many of these frames are being learned separately and not initially as part of a more general system. This is despite the fact that all three main auxiliaries together with two modals are represented in the frames in Table 4. There is also a *yes/no*-question (**Can X -?**) and a number of negated frames. The implication is that the mere presence of large numbers of utterances containing a wide range of auxiliaries and syntactic structures does not guarantee the existence of a fully abstract auxiliary syntax in these children's grammars.

2.4.3 *Evidence for developing schematicity and generalization*

Subjects and verbs

In a usage-based account, constructions can be productive while still being only partially schematic. Many of the children's early auxiliary frames are indeed highly productive with a wide range of verbs being used. There are a number of possible indications of increasing schematicity of these constructions and of low-scope constructions building up towards a more auxiliary-wide syntax. For instance, increasing schematicity can be seen in the development of the subject slot in the frames in Table 4. Those frames with the highest ranks almost all come in initially either without a subject or with a fixed subject, usually *I*. Frames with lower ranks that come in later, together with those in Table 5, are more likely to show subject variation in the three utterances that go up to make the frame: 54% of the frames in Table 4 come in with variable subjects as opposed to 67% in Table 5. Thus in using these early low-scope frames, children are showing a developing knowledge of the range of subjects and of verbs that can be placed in and across the frames.

Errors

Errors can also be informative as to what is formulaic and which parts of the system may be developing. Errors were noted if they concerned the subject, auxiliary form, main verb form or tag. All the children's non-tag question errors are listed in Table 6, though I will only discuss those that show some systematicity. Errors in the first utterances contributing to a frame are also indicated in Tables 4 and 5. Although the relative thinness of the sampling makes it difficult to draw hard and fast conclusions about how systematic these errors are, we will briefly consider them as possible indications for developing generalizations and for possible links between different auxiliaries. First we should note that, of the 62 frames in Table 4, only two have errors in the utterances that contribute to the frame being classed as productive.[10] On the other hand, 20 of the 57 frames in Table 5 have some kind of error in their initial three utterances and these errors are divided almost equally between question frames (37.5% errors) and non-question frames (36% errors). This difference suggests that, as the later frames were developing, the children may indeed have been starting to grasp some of the more general aspects of the auxiliary system and be groping for the correct form for both the auxiliary and for the main verb while having available a variety of more or less entrenched lexically-specific constructions with auxiliaries. We can look at this in a bit more detail by consulting Table 6.

I have divided the errors in Table 6 into five types together with a miscellaneous column that includes a number of *wh*-inversion errors. The first two columns show errors in the form of the main verb following auxiliaries BE and HAVE respectively and the third shows errors where the children appear to have used BE for HAVE or vice versa. The fourth column lists errors with DO including the wrong form of the main verb, some 'over-tensing' errors and some possibly emphatic uses of DO. The fifth lists all agreement errors.

One possible way to think about the errors in Table 6 is in terms of what they tell us about (a) the open slot in the construction and (b) the child's knowledge of the auxiliary system beyond any particular lexically-specific construction. Thus April, Les and Mavis' errors with HAVE in column 2 involve using an incorrect past participle, often of an irregular verb, *blowed* for *blown*, *flied* for *flown*, *drank* for *drunk*, *maked* for *made* (as noted by Pinker 1984) which suggests that the slot in this frame is already linked to some meaning associated with immediate past. On the other hand, the errors in the verbs that Charles uses with this construction are less clearly marked for past which may mean that he is still groping for the correct form-function mapping for this slot. A further example is the 'double tense-marking' errors of April and Ivan with *did* (column 4). These were also noted by Pinker (1984). Again the use of past tense on the main verb suggests that the children have identified the meaning of the slot with past and probably also the frame. Here, though, they have not coordinated between the two, presumably because a more abstract ability to manipulate finiteness is still developing.

10. Charles: *Peter's broke my gun.* Ivan: *Can't get him out, in't he?*

Table 6. The Children's Non-Tag Question Errors

Child	Wrong main verb form with is	Wrong main verb form with have	Is for have or *vice versa*	Non-agreement errors with do	Agreement errors	Other
April	2;6 – My Daddy's do that – He's not go fast	2;10 – He's blowed that candle out – He's flied away	2;11 – Mine is dropped off	2;11 – I did found a mouse – I did found a crab		
Charles	2;10 – Brian is go on – I'm go be Joe Lean	2;7 – Peter's broke my gun			2;8 – F.Xmas haven't got a key	2;7 – Why that car wouldn't go? 2;10 – Them haven't made a big one
		2;8 – Haven't read (present tense) it before				
		2;9 – I haven't march anymore		2;11 – It doesn't crossen that – Where this one goes, this goes in here and does this one goes in here?	2;10 – He's haven't got a digger – We's having dinner	2;9 – What Brian is going?

Child	Wrong main verb form with is	Wrong main verb form with have	Is for have or *vice versa*	Non-agreement errors with do	Agreement errors	Other
Ivan		3;0 – Have you eat yours?	2;9 – Are you got another car? – Are you mended that?	2;9 – Don't got a hanky	2;9 – Has you got another car?	2;10 – This one's need sharpen
	2;11 – Are you make some more blutack?		2;11 – What are you made? – What is you made?	2;11 – D'you bought it? – Did you broke it? – I did fall out	2;10 – Has you got that much?	
					2;11 – Had (for have) you got two cars? – Has you got lipstick on? – Has you got windows in your car?	
Kathy	2;6 – I'm colour					2;11 – Where's he can't get?

Child	Wrong main verb form with is	Wrong main verb form with have	Is for have or *vice versa*	Non-agreement errors with do	Agreement errors	Other
Les	2;8 – Is he bang his head on the floor?	2;9 – Have you drank your coffee?	2;7 – Are you finished your coffee? – Are you get one tomorrow? – Are get a blue one? – Are you finished nearly?	2;8 – Did it went off?	2;7 – He haven't got any sugar	2;10 – What's this here doing? – What's here doing?
		2;10 – Have fell down the stairs	2;8 – This is got toys in here – This is got some toys, great toys – Is he fallen? – Are you got one of them?			
		2;11 – I've maked a tunnel	2;9 – Are you want some breakfast? 2;10 – Are you get one from the shop? 3;0 – Are you have your hair cut?			

Child	Wrong main verb form with is	Wrong main verb form with have	Is for have or *vice versa*	Non-agreement errors with do	Agreement errors	Other
Mavis	2;6 – I'm want to come with you	2;11 – Have you fell in work?		2;11 – He did hurt me toe	2;11 – Do me Dad smoke?	2;5 – I'll had a phone call] 2;11 – Where's you gone?
	2;7 – I'm give him a nose		2;11 – I've gonna have a look	– Does he chews it?	2;11 – Have he got them? – Have me Mum got another kettle? 3;0 – Only babies does go on the stations – Do it go in here now?	
	2;8 – I'm fasten them – Am I go with you shops?					

The errors in column 1 all involve a missing *–ing* on the main verb form. In one sense these are likely to be 'slips of the tongue' in that they occur well after each child has already produced the relevant frame (Mavis's: *Am I go with you shops?* at 2;8 is the exception). For instance Kathy at 2;6 said *I'm colour* and later in the same session *I'm colouring*. However 'slips of the tongue' arise under performance constraints and indicate competition between forms. As other frames get established and the relationship between the frame, the form of the main verb that goes with it and the full form of the auxiliary develop, competition may arise between the different representations. The errors in column 3 do indeed suggest that there can sometimes be overlap between some forms of auxiliaries BE and HAVE. The two types of error are Ivan and Les' use of *are* for *have* and the use of *is* for *has* (April, *Mine is dropped off*; Les, *This is got some toys in here, Is he fallen?*). Competition between IS and HAVE could arise from a number of sources. First, there may be specific uses in the input that may cause the representations to overlap. For instance mothers say *Are you finished?* as well as *Have you finished?* and *Is it gone?* as well as *Has it gone?* We can see from Table 5 that, for those children who produce it, **Are you X?** is the earliest frame with a full auxiliary to emerge (probably as a result of its frequency in the input, see below) and that the **Have you X?** frame is considerably later. So **Are you** starts off as a lexically-specific string and the **Are you X?** construction may not be closely related to other forms of aux BE, allowing forms of the main verb other than the progressive to be placed in the slot. The meaning may also overlap with the meaning of the **Have you X?** construction, increasing the likelihood of these errors (see below). Something similar may happen for newly emerging frames with the full form *is*. Since the *'s* clitic is the same for BE and HAVE, once children start to segment these frames and to connect the newly identified form to the full form of the auxiliary, the fact that the form is the same may bring the two representations closer together, leading to occasional errors (for instance Les says: *Is he bang his head?* and *Has he hit his head?* in the same session. Interestingly Theakston and Lieven (2005) also found BE for HAVE substitutions in their auxiliary elicitation study, but not vice versa, perhaps because the BE form is more entrenched.

Charles, Ivan and Mavis make a number of agreement errors (see column 5). One possible explanation relating to the existence of lexically-specific frames is that the child has not yet fully analysed the frame and therefore does not always coordinate the person marking on the frame with that on the main verb. Thus when Charles says *He's haven't …* and *We's having…*, his **Pn's** --- frame may have been competing with other, possibly more correct, ways of saying what he wants to and, because of its relative strength, the construction may have 'won out'. Ivan's errors of the form *Has you got…?* are also clearly in competition with the correct *Have you ….?* since at 2;10 he also says *Have you done nice colours* and at 2;11, *Have you got light in your car?* These *Has you…?* errors are interesting because, on the one hand, the construction looks somewhat entrenched and, on the other, he is very unlikely to have learned it from the input. This may be an occasion where the child's own erroneous productions have entrenched an incorrect construction, if only very temporarily. Alternatively, or as well, since Ivan produces *Have you got ...?* a number of times and then also *Has you got ..?* and *Had you got ...?*, it may be that the fixed form of *you got* allows him to notice potential variation in the form of the initial auxiliary. Mavis makes the opposite error to Ivan, using *Have ...?* and *Do --?* each twice in 3rd person singular contexts. At 2;11, she has a productive **Have Pn ---?**, which includes these errors but by 3;0, she has produced a correct **Has Pn ---?** construction. This reflects a possibly interesting point about many of these errors, namely that they seem to occur together and be relatively short-lived. We will see this again when we consider Kathy's errors with tag questions.

I have attempted to indicate how errors might reflect some of the processes underlying both the initial formation of constructions and their development into a more fully analysed interconnected grammar. Clearly with such relatively small numbers, it is not possible to make definitive statements but there are a number of studies that support the suggestions made here and are based on stronger data. For instance Rowland (2007) has shown how high frequency *Wh*-aux frames in the input can protect the child from uninversion errors while Freudenthal *et al.* (2007) have shown how the learning of utterance-final strings can also lead to error, namely optional infinitive errors. The children in the present study initially make rather few errors since they are using well entrenched, error-free constructions learned from the input. Occasionally when they do not know the correct form or when it is in competition with another entrenched form, errors will occur. Finally, as the system becomes gradually more schematic and abstract, children will have to develop constructions for agreement, tense marking and finiteness and some of the errors noted above indicate that these developments are underway for some of the children.

Relationship between different forms of the same auxiliary

Although, different forms of the same auxiliary may often come in as separate frames with initially unrelated meanings, links between them will develop. Juxtaposition of the different frames in discourse and developing associations between overlapping meanings and/or overlapping forms may contribute to establishing these links. Links may also develop between frames with different auxiliaries, for instance a more general schema for inversion or for tag questions, also considered below.

CAN is the only auxiliary that occurs in three different frames in Table 4. In what follows, I will take the emergence of the three CAN frames as a 'temporal baseline' for looking at a number of linguistically defined 'operations' in which a wide range of other auxiliaries take part: ellipsis, inverted *yes/no*-questions, tense-marking, tag and *wh*-questions. The results are summarized in Table 7 which shows the age at which each child produced their first frame, the age at which all three CAN frames were produced and the ages at which two examples each of ellipsis and of tag questions are attested. The last three rows show the ages at which each child produced two *yes/no*-inversion frames, two *wh*-frames and two sets of frames contrasting in tense (e.g., *is/was; do/ did*).

Table 7. Age at which different structures are attested

	April	Charles	Ivan	Kathy	Les	Mavis
First Frame	2;3	2;2	2;8	2;4	2;2	2;2
3 CAN Frames	2;10	2;9	2;11	2;8	2;7	2;5
Ellipsis (2)	2;7	2;4	2;8	2;8	2;7	2;5
Tag Questions (2)	–	–	2;8	2;11	2;10	2;9
Yes/no-Inversion Frames (2)	–	2;9	2;9	2;9	2;7	2;9
Wh-Frames (2)	–	–	–	2;11	2;9	3;0
Tense Contrasts Between Frames (2)	–	–	2;11	–	–	2;11

From Table 6 we can see that 3 to 7 months elapsed between the production of each child's first frame and the point at which all three CAN frames were produced. All 4 children who produced tag questions produced them with CAN as well as with other auxiliaries and we can see that correctly formed tag questions with reversed polarity appear late (2;10–3;00, see Appendix A for all the children's tag questions). In the case of all but Ivan, this is 3–6 months after the appearance of 3 frames with CAN. In principle, successive utterances in discourse can be used to provide evidence of the child's grasp of the relationship between the different forms. In fact, however, there are only a few examples of such juxtapositions with CAN all shown in Example 2. This could be due to sampling but it is interesting to note that all of these come at, for Mavis, or after, the point where each child has produced all 3 CAN frames, possibly suggesting that linking them is indeed a later development.

Example 2: Contrasting uses of CAN in discourse [11]

(a) April: 3;0
M. I can hear where it is.
C. Can you hear it?

(b) April: 3;0
C. A boy can't go…. A boy can go on it (restart)

(c) Kathy: 2;10
I. Can't see any moocow
C. I can see one

(d) Les: 2;9
C. I can't open this, Graeme. Can you open it?

11. M=mother; I=investigator; C=child.

(e) Mavis: 2;5
M. Can I draw with you?
C. You can draw with me

The two children for whom the production of the three CAN frames takes the longest (April and Charles) also seem to be the ones who show least evidence of producing more complex structures of tag questions, *wh*-frames and tense contrasts. These structures are produced late in the year by the other four though Kathy and Les do not meet the tense contrast criterion. We may tentatively conclude that these criteria are more demanding, either because of the semantics involved or because they reflect the development of a more abstract and system-wide grasp of auxiliary syntax. On the other hand, the earlier ages for the production of two examples of ellipsis and two *yes/no*-question frames suggest that these may be less demanding achievements.

Ellipsis
Table 8 shows the first two examples of ellipsis found for each child. As noted ellipsis appears to be early compared to the production of tag questions, *wh*-frames and tense contrasts, Ivan, as always, being the exception.

Table 8. The first two examples of ellipsis for each child

Child	Age	Adult utterance	Child ellipsis
April	2;7	M. I bet you can't do this	A. I can
		I. They go there	A. No, don't
Charles	2;4	M. You've got an ear on top of your head	C. I haven't
		M. You can be Dick Turpin	C. No I can't
Ivan	2;8	M. No, 'cos I haven't got any	I. Yes, you have
		M. You'd be dead	I. Won't
Kathy	2;8	M. Mind you don't burn yourself	K. I'm not
		I. I can't draw Bongo	K. You can
Les	2;7	M. Who drives the tractor?	L. Peter does
		M. Who goes every day to the pub?	L. Daddy does
Mavis	2;5	M. You'll have to find the other one	Ma. I can't
		M. What are you shouting at me for?	Ma. I'm not

These examples of ellipsis, containing, as they do, reversed pronouns, reversed polarity auxiliaries, full forms of contracted auxiliaries and DO-support could be analysed as demonstrating the early presence of full auxiliary syntax, despite the evidence I have presented above that these are slowly developing achievements. On a usage-based account, however, explanations would focus on children learning ways of producing highly pragmatically relevant utterances in discourse (mainly relating to contradiction and resistance, e.g., *I can, won't, don't, I'm not*) together with the modelling of these exchanges by adults (e.g., i.e. for Les, the adult 'display' question followed by a semi-formulaic answer *X does*). Children often use *I can't* and *Don't* as isolated utterances before they produce utterances with these auxiliaries and a main verb. Caretakers, too, use these types of utterances to children '*Oh no you won't*', '*Yes, you can*' and many use tag questions from which children may have isolated the tag (e.g., *You've finished, haven't you?*). If children understand the semantics of the interlocutor's utterance, they know what it is they are unable or refusing to do and can produce a response that is pragmatically appropriate.

Yes/no-questions

Although **Can X --?** is the only *yes/no*-question frame to occur in Table 4, all the children except April, produce either **Will X --?** or **Shall X--?** at relatively high ranks in Table 5, suggesting that these frames may be lexically-specific. All the other *yes/no*-question frames are with main auxiliaries rather than modals and come in relatively late. For instance, despite Mavis's early start with producing auxiliary frames, inverted question frames with main auxiliaries only appear at 2;11. As I noted above, these *yes/no*-questions with main auxiliaries involve a lot of errors. If we refer back to Table 5, two of the three children who produce **Are X –ing?**, **Do X --?** and **Does X --?** and all the children who produce **Have X--?** and **Did X --?** make errors (see Appendix A). The relatively late emergence of most *yes/no*-question frames together with the errors again suggest that the children are developing a more integrated grammar.

Both Les and Ivan use an incorrect **Are you X?** frame though the errors that they make are not identical. The frame itself may have been learned from the input in both cases (it is the most frequent frame in adult speech to children, see below and Appendix C) and misapplied. In Ivan's case **Are you X?** and **Has you X?** coexist and the alternation between *Are you got another car?* and *Has you got another car?* in close juxtaposition at 2;9 suggests that they overlap in meaning. Les seems to use **Are you X?** more as a 'generic' *yes/no*-question which in adult speech would sometimes be **Are you X-ing** with a future meaning (*Are you getting one tomorrow?*) and other times **Do you X?** (*Do you want some breakfast?*). *Are you finished?* is probably also said by adults (to mean something similar to *Have you finished?*) again creating overlap between the two forms. As well as these errors at 2;7, Les also says *Are you going--?* and *Are you getting--?* suggesting that he has a considerable inventory of *yes/no*-questions but has not yet fully worked out the relationships between them and their internal structure. Here, again, we may be able to see two processes at work in the children's learning: first the learning of a highly frequent construction with a relatively global meaning **Are you X?**, and, second, the beginnings of links between different frames leading to confusion about which participle to use and errors in agreement.

Tag questions

The production of syntactically correct tag questions is often taken as indicating that the child has a general category of 'auxiliary' (Richards 1990) because if indeed a fully general schema (rule or set of checking relations) exist for the production of grammatically correct tag questions, it requires understanding of the relationship between the affirmative and negative forms of the same auxiliary which are often not transparent (*You'll be doing that, won't you?*; *You've been there, haven't you?*; plus the use of 'DO-support' for main verbs: *You got that out, didn't you?*). Whether or not one should think in terms of a single schematic construction underlying the production of tag questions in the adult system, it is interesting to consider what might contribute to the learning of tag questions. Of the four children who produce tags (see Appendix A), two (Les and Mavis) get them largely right from the beginning so it is difficult to identify any learning processes. Les produces 10 tags and Mavis 27, and the first five for each show subject agreement, reversed polarity and DO-support, together with tag questions involving modals. Note, however, that the bulk of them occur late in the year, that some of them are missing the auxiliary in the matrix (Mavis, 3;0: *You going on that, aren't you?*) and in some others there is not a match between the auxiliary in the matrix and the tag (Les, 3;0: *We haven't got a tv, hasn't it?*; *You have to put that on, will you?*).

Ivan and Kathy's tag questions are more interesting (they total 30 and 23 respectively). Ivan's first 5 tags (at 2;7) all contain errors, usually missing the subject and auxiliary in the matrix and/or with the incorrect form of the main verb. The next set of nine tag questions at 2;8 includes two that are correct, one with DO-support and one with a modal. However four more are without reversed polarity and, of these, two could be analysed as right dislocations (*It ring, did it?* and *Buying another car, are you?*) and in two, the auxiliary form in the matrix and the tag is the same. Some of Ivan's tag questions between 2;9 and 3;0 are similar to these, others have errors of person and tense agreement between matrix and tag and six are fully correct. There may be a number of different processes involved here. In terms of pragmatics, Ivan may have learned that some kind of tag at the end of utterances is a good way to extract a response from his interlocutor, as well as also learning that he can do this by repeating the auxiliary form of the matrix (without reversing the polarity). In turn, this could then make the underlying structure of reversed polarity tags more salient and allow him to start working out the correct relationship between the matrix and tag. As we can see this takes some time.

Kathy's tag questions at 2.11A[12] capture aspects of this process at one time point. All her tags are variants of the auxiliary HAVE. Four are fully correct, with reversed polarity, tense and person agreement. Three do not reverse the polarity and one of these has a non-matching auxiliary in the tag. On the tape, all these utterances occur in close proximity to each other and it is seems that Kathy has a less than full representation of the correct structure and is groping towards it. She obviously has some understanding of the pragmatics of tag questions and of the relationship between the matrix auxiliary and the tag, but seems to have an 'all-purpose' tag (*han't you*), which

12. Two of Kathy's sessions were in the month of 2;11 and for most analyses were combined. Here it is important to separate them, however.

she attaches in case of doubt. This seems on the way to resolution by the next recording session although there are still a number of failures of coordination between the matrix sentence and tag.

A brief look at these children's early ellipsis, *yes/no*-questions and tag questions suggests that developing anything like a system-wide syntax that would represent auxiliaries as a class takes some time. Rather than being a process that builds on an already existing auxiliary-wide syntax, it depends on coordinating a number of different and strengthening representations and includes the learning of pragmatically appropriate responses.

2.5 Relationship to input

Finally, I briefly consider the relationship between the production of these frames and the same frames in adult speech to children. For the reasons mentioned above, the amount of speech addressed by the mothers of the children in this sample was too variable and, in some cases, too sparse, to allow for meaningful comparison. Instead I have correlated the order of emergence of the frames of these six Manchester children with the relative frequency of frames in a different sample of Manchester mothers – four of those of the Manchester corpus on CHILDES (MacWhinney 2000). The families in the two groups come from the same geographical area but there is a more lower and working class balance in the families of the children in the present study and a more middle-class balance in the families of the Manchester corpus.

The Manchester corpus was a longitudinal study of 12 children between 2;0 – 3;0 (Theakston, Lieven, Pine and Rowland 2001). For the present purpose, eight hours of recording was used for each mother starting from the second recording session and following on consecutively. This yielded a mean of 1213 maternal utterances containing an auxiliary and a main verb per mother (range 970 – 1607). The definition of a frame was the same as for the children, namely the same auxiliary form used with at least three different verbs. If the same sentence subject appeared in all three examples, this was included in the frame; otherwise, the presence of a variable subject was noted. The mean rank order of the frequency of each frame in the mothers' data was calculated and correlated with the mean rank order of emergence of the children's frames (tables 4 and 5). Frames that the children did not produce were all given a filled rank one lower than the lowest mean rank in the child data (all frames are listed in Appendix B). The results, using a Spearman's rank correlation were significant ($r = .71$, $p < .001$ two-tailed). Despite the fact that the mothers and children came from different samples, this does suggest that the relative frequency of subject-auxiliary combinations in the speech that the children are hearing may play a part in the order in which they learn these frames. However, frequency is unlikely to be the only factor as we can see by examining Table 9 which lists all the frames used by the mothers and not produced by the children.

Table 9. Frames used by the mothers in the Manchester CHILDES corpus and not produced by the children in the present study

Be V-ing
Why are you V-ing?
X were V-ing
Were you V-ing?
Where are x V–ing?
Don't you VP?
What do you VP?
What do x?
What does x?
Where did x?
Which x do?
Who did you x?
Who do you x?
What x do?
Where do x?
X have
What have you x?
Shouldn't x?
Shat shall we x?
X shouldn't
Where shall x?
Where should x?
Won't it x?
X wouldn't
You'd x
I'd x
X would
Can't you x?
X could
What can x?
X must

To a large extent the characteristics of these frames show a level of complexity that we already noted the children moving toward in their later acquired frames in Table 5, namely, large numbers of *wh*-question frames including many with DO-support. There are also frames with *could, would,* and *should* that express rather more subtle modality than *can, can't, will, won't, shall* and *shan't*. Finally there are a number of frames with either *you* or *we* as subjects that may well characterize the interests of mothers more than that of children.

3. Discussion

The results from this study support previous research findings which suggest that the early utterances of children that contain auxiliaries are likely to be low-scope formulae and not part of an auxiliary-wide knowledge of syntax. However they extend these results by using a systematic definition of productivity and by showing that, despite being formed around particular auxiliary forms, these frames can be highly productive. In addition, they account for a major proportion of the children's utterances between 2;0 – 3;0. The results also support previous research in suggesting that the development of tag questions, tense contrasts on auxiliaries and non-copula *wh*-questions, particularly those requiring DO-support, may be relatively complex and late, while children may be able to learn various forms of ellipsis without auxiliary-wide knowledge. However, the study suggests that the mere fact that children produce *yes/no*-questions or utterances with DO-support cannot be taken as unequivocal evidence of an auxiliary-wide syntax. A usage-based approach starts from the actual forms that children produce and then looks for evidence of the level of schematicity at which the construction is operating. Thus it is important not to treat the presence of a form as evidence for the existence of the underlying abstract category. As I have tried to show, this evidence can come from comparisons of provision of the same form in other constructions, from the errors that children produce and from discourse substitutions.

3.1 Frequency and sampling

Frequency in the speech that children hear seems to be one important factor in their early production of these frames but the complexity of the syntax involved and the semantics of the frame may also mean that children do not produce it early. One possible objection is that these results might merely reflect that fact that sampling is picking up the children's most frequent frames first and so what has been shown is not an order of development but rather the relative frequency of different forms and that this is where the correlation with the input is coming from. There is bound to be an element of this, since sampling is critical to the likelihood of rare events being detected (Tomasello and Stahl 2004). Recently there have been a number of important suggestions as to how one might try to control for the effects of sampling including Rowland *et al.*'s chapter in this volume. I have not attempted to use these methods here because the most relevant would have been to control the input data down to the size of the children's samples. But, given that the latter are rather small, this is likely not to give very reliable results and, in addition, the input samples are not from the children's own mothers. It is interesting to note, however, even given the relative thinness of sampling, that a number of related errors were picked up in the same session, suggesting that they could be reflecting a systematic change in the child's grammar. On the other hand it is sobering to reflect that recording on a different day or perhaps even at a different time might have missed these interesting but seemingly short-lived errors completely! Developing sophisticated methods of dealing with the problem of sampling in naturalistic data is of essential importance in moving the field forward.

3.2 How abstract is the child's knowledge of auxiliaries?

However it is unlikely that these results are simply a reflection of how frequently the child produces utterances fitting the particular frames and that children actually have the relevant abstract knowledge from the outset. First, the order of production of different types of frames broadly fits with the predictions as to their complexity made by other researchers thoroughly hostile to the theoretical perspective of this article, both in terms of those frequently defined as non-productive and those thought to require more complex syntax. Second the results of both studies with denser data (Theakston *et al.* 2005) and experiments (Theakston and Lieven 2005) also suggest that there is variation in how productive different subject-auxiliary combinations are and that children can vary in their control over different forms of the same auxiliary (for instance they are usually more competent with singular than plural forms, even when they can produce the plural).

Most importantly, what would it mean for children to have the relevant abstract knowledge from the outset? The most extensive account is Pinker's (1984) which suggests that children already have some innate understanding of complementation, of the auxiliary class as a 'broken' paradigm, of its position towards the edge of the sentence and of the abstract notions of tense, modality and agreement. Other researchers from within a UG framework might well agree with this list while varying in the details. For instance, in Santelmann *et al.*'s (2002) account, the problem with auxiliary inversion only applies to questions requiring DO-support, a special feature of English. But, while the present study bears out the difficulty that some of the children have with *yes/no*-questions starting with some forms of DO, other *yes/no*-questions also show errors as the children have to coordinate the frame they are learning with the form of the main verb, or as they seek to change the person reference of the frame. What is really at issue, I think, is the contribution of item-based constructions to working out the more general aspects of the system and whether or not more abstract syntactic knowledge is required to go from the input data via these constructions to a more general syntax of auxiliaries. These children have a more or less lengthy period when they are producing large numbers of correctly formed and productive utterances containing auxiliaries and main verbs. The early absence of errors and the way in which the errors that occur later seem to indicate partial representation of different operations and to interact with pre-existing frames, is suggestive of a slow build up of different constructions and relations between them. Initially the children's constructions are relatively 'island-like', though variable slots for verbs and subjects appear quite quickly. The placement of the different auxiliaries could, therefore, be learned from the frames. However relating different constructions to each other as well as to the development of tense and agreement marking takes considerable time and depends on developing more complex semantic and pragmatic representations of the auxiliary constructions that will include tense and agreement marking. Dividing auxiliary development into either 'rote-learned' or 'syntactic' does not seem to capture this developmental picture.

However, it is also important to point out that much more work needs to be done from a usage-based approach to show how this build-up to more system-wide operations occurs. Can we identify a point at which children seem to be able to fully coordinate the tense and person agreement forms of the subject, auxiliary and main verb and, if so, is this a sudden reorganizational change of the general type suggested by Karmiloff-Smith (1986) and more specifically by Jordens (2002) for auxiliary provision as a function of the development of finiteness marking? Or does children's development continue to proceed in a piecemeal way as each part of the system gradually becomes more fluent and error-free? In my view, no one methodology on its own is going to be able to arrive at a fully satisfactory answer.

3.3 Using different methodologies

The limitations of longitudinal sampling have already been mentioned. Depending on the frequency of the phenomenon, denser sampling is, of course, better, and it will be important to track the emergence of productive auxiliary frames in the dense data that we have collected in Leipzig to see whether the general pattern suggested here is supported by much denser data. However we have to recognize that even with denser data there is an element of luck involved in managing to pick up the short-lived, groping and error patterns that can give evidence of developments in the child's system. One way to address this problem is through detailed diary studies focussing on one part of the system as for instance Rowland (2007) did in her study of her daughter's *wh*-question development. This too has its limitations, of course, in terms of the volume of what can be recorded and the dedication of the diarist.

However both experimental and modelling methods could also be used to investigate the issues raised here. For instance, if children are successful in coordination between subject, auxiliary and main verb in the constructions identified as early and low-scope, can we show experimentally that they have greater difficulty when presented with other forms of the auxiliary or other auxiliaries (Theakston and Lieven 2005)? Or if they can produce inverted *yes/no*-questions with one auxiliary (e.g., *can*) can they do this for the negated form as well (*can't*) (Ambridge and Rowland submitted; Guasti, Thornton and Wexler 1995)? Finally is children's ability to produce both the affirmative and negated form of one auxiliary related to their ability to negate other auxiliaries? While some experiments that bear on these questions have been conducted over the years, it is only rather recently that experiments have been designed specifically to test the ability to operate at a more general level than a particular auxiliary form (Ambridge *et al.* 2006).

I also suspect that some of these questions could be highly amenable to modelling. For instance, we know that there are relationships between the frequency of various constructions in the input and their emergence in the child's speech and that constructions with the same auxiliary do not necessarily emerge simultaneously. It would be interesting to see whether the similar disjunctions between different constructions would arise over time in a model with CDS input. One could also see whether the model produced errors after a period of relatively error-free learning and whether there was any evidence of a 'cascade' effect for, for instance, correct subject-auxiliary agreement across the different main auxiliaries and their forms or across different yes-no question constructions as suggested by Kuczaj and Maratsos (1983).

Despite the problems of sampling, naturalistic data collection is central to the study of children's language development and not only because it can identify important questions to be investigated with these other methodologies. Experiments can control variables and give insight into group performance but many experimental methods require estimates of relative frequencies of forms within and across constructions in order either to control for, or to investigate, frequency effects. Corpora tell us about language use and allow us to make these quantitative estimates of the proportional use of different constructions and forms in both the children's speech and that of the speech directed to them. Furthermore, we can only gain a detailed picture of development and of individual differences between children through the analysis of longitudinal corpora.

3.4 Individual differences

There are, in fact, some interesting individual differences between these children. In general, they showed a fairly orderly progression from relatively early production of 3 CAN frames and ellipsis through to later production of tag questions, *wh*-frames and tense contrasts on auxiliaries. However one child, April, despite producing at least the same number of utterances with auxiliaries as two of other children, did not have any productive frames with these more complex features by 3;0. Mavis, the only child to produce all the complex structures listed in Table 6, made steady progress throughout the year. Ivan contrasted in a different way, starting very late and with a much higher MLU than the other children and producing tag questions at roughly the same point as he produced two or more *yes/no*-question frames. Once he started to produce utterances with auxiliaries, Ivan showed the most rapid development. A contributing factor may have been his discovery that questions are an excellent method of maintaining an interlocutor's attention and getting a response, hence his early production of *yes/no*-frames and tag questions. It is possible that other aspects of his grammar were not so well developed, leading to the errors he made. Given how late Ivan started compared to the other children and the rapid development he made, one also has to consider the role that comprehension may have played in establishing constructions and partial relationships between them before he produced them.

It is worth mentioning that factors often implicated in accounting for differences in language development, namely class background, gender and sibling order will not do the job here. April was first-born and from a relatively middle-class background, Mavis had a number of older siblings and came from a much more working-class background. Ivan also had older siblings close in age. There is also no evidence for gender differences. I am not here disputing the results of studies based on proper comparison between large numbers of children, only pointing out that individual children can always be the exceptions.

Accounting for differences between individual children is always going to be difficult because so many different factors may be involved. One important point about a usage-based approach, however, is that it is not in principle hostile to individual differences either in the order in which learning of different constructions take place or in the particular forms of the grammar of different adults. Differences in the overall amount of input and in the relative frequencies of different structures and forms will be important, and this will always be read through the current state of a child's grammar in terms of the form-meaning mappings that are already represented, the relationships between different constructions and the extent to which they are entrenched. The collection of denser corpora from a number of children, together with attempts to model some of these factors may help us see how they can interact to produce a particular pattern of development.

4. Conclusion

In this paper I have suggested how a usage-based framework for understanding children's language development would approach the question of how children build up auxiliary syntax by tracking the development of 6 children's productive auxiliary syntax between the ages of 2;0 – 3;0. I have shown that this development can be seen as the initial establishment of highly productive, but low scope frames based around particular auxiliary forms, followed by working out relationships between different frames and the integration of tense and agreement into them which in turn leads to a grammar that looks more 'system-wide'. I have argued that a usage-based approach to syntactic development may fit more naturally with the evidence than one based on pre-existing representations of abstract linguistic categories.

Appendix A.
The children's tag questions

Les	Mavis
2;9 You like playing football, don't you? 2;10 Can't read it, can you? Fallen over, didn't it? I kicked it over, didn't I? See if it's working, will we? 2;11 Can't eat it, can you? You'll have to get me a ghost buster fun, won't you? You have to get me a ghost buster laser, won't you? 3;0 We haven't got a tv, hasn't it? Can wind it up, can't you? You have to put that on, will you	2;4 It's working, isn't it? 2;9 I just got one out, didn't I? Just dropped a purple, didn't I? 2;10 Mummy aren't you coming, are you? 2;11 And I'll be dead, won't I? We've got the same, haven't we? You forgot, didn't you? I will buy you a pressie, won't I? And we clean ou(t) coats, didn't we? We're going home on Monday, aren't we? And you're coming, aren't you? I do, don't I? Yeh, he will, won't he? Yeh it is, isn't it? Can have your watch on now, can't I? Yeh I will, won't I? I had one of those we had, han't we Mum? Mum you had one of those, Helen (investigator), didn't you? Hey, you can have one of those, that, can't you? Mum I can play with them games, can't I? 3;0 It used to, doesn't it? That one walks and it talks, doesn't it? Lisa's (sister) going on that one, aren't you? You going on that, aren't you? We got one last night, didn't we? I fell an' all, didn't I? Said byebye Mummy, didn't I?

Ivan	Kathy
2;7	2;10
Going up there, aren't you?	Where does that go there, doesn't it?
Have take that back, won't we? (matrix imitated)	Put it there, shall we?
	2;11A
Go there, does it?	You don't like dohdi (=dummy), han't you?
uh eat boy int he?	You've not seen that, han't you?
He get em in int he?	You've not seen that bit, have you?
2;8	You han't seen my pram, han't you?
Fell out there, didn't she Mummy?	You've not seen that, have you? (x2)
It won't come off, will it?	She's seen that (toM) Han't you? (to I)
Buying another car, are you?	You've not seen this one, han't you?
It ring, did it?	You not seen it (be)for, han't you?
Panther getting eat boy int he??	Mummy's lost the pictures hasn't she?
These are for the window, are they?	
	2;11B
That got no shoe, han't?	You want see Father Xmas, don't you?
We didn't Mummy, didn't we?	Shall I show, shall we?
2;9	He can't get in, can't she??
Don't want sellotape there, do I?	The mouse has got # han't she?
Lost that,are you?	Nobody can jump, can't they?
Do go on there, did it?	Don't let him have it, do you?
Did you get that out, did you?	I'll bring all my dohdis (=dummies), don't I?
	Read it, won't it?
2;10	You seen that, han't you?
Want this tuna, do you?	Been to see that, han't you?
Can't get past, can you?	
You scribbling on, int yer?	
I dropped them all, don't I?	
That go there, didn't it?	
Betty (sister), are you scissors in the drawer, are they?	
Can I see it, can I?	
2;11	
It's come out, hasn't it?	
Lelena (investigator) borrow that, does she?	
3;0	
I can undo it, can't I?	
Got two bedrooms, hant we?	
We have got two bedrooms hant we?	
Can't find that one, can you?	

Appendix B.
Mean rank order of frequency of mothers' frames (Manchester corpus)

Are X – ing	67.75	X is – ing	31.25
Do X –?	66.5	X might be -	30.125
Can X –?	66.25	Where did X -?	29.875
Shall X –?	66	X have -	29.625
X don't -	65.75	What can X -?	27.75
X can –	63.5	I'm – ing	26.5
X can't –	59.5	You'd -	24
Have X –?	59	X been – ing	23.125
X're – ing	57.125	What do X -?	22.375
Don't – [IMP]	56.5	X did –	22
Is X – ing?	56.375	How do X –?	20.625
What do you –?	54.625	Where are X –ing?	20.25
X've -	54.5	X be -ing	19.75
X doesn't -	54.5	What have you –?	19.75
X won't -	53.75	Why are you –ing?	18.625
X'll –	53.625	X wouldn't -	18.5
Did X –?	52	Where do X -?	18
X 'is – ing	47.875	Where shall X -?	17.625
What did X –?	47.5	Who did you -?	17.25
Has X –?	46.875	Can't you?	17.25
Does X –?	46.375	Won't it -?	17.125
X didn't -	45.5	X must -	16.5
X were -ing	43.625	Which X do -?	16.375
X haven't -	43.125	Who do you -?	15.75
X will -	42.375	What X do -?	15.625
What are X – ing?	42.25	X do –	14.875
X 'has -	41	Where should X -?	14.75
X could -	40.5	I'd -	14.75
Will X –?	39.875	Shouldn't X -?	14
X might -	37	Were you –ing?	14
X was – ing	36.25	X shouldn't -	13.875
What does –?	32.875	Who's –?	13.125
X hasn't –	32.75	What's X – ing?	12
What shall we –?	31.875		
X would -	31.75		
Don't you –?	31.375		

Using corpora to examine discourse effects in syntax

Shanley Allen, Barbora Skarabela and Mary Hughes

1. Introduction

A growing body of evidence shows that children's acquisition of at least some aspects of syntax is affected by their understanding of information flow in discourse. Specifically, children choose whether and in what form to realize arguments in their speech depending on their determination of how cognitively accessible the referent is to the listener. In this chapter, we argue that studies of naturalistic corpora are essential for understanding this process. We discuss recently developed methods for these studies, recent findings, the complementary contribution of experimental studies, and directions for further research.

Argument realization entails the selection of a particular linguistic form – full noun phrase, demonstrative, pronoun, or zero anaphora (omission) – to express a referent as the subject or object of a verb. In English, for example, one can describe an event of hugging using any of the following utterances depending on the context: *I hugged Marion*, *I hugged the girl*, *I hugged this one*, or *I hugged her*. In null-subject or null-argument languages which allow ellipsis (e.g., Italian, Japanese, Inuktitut), the subject and sometimes the object can also be omitted.

It is well-documented that children omit arguments more frequently and in different contexts than adult speakers of their language, regardless of the typology of their language (e.g., Allen 2000; Bloom 1990; Gerken 1991; Greenfield and Smith 1976; Grinstead 2000; Hyams 1986; Kim 2000; Serratrice 2005; Skarabela and Allen 2003; Valian 1991; Valian and Eisenberg 1996). Accounts of this phenomenon abound from various theoretical perspectives, some claiming that early non-target-like argument omission is grammatical for the child (e.g., Hyams 1986; Hyams and Wexler 1993), and others claiming that it derives from early processing limitations (e.g., Bloom 1990; Gerken 1991; Valian 1991). This work has focused on the general conditions under which argument omission is permitted or likely to occur – i.e. why children omit arguments at all. However, although it is widely acknowledged that children do not omit all or often even most of the arguments that meet those general conditions, work from these theoretical perspectives does not tend to seek explanations for which arguments are actually omitted out of the many ones for which omission would be allowed under the general conditions. In addition, this work has focused on argument realization in languages (like English) in which arguments are typically required in adult speech, and has pursued the question of why children *over*-omit arguments. Very few if any studies from these perspectives have investigated argument realization in null-argument languages.

In the past 15 years, a different perspective on child argument realization has emerged, largely growing out of work on discourse-pragmatics in adult speakers of null-argument languages (e.g., Ariel 1990; Bock and Warren 1985; Chafe 1987; Du Bois 1987; Givón 1983; Gundel, Hedberg and Zacharski 1993; Prince 1985). This new perspective focuses on what factors are relevant in a speaker's choice to realize an individual argument as lexical, pronominal, or null (e.g., Allen 2000, 2007; Cho 2004; Clancy 1993, 1997, 2003; Guerriero, Cooper, Oshima-Takane and Kuriyama 2001; Guerriero, Oshima-Takane and Kuriyama 2006; Hughes and Allen 2006; Narasimhan, Budwig and Murty 2005; Paradis and Navarro 2003; Serratrice 2005; Serratrice, Sorace and Paoli 2004; Skarabela 2006; Skarabela and Allen 2002). For example, speakers often omit arguments which have just been stated in the previous utterance, but tend to overtly realize arguments which are new to the discourse. Research identifying particular features of information flow and analyzing the effect of these in various sets of child data can allow us to come much closer to understanding and predicting the form in which a child will realize a particular argument, what factors children attend to most, and how children come to realize arguments in an adult-like way. This work has focused primarily on null-argument languages and whether children follow the same patterns as caregivers in which arguments they omit. Extending to non-null-argument languages such as English, we can further investigate which particular arguments that meet the general omission criteria established from grammatical and processing perspectives (or other criteria yet to be discovered) are likely to actually be omitted, based on children's understanding of information flow in discourse.

But what type of data is best suited for answering these questions? The growing sophistication of experimental paradigms might tempt one to believe that experiments are the obvious answer. As argued by Valian and Aubry (2005), experiments in this area can offer several advantages: high frequency of occurrence of variables which may be rare in spontaneous speech, control of the contexts of interaction to single out the effects of individual variables, systematic manipulation of variables, comparison of one variable against another in a constrained setting to test the relative influence of each, a relatively large and representative sample of children, and systematic comparison of children with different levels of linguistic ability (e.g., by MLU). As discussed later, experiments clearly have made valuable contributions to research on argument realization.

We argue in this chapter, however, that naturalistic corpus research in this area is essential for three reasons. First, it allows us to identify individual factors that are relevant in natural child discourse, on the basis of children using language in contexts of their choice, to extend our understanding derived from theorizing and adult studies. Spontaneous speech is a linguistically and cognitively inexpensive task, revealing children's standard ability to select argument forms to realize intended referents, and allowing us to see which factors influence the way that children realize arguments under natural conditions. Relevant factors are obviously identified through experimental work as well, but arguably the naturalistic data allows identification of factors in more natural settings. In addition, information from the two approaches allows for triangulation by showing that the factors are relevant in a variety of situations. Second, naturalistic corpus research allows us to see how a variety of factors work together in influencing argument realization, rather than looking at only one or two carefully controlled factors in the typical experimental situation. Examples of complex interactions between the features of accessibility and argument form that occur in naturalistic communication situations can then be used as the basis for designing experiments to further explore these interactions. Third, it allows us to see how children learn and use the accessibility factors in the flow of long stretches of natural discourse as opposed to in the short interchanges typical of elicited production tasks and other experimental contexts. This includes following certain grammatical patterns across discourse (Du Bois 1985, 1987), building on patterns modelled in caregiver speech (Clancy 2003), and managing miscommunication (Skarabela 2006).

That said, the study of spontaneous speech corpora in this domain is not easy. Since the structures under investigation are often relatively rare, a large amount of data from several children is needed to provide enough power for statistical analysis. Transcript data available publicly is typically insufficient for looking at contextual and interactional determinants of cognitive accessibility such as presence/absence of the referent, contextual disambiguation of the referent, and joint attention; only videotaped data provides the necessary information. Finally, selecting which features to study, coding them in a consistent and replicable way within a study, and comparing across studies are all very challenging because of the large number of features involved and the myriad ways of defining them. Discussion in this chapter focuses on the latter, reporting on recently developed methods for coding and analyzing large corpora, and discussing the relative merits of corpus-based research for studying the effects of discourse on the acquisition of syntax.

The remainder of the chapter is structured as follows. After beginning with a brief outline of research on the effect of information flow on argument realization in adult speech to establish a context for the child studies, the most substantial part of the chapter provides an extended overview and (meta-)analysis of several aspects of the study of argument realization in naturalistic corpora. We first describe and define several individual features of information flow which have been identified in naturalistic studies, highlighting differences in definition or application across studies where relevant, and showing that children are sensitive to each of these features in their argument realization. We also touch on developmental results relevant to individual features, although this has not been a focus of naturalistic work for various reasons. Next, we examine the various ways in which the interaction between the features has been assessed, including studies which group features together as well as those which compare individual features to each other. Finally, we present three examples of insight gained by looking at information flow across utterances within a stretch of discourse. In the last portion of the chapter we turn to an assessment of representative experimental studies, discussing their strengths and difficulties and showing how they provide complementary information about the role of cognitive accessibility in argument realization to that gleaned from naturalistic studies. We see how a reduced set of features have been studied in experiments, carefully controlled and typically not in interaction with each other, and also how studying development has been an important focus. We finish the chapter by summarizing the values of naturalistic corpus analysis in this area, and providing directions for further research.

2. The effect of information flow on argument realization in adult speech

Our understanding of the effect of information flow on argument realization is rooted in a by now ample literature based on adult spontaneous speech data in a variety of discourse contexts. The modern wave of research on this topic dates back some three decades (e.g., Ariel 1988, 1990, 2001; Arnold 1998; Arnold and Griffin 2007; Bock and Warren 1985; Brennan 1995; Chafe 1976, 1987, 1994, 1996; Clancy 1980; Clark and Haviland 1977; Clark and Marshall 1981; Du Bois 1985, 1987; Du Bois, Kumpf and Ashby 2003; Fretheim and Gundel 1996; Garrod and Sanford 1982; Givón 1983; Gordon, Grosz and Gilliom 1993; Grosz, Joshi and Weinstein 1995; Gundel 1985; Gundel *et al.* 1993; Marslen-Wilson, Levy and Tyler 1982; Prince 1981, 1985). This work is broadly organized around the notion of accessibility of a referent within the flow of discourse. Bock and Warren (1985: 50) define conceptual accessibility as "the ease with which the mental representation of some potential referent can be activated in or retrieved from memory." A variety of discourse factors are investigated in the literature mentioned above and shown to feed into this accessibility. These include recency of prior mention of the referent in discourse, number of other potential competitor referents in the immediate discourse context, number of utterances that the referent persists in the discourse after its initial mention, extent to which the referent is the topic of current discourse, degree to which the referent is the focus of attention in the physical context, presence of the referent in the physical context, degree of animacy of the referent, degree to which the referent is uniquely identifiable for all in a given setting or social group (e.g., *the sun*, *the floor*, *the queen*, *the boss*, *John*), and degree of imageability of the referent. Several researchers have elaborated scales or hierarchies indicating how accessible a referent is on the basis of some or all of these characteristics. In general, a highly accessible referent tends to be recently mentioned, with no competitors, persistent after initial mention, the topic of current discourse, the focus of attention of the interlocutors, present in the physical context, highly animate, uniquely identifiable, and highly imageable. In contrast, a referent with a low degree of accessibility tends to be newly mentioned, with several competitors, not persistent after initial mention, not the topic of discourse or focus of attention, absent from the physical context, inanimate, not uniquely identifiable, and not easily imageable. Obviously few if any referents have all of these characteristics at once, so most referents lie at some intermediate point on an accessibility scale.

With respect to argument realization, Ariel (1994: 99) proposes that speakers "direct their addressees' retrieval of the intended referents by signalling to them how accessible those mental entities are" through use of particular forms in speech to express those referents. Again, several researchers propose scales of argument forms ordered by the degree of information about the referent provided in the form, indicating correspondence between each form and the level of referent accessibility it is used to express (e.g., Ariel 1990; Givón 1983; Gundel *et al.* 1993). At one end of the scale, the most accessible referents are realized by forms that provide very little information about that referent: zero anaphora, agreement markers, and unstressed or bound pronouns. The speaker signals the fact that the referent is known by providing little additional information in the linguistic expression. At the other end of the scale, the least accessible referents are realized by forms that provide substantial information about that referent: stressed or independent pronouns, demonstratives, definite and indefinite full noun phrases. Here the speaker signals that s/he does not expect the hearer to be able to identify the referent from the already-existing linguistic and physical context of discourse by providing more complete information in the current linguistic expression. Ariel also notes that speakers may sometimes choose a high information form (e.g., full noun phrase) for a highly accessible referent in order to combat the effect of natural decay or to reduce the possibility of interference from other possible referents. As Gundel *et al.* (1993) and others point out, the overall strategy of matching level of information in the linguistic form with referent accessibility corresponds with Grice's (1975) Maxim of Quantity which states that the speaker should be as informative as required but no more informative than needed.

These relationships between referent accessibility and argument realization have been upheld in many studies of adult discourse across a wide range of languages of varying typologies, although languages differ in exactly which forms are used to realize referents at different levels of accessibility depending on the inventory of forms available in each language. In addition, Du Bois (1985, 1987) has shown that argument form and accessibility (as revealed by recency of mention of referent) have reflexes in the grammatical structure of discourse, which he labels Preferred Argument Structure. Only one lexical argument (i.e. full noun phrase as opposed to pronoun or zero anaphora) and one new argument typically appear in a verbal clause, regardless of the number of arguments present in the clause (intransitive, transitive, ditransitive). Further, both lexical and new arguments tend not to appear in A position (subject of transitive verb), and rather appear in S (subject of intransitive verb) or O (object) positions. Subsequent research across many languages of different typologies has upheld these observations, although languages differ in details such as how lexical and new arguments are distributed across S and O positions (e.g., Du Bois *et al.* 2003).

Given that it is well established that these features of information flow affect argument realization in adult speech, it is appropriate to ask how and when this develops in children. Are children sensitive to accessibility features from their earliest speech, or does this take time to develop? Are they sensitive to the same kinds of features as adults? Are they sensitive to the features in the same way as adults? Which of the features are most salient for children, and are reliably encoded in children's speech? How do the features interact with each other, and with other aspects of grammar?

The answers to these questions will lead us to a deeper and more thorough understanding of what drives argument realization in children, and ultimately to a more complete theory of what drives the development of grammar in children, as hinted at in the following examples (see Allen 2006 for an extended discussion of this question). As noted earlier, explaining the child-adult differences in argument realization has been a major question in the field of language development over the past 30 years, and has served as a microcosm for exploring the various factors that feed into language development and how (if at all) they interact. The predominant theoretical explanations of child-adult differences in argument realization focus on identifying the general grammatical (e.g., Hyams 1986; Hyams and Wexler 1993) and processing (e.g., Bloom 1990; Gerken 1991; Valian 1991) conditions under which children are expected to omit arguments. But these approaches do not have the tools to explain which of the many arguments meeting those conditions are actually omitted. For example, versions of the grammatical approach claim on the basis of syntactic principles that subjects can be omitted in matrix but not subordinate clauses (e.g., Rizzi 1993/1994) or with non-finite but not finite verbs (e.g., Wexler, Schütze and Rice 1998), and versions of the performance approach claim that subjects are much more likely to be omitted when they occur with long VPs than with short VPs due to children's limited processing resources (Bloom 1990). However, clearly not all subjects of non-finite verbs, subjects in matrix clauses, or subjects with long VPs are omitted. Understanding how cognitive accessibility contributes to argument realization can enable us to predict which subjects meeting these grammatical and processing conditions will be omitted. We may also find that the dynamics of information flow in fact underlie these grammatical and performance patterns: perhaps subjects of non-finite clauses are significantly more accessible overall than subjects of finite clauses, or subjects of long VPs are significantly more accessible than subjects of short VPs! In addition, the cognitive accessibility approach can serve to uncover new patterns of argument omission in children. For example, research on adult speech from this perspective predicts an asymmetry in child argument omission between subjects in the A vs. S positions, a pattern not yet revealed in the extensive literature from the grammatical perspective.

An understanding of when and how children hone their sensitivity to the relationship between accessibility features and argument realization could also help us understand how children retreat from early over-omission of arguments or why children increase their use of strong pronouns and lexical arguments, questions that have largely been left unexplained in literature from the grammatical perspective. Further, developmental data from corpora coded for accessibility features could help resolve an apparent conflict between the grammatical and performance approaches identified by

Hyams and Wexler (1993). At least one version of the grammatical approach predicts that arguments omitted by young children in non-null-subject languages are those arguments that would be realized as pronouns by older children and adults. However, the performance approach predicts no such continuity since subjects are omitted on the basis of processing resources and not any discourse-based properties. A developmental assessment of argument form based on referent accessibility would clarify which of these predictions is consistent with the data.

With these ultimate motivations in mind, we now turn to a detailed overview and analysis of the effect of the dynamics of information flow on argument realization as revealed through research on naturalistic spontaneous child speech.

3. The effect of information flow on argument realization in child speech

Over the past 15 years, a growing number of studies have appeared in the language development literature using naturalistic data to investigate the relationship between information flow and argument realization (Table 1). As noted earlier, these studies have an advantage over experimental studies in that they view the workings of information flow in naturalistic contexts, typically in the child's own home with familiar interlocutors (parents, siblings, friends, and/or familiar researchers). The situations of interaction are not contrived, and thus researchers can be more assured that children produce their utterances as they typically do, influenced by conditions of interaction that they encounter and use regularly in their daily life. In addition, the child may have a better knowledge of objects that are typically present in the home setting and thus be more free to show the full extent of their linguistic ability; it may be difficult to take in all the nonlinguistic information in an unfamiliar lab setting.

In most studies, data is collected in sessions from 20 to 60 minutes long, at a frequency of every two weeks to every four months, over a period of six months to two years. This allows one to observe development within a single child, and to check the stability of the use of information flow features over a period of time. Because of the intensity of data collection, however, usually only a few children are studied, thus compromising the generalizability of the work to some extent.

The first study along these lines, conducted by Greenfield and Smith (1976), shows that children at the one-word stage tend to select for production, based on their assumed target utterance, the one word that conveys the most essential information of their intended message. That word, in combination with contextual information, encodes the communicative intent of a full utterance in adult speech. Greenfield and Smith (1976) call this tendency the Informativeness Principle: children tend to omit presupposed information that can be taken for granted, and they tend to select the word that expresses what is new or changing in the situation, representing information that is not already shared in some way between the speaker and interlocutor.

Table 1. Studies investigating referent accessibility and argument realization

Study	Language	Age	Source of data	Features
Allen (1997, 2000, 2007)	Inuktitut	2;0–3;6	Videotaped data (Allen 1996)	absence, newness, contrast, differentiation in context, differentiation in discourse, inanimacy, person, query
Allen and Schroeder (2003)	Inuktitut	2;0–3;6	Videotaped data (Allen 1996)	newness
Cho (2004)	Korean	1;8–3;0	Audiotaped data	newness
Clancy (1993, 1997)	Korean	1;8–2;8	Audiotaped data	absence, newness, contrast, animacy, person, query
Clancy (2003)	Korean	1;8–2;8	Audiotaped data	newness, animacy, person
Guerreiro, Oshima-Takane and Kuriyama (2006)	Japanese, English	1;9–3;0	Videotaped data (Oshima-Takane, Goodz and Derevensky 1996)	newness
Hughes and Allen (2006)	English	2;0–2;1	Videotaped data (Lieven, Behrens, Speares and Tomasello 2003)	absence, newness, differentiation in context, differentiation in discourse, inanimacy, person
Mishina-Mori (2007)	Japanese, English Japanese-English bilingual	2;6–3;2	Audio- and/or videotaped (Brown 1973; Mishina 1997; Miyata 1995)	newness
Narasimhan, Budwig and Murty (2005)	Hindi	2;10–4;3	Audio- and videotaped data (Budwig and Chaudhary 1996)	animacy, contrast, newness, query

Study	Language	Age	Source of data	Features
Paradis and Navarro (2003)	Spanish, English, Spanish-English bilingual	1;0–2;0	Transcribed data (Deuchar and Quay 2000; López Ornat 1994; Serrat Sellabona unpublished)	newness, contrast, absence, query, emphasis
Serratrice (2005)	Italian	1;5–3;0	Transcribed data with rich contextual notes (Cipriani, Pfanner, Chilosi, Cittadoni, Ciuti, Maccari, Pantano, Pfanner, Poli, Sarno, Bottari, Cappelli, Colombo and Veneziano 1989)	activation state, referential ambiguity, person
Serratrice, Sorace and Paoli (2004)	Italian, English, Italian-English bilingual	1;7–4;7	Transcribed data with rich contextual notes (Serratrice, no date given, for Italian-English bilingual child; Cipriani et al. 1989 for Italian monolinguals and Brown 1973; Sachs 1983; Suppes 1974 for English monolinguals)	person, absence, activation (=newness), contrast, differentiation in discourse, query
Skarabela (2006)	Inuktitut	2;0–3;6	Videotaped data (Allen 1996)	physical absence, linguistic newness, contrast, interference, lack of joint attention
Skarabela (2007)	Inuktitut	2;0–3;6	Videotaped data (Allen 1996)	joint attention
Skarabela and Allen (2002)	Inuktitut	2;0–3;6	Videotaped data (Allen 1996)	newness, joint attention

More recent studies in this domain have focused on identifying individual features of accessibility in information flow from adult discourse that are relevant to children, and determining how to code them in child data (which is often more challenging than adult data). Once the features are coded in naturalistic corpora, they are assessed both qualitatively and quantitatively to determine how they shape children's realization of arguments. Table 1 lists many of these recent studies, including the languages and ages dealt with, and the accessibility features studied. We do not include studies based on narrative data since they do not involve large spontaneous speech corpora which is the theme of this volume. It should be noted, however, that several narrative studies have been published focusing at least partly on the relationship between referent accessibility and argument realization (e.g., Clancy 1992; Hickmann and Hendriks 1999; Karmiloff-Smith 1985).

As shown in Table 1, at least 11 studies to date (some reporting results in more than one paper) have investigated the effect of one or more accessibility features on argument realization across seven languages (English, Hindi, Inuktitut, Italian, Japanese, Korean, Spanish). All studies have found at least some evidence that children use relatively more informative linguistic forms (full noun phrases, demonstratives, stressed or independent pronouns) to realize referents which have a low degree of cognitive accessibility, and relatively less informative forms (unstressed or bound pronouns, omission) to realize referents which are highly accessible. Some studies have also looked at how this sensitivity develops in children, although this has not been a major focus of naturalistic work. In the next sections we focus on the different features used in these studies, how they are typically defined and coded, whether the different features are tapping into accessibility in the same way, and what developmental patterns are apparent.

4. Individual accessibility features

A total of nine different accessibility features have been investigated across the different studies listed in Table 1, although they are labelled and defined somewhat differently across studies. They are all derived from the features used in the adult studies mentioned earlier, but not all the features studied for adults have been studied for children. Although each of the features is in reality both continuous and complex, in most studies each is treated as binary (accessible, not accessible) for purposes of the studies of argument realization discussed here. This enables assessment of the statistical relationship between the accessibility of the referent and the form of the argument in a way that using a continuum to code degree of accessibility would not. Further, it substantially simplifies the task of determining degree of accessibility of a referent for each feature. The "not accessible" value for each feature indicates that a referent would not be accessible to the interlocutor in a conversation solely on the basis of the discourse or situational information from that feature, such as a referent newly introduced into discourse or absent from the physical context of interaction. The "accessible" value, in contrast, indicates that a referent would be accessible on the basis of information from that feature, such as a referent already recently referred to in the discourse or present in the physical context. However, it is clear that some features are stronger than others in their influence on argument realization, and that most features are not symmetrical in their effect. Each of the nine features is discussed in some detail in the following paragraphs. Developmental trends with respect to individual features are noted after the features are discussed.

4.1 Newness

The most widely studied feature is the recency of mention of the referent in the discourse. Indeed, this is the one feature that is regularly referred to as undoubtedly having some effect on child argument realization, even by researchers from theoretical perspectives not related to discourse-pragmatics (e.g., Bloom 1990, 1993; Hyams and Wexler 1993). The "not accessible" value for newness characterizes a referent which has not been mentioned in the prior discourse and is predicted to be realized by a high information form, while a referent that has been previously mentioned (i.e. "accessible") is predicted to be realized by a pronoun or null argument. This is one of the two features for which both binary values of accessibility are assumed to have a strong influence on argument form.

The criteria for evaluating whether a referent is new or given vary substantially across studies. Most studies restrict the definition to explicit linguistic mention in prior discourse. However, different cut-off points are used across studies to distinguish new vs. given, reflecting in part a poor understanding of the psychological mechanisms underlying the contribution of newness to overall accessibility. Based on criteria laid out in Chafe (1976) and Du Bois (1987) for adult research on elicited narratives, some child studies (e.g., Clancy 1993) recognize three categories of newness: *non-new* (mentioned in the preceding utterance), *accessible* (mentioned in the preceding 2+ utterances), and *new* (never before mentioned in the interaction). This classification works well for elicited narratives which do not typically exceed 100–200 utterances, and in which participants are focused on the same storyline throughout the interaction. It seems much less useful, however, for spontaneous speech interactions in which the topic of conversation changes frequently and in which one session could easily include 1000 or more utterances. Therefore, most studies of newness in child spontaneous speech collapse the accessible and new categories together into one category leading to the application of a binary distinction between new and given referents. Studies following the earlier-mentioned adult work consider a referent as new when it has not been explicitly mentioned in the preceding 20 utterances, and given otherwise (e.g., Allen 2000; Guerriero *et al.* 2006; Hughes and Allen 2006; Mishina-Mori 2007; Skarabela 2006). However, some studies apply a much earlier cut-off point ranging from three prior utterances (Narasimhan *et al.* 2005) to 5–10 exchanges (Paradis and

Navarro 2003), while others do not specify any particular cut-off point (Serratrice *et al.* 2004). In an attempt to clarify the underlying motivation for the boundary between new and given in child speech, Skarabela and Allen (2003) analyzed in their corpus of Inuktitut child speech how frequently a target referent was mentioned one utterance prior, two utterances prior, and so forth, up to 21 or more utterances prior. They determined that very few arguments have preceding references more than 5 utterances prior, suggesting that the difference between a cut-off of 5 versus 20 preceding arguments is minimal, and that an earlier threshold between new and given information (i.e. a distance of 5 utterances to encode a referent as new) might be more appropriate for child spontaneous speech.

Another area of difference across studies is the relationship between *newness* and person of the referent. Following Chafe (1976) and Du Bois (1987), most studies consider first and second person referents as given because they always encode reference to speech participants ('I', the speaker, and 'you', the listener), while third person referents are classified as either new or given depending on the context (e.g., Allen 2000; Guerriero *et al.* 2006; Hughes and Allen 2006; Mishina-Mori 2007; Serratrice *et al.* 2004, Skarabela 2006). Some researchers are more cautious, classifying all first introductions of first and second person referents as new (Clancy 1993; 1997, 2003; Narasimhan *et al.* 2005), although they acknowledge that the effect is slight since there are few first introductions of such referents.

4.2 Topicality

Topicality refers to whether the referent is or is not the focus of the current conversation (e.g., Givón 1983; also widely discussed in the generative literature), usually termed "accessible" and "not accessible" respectively. It overlaps substantially with *newness* to the extent that the two are often not easily distinguishable. One difference is that *topicality* takes as a reference point both extralinguistic and linguistic contexts, whereas *newness* is typically restricted to only linguistic contexts. Serratrice *et al.*'s (2004) feature *activation* is very similar if not identical to *topicality*; they consider a referent "accessible" for *activation* if it is associated with topic maintenance, and "not accessible" for *activation* if it has not been previously introduced in discourse or signals a shift of topic. Narasimhan *et al.* (2005) formulate their feature *prior mention* in terms of whether or not the referent is being *talked about* rather than in terms of purely linguistic mention of the referent – again consistent with the concept of *topicality*. This enables them to capture the tendency for referents to be talked about more frequently than they are explicitly mentioned. Cho (2004: 37) identifies a referent as topical if it "had been mentioned in the immediately preceding clause, or was present physically in the discourse context." Other researchers define *topicality* in terms of a referent's salience in the discourse context (Clark 2003; Kayama 2003). The coding of *topicality* is much less objective than that of some of the other features since it depends on one's impression of salience rather than on anything quantifiable. As is the case for *newness*, both the "accessible" and "inaccessible" values of *topicality* are assumed to have strong influence on argument form.

4.3 Absence

The feature *absence* refers to whether a referent is present in or absent from the physical context of the conversation, sometimes narrowly defined as the visual field/space of the discourse interaction (Paradis and Navarro 2003). *Absent* referents are considered less conceptually accessible to the hearer than *present* referents and thus are more likely to be realized by a high information argument form, as has been confirmed by all of the relevant studies listed in Table 1. There is much less strength in the reverse prediction, however: just because a referent is present in the physical context does not constitute grounds for realizing the associated argument with a low information form because mere presence of a referent does not make it particularly salient to the hearer. For this reason, Narasimhan *et al.* (2005) do not include *absence* as one of the indicators of accessibility (which they refer to as "pragmatic prominence") in their study. Note that several researchers have coded *absence* on the basis of contextual notes in transcript data (e.g., Paradis and Navarro 2003; Serratrice *et al.* 2004). This is less than ideal for obvious reasons.

4.4 Query

The feature *query* indicates whether or not a referent is the subject of or the response to a question. The underlying assumption is that (information about) the referent is either not yet identified or newly identified in an instance of *query*. As a result, the listener has less than complete knowledge of the referent, and thus the speaker is likely to realize it using a high information form. As with *absence*, the reverse is not true: the failure of a referent to be the subject of or response to a question does not make it salient to the hearer and thus use of a low information form is not expected on that basis alone.

The way that the definition of *query* plays out in actual coding differs substantially across studies. Allen (2000) and her colleagues (Hughes and Allen 2006; Skarabela 2006) define *query* quite narrowly such that in the interaction *Who ate the cake? John did!*, only *who* and *John* would be coded as "not accessible" for *query*. Serratrice *et al.* (2004) would have coded both *cake* (since information *about* the cake is queried) and *John* (they did not code question words for discourse-pragmatic features at all) (Serratrice personal communication, April 2007). Narasimhan *et al.* (2005) would have coded only *John* since they limited the definition of *query* to responses only. Paradis and Navarro (2003) coded "not accessible" for *query* "when the referent was being questioned (in an intonational interrogative) or used in response to a question" (note that they did not code any arguments in structurally interrogative utterances), so they would have coded only *John* as "not accessible" in the above example. Clancy (1993,

1997) would have coded *John* in both the response *John did!* (with a verb) and *John!* (without a verb); all other studies coded only referring expressions which were arguments of overtly expressed verbs.

It is not surprising, therefore, that different studies have found quite different results about the role of *query* in argument realization. Clancy (1993, 1997) and Serratrice *et al.* (2004) both found that children were more likely to use a high information argument form to realize a referent which was the subject of or response to a question. In contrast, *query* did not have a significant effect on argument form in child Inuktitut (Allen 2000). Paradis and Navarro (2003) did not assess the significance of the effect of *query* in their analysis, and Narasimhan *et al.* (2005) analyzed its effect only in combination with other discourse-pragmatic features so the unique effect of *query* is not discernable. More research following a consistent method will reveal whether this feature indeed affects argument realization.

4.5 Disambiguation / contrast / interference

Several researchers assess whether a particular referent has potential competitor referents in the linguistic or physical context that could be easily confused with the target referent. Note that it is not necessary for the speaker to explicitly draw attention to this potential ambiguity; it is only necessary that the potential ambiguity exist. The prediction is that the speaker will more likely realize a potentially ambiguous referent with a high information form to make its identity clear. As with the previous two features, the reverse prediction does not hold. Just being unambiguously identifiable in either discourse or physical context does not make a referent salient, and thus does not by itself encourage use of a low information form to realize that referent.

This feature has appeared in the literature under several different names, and with different definitions. Both Clancy (1993, 1997) and Narasimhan *et al.* (2005) refer to it as *contrast*. They take the verb semantics as the main criterion, coding the target referent as "not accessible" for *contrast* if there is one or more other possible referents "bearing the same relation to the same predicate … or bearing a parallel relation to a similar type of predicate" (Clancy 1997: 641). Paradis and Navarro (2003: 379) similarly ascribe *contrast* to an argument "whose function [is] to disambiguate between two possible referents." Allen (2000) and Hughes and Allen (2006) separate the effects of linguistic and physical context into two features, termed *differentiation in discourse* and *differentiation in context*. The former refers to a referent which has one or more potentially competing referents in the previous 5 utterances; the latter refers to a referent which has one or more potentially competing referents in the immediate physical context. Serratrice *et al.* (2004) and Serratrice (2005) restrict themselves to disambiguation in the linguistic context (termed *differentiation in discourse* and *disambiguation* respectively); they could not analyze the physical context since their analyses were based mostly on transcript data. Skarabela (2006) only investigates disambiguation in the physical context, using the term *interference*.

All of the mentioned studies confirm the relevance of *disambiguation* (as they construe it) to argument realization. Allen (2000) and Hughes and Allen (2006) show in separate studies of Inuktitut and English data that *differentiation in context* has a significant effect while *differentiation in discourse* does not when both are assessed together to determine their relative contribution to a logistic regression model. Allen (2000) suggests that this is due to confounding between these two features, as well as between these features and *explicit contrast* (see next section). Since other researchers either analyzed only one of these features or treated the two together as one feature, it is not surprising that the discrepancy in Allen (2000) and Hughes and Allen (2006) did not show up in those studies.

4.6 Explicit contrast / emphasis

Allen (2000), Paradis and Navarro (2003), Serratrice *et al.* (2004), and Skarabela (2006) investigate the effect on argument realization of a contrast made explicit or emphasized by the speaker. This is different from the factor disambiguation / contrast / interference just discussed because in addition to the ambiguous situation being present in the linguistic or physical context of discourse, it is actively resolved by the speaker through some type of emphasis. A referent that is explicitly contrasted with another potential referent is more likely to be realized with a high information form since there is more than one potential referent in the context. However, a referent which is not being explicitly contrasted would not pull for a low information form since it is not particularly salient. This feature is different from the others discussed so far in that it depends to some degree on assessing the speaker's intent rather than simply the situation presented by the discourse and physical context.

Allen (2000) and Skarabela (2006), both using the term *contrast*, employ both non-linguistic and linguistic means to assess whether the speaker is explicitly contrasting a referent, including stress, tone of voice and gesture. Allen (2000: 488) describes typical situations of explicit contrast as a child "wanting to prohibit others from doing something he or she is doing, or when a child wants to do something someone else is doing". Serratrice *et al.* (2004) (also under the term *contrast*) use the preceding and following discourse context to determine the child's intention or assumption of contrast (since their data is mostly in the form of written transcripts, they have no access to intonation information). Paradis and Navarro's (2003) definition of *contrast* partly includes this idea of explicit contrast in that they use it to code an argument whose function is to focus on a particular referent. Their feature *emphasis*, used to code arguments that "could be read as if they had more prosodic prominence, in other words, the speaker seemed to intend to highlight that [argument]," also is similar to the notion of *explicit contrast* although not completely identical. All these studies find, as expected, that children use more informative forms to realize referents which they explicitly contrast with others.

Hughes and Allen (2006) purposefully leave *explicit contrast* out of the list of features coded in their study because it functions differently from the other features. Since it is most often indicated by prosodic prominence, the argument must be realized using a high information form (e.g., stressed pronoun, full noun phrase) for the feature to apply, and thus all arguments which are explicitly contrastive are realized with high information forms almost by definition. As noted earlier, the feature *explicit contrast* often overlaps with the various types of *disambiguation* coded across studies. The confounding between these features should be sorted out in future research.

4.7 Person

The person of referent is often included as a discourse-pragmatic feature since, following Du Bois (1987) and others, third person referents (e.g., *he*, *she*, *it*, *they*) have different discourse-pragmatic status than first and second person referents (e.g., *I*, *we*, *you*). The search space for the latter tends to be quite restricted, particularly in child discourse (Allen 2000), because there are relatively few participants in a typical conversation. In contrast, it is much more difficult for the hearer to identify the referent of a third person argument since there is a potentially unlimited number of third person referents in the search space. Thus, child speakers are predicted frequently to realize first and second person referents with low information forms. Most languages only allow first and second person referents to be realized as low information forms: pronouns, agreement markers or null forms depending on the language (e.g., Inuktitut does not permit first and second person pronouns in argument position). However, children are predicted to select the lowest form available in their language if more than one option is available. Third person referents can be expressed in most languages using a wide variety of forms – full noun phrases, proper names, demonstratives, independent and bound pronouns, verbal agreement markers, and null forms – although the exact forms possible depend on the language (e.g., Inuktitut allows all but pronouns, English has no plural agreement markers and severely restricts null forms). Just the fact of being third person does not make the referent strikingly inaccessible to the hearer, however, so it does not command use of a particularly high information form. Thus, the effect of *person* is the converse of that for the previous four features discussed; here, the "accessible" value pulls for using a low information argument form because being first or second person makes the referent quite salient to the hearer, but the "inaccessible" value does not by itself pull for a high information form.

The tendency for first and second person referents to be realized with the lowest information form possible in a language, and to do so more frequently than third person referents, is confirmed by all the studies in typologically diverse languages listed in Table 1. Although no effect of person was found in data from one English-Italian bilingual child, the authors claim that that is due to interaction between *person* and other features (Serratrice *et al.* 2004). Indeed, *person* clearly overlaps considerably with *newness* (first and second person referents in most studies are assumed to be "accessible" for *newness* by definition), *absence* (first and second person referents are virtually always present in the physical context of the conversation), *disambiguation* (it is almost always clear who the speaker and hearer are in a conversation), *animacy* (first and second person referents are always animate), and *attention* (first and second person referents are assumed to always be jointly attended to). Because of the powerful effect of person in argument realization, and because of the high degree of overlap between *person* and other features, some researchers have restricted some or all of their analyses to third person only (e.g., Allen 2000; Hughes and Allen 2006; Skarabela 2006, 2007; Skarabela and Allen 2002, 2003).

4.8 Animacy

The feature *animacy* has also been studied frequently in the context of argument realization in both child and adult language. Animacy refers to how alive or sentient an entity is, with first person humans at one end of the continuum and abstract entities at the other. Adult studies often elaborate detailed animacy hierarchies with 8 or more levels, which are crucial in many languages for understanding the intricacies of such phenomena as ergative marking, noun classification, and word order (e.g., Comrie 1989; Silverstein 1976). In the child studies discussed here, animacy is applied as a binary feature that differentiates between animate referents (human, animal) as "accessible" and inanimate referents as "not accessible." As noted earlier, there is substantial overlap between *animacy* and *person* because all inanimate referents are third person, and all first and second person referents are animate.

Although animacy is often used as an accessibility feature, it is distinct from other such features since it is an inherent semantic property associated with individual referents. Unlike *newness*, *absence* and *person* which are determined by a particular discourse-pragmatic context, *animacy* is an inherent property that is stable across different discourse-pragmatic contexts. In certain contexts in child discourse, however, inanimate referents such as dolls, stuffed animals, and certain toys assume the characteristics of humans and are thus typically coded as animate.

What, then, is the relationship between animacy and argument realization? The logic is very similar to that just described for *person*. In typical child discourse, the number of inanimate entities (e.g., food, cup, television, furniture, clothes) outweighs the number of animate entities (e.g., mother, father, sibling, friend, dog). Thus, reference to an inanimate entity is potentially more ambiguous than to an animate entity, such that inanimate entities are predicted to be realized more frequently by high information argument forms than animate entities. Previous studies in this area yield controversial results, however. While animacy is found to influence argument realization in the expected way in some languages (e.g., Korean: Clancy 1993, 1997, 2003), it does not have a significant effect on the linguistic form in others (e.g., Inuktitut: Allen 2000; English: Hughes and Allen 2006). Although Narasimhan *et al.* (2005) include *animacy* in their analysis, its effect cannot be separated from that of others included in the designation "pragmatically prominent". It is thus unclear to what extent animacy alone influences the choice of argument form. In addition, differences in the reported findings may originate in slightly different coding strategies (e.g., coding dolls as animate versus inanimate entities). Finally, the link between this inherent semantic property and argument realization may be too weak. Being animate does not make a referent particularly salient in discourse, and being inanimate does not make a referent particularly non-salient. Therefore, although there is a difference in relative salience between animates and inanimates, the effect is not especially strong, and probably not strong enough to have a significant effect on argument realization.

4.9 Attention

The feature *attention* assesses whether or not a speaker and listener are focused on the same referent while they are aware of each other's attention (Tomasello 1999). The basic prediction is that referents produced in the context of joint attention are more likely to be realized by low information forms than those produced in the absence of joint attention, because the former are particularly salient in discourse. Referents produced in the absence of joint attention are not particularly non-salient in discourse, however, so there is little reason to expect them to be necessarily realized by high information argument forms. To assess whether or not joint attention is in progress for a particular referent, videotaped data are examined for eye gaze, body direction, head direction and gesture (including pointing) of both interlocutors. First and second person referents are automatically considered instances of joint attention in progress since these refer to the speech participants. Further, referents not physically present in the context of the ongoing conversation cannot be coded for joint attention. However, the presence of the target referent in the physical context of the interaction *does not* automatically imply that the speaker and listener are involved in joint attention, i.e. a speaker and listener may be involved in "joint activity" (Clark 1996) without joint attention being established.

Analyses of data from 2- to 3-year-old learners of Inuktitut (Skarabela 2006, 2007; Skarabela and Allen 2002, 2004) show that the predictions are realized. In addition, a recent study of the role of joint attention in argument realization in Mandarin child-directed speech shows that Chinese caregivers are more likely to omit arguments of transitive verbs when they are jointly attending to the referents of those arguments with their children (Lee 2006). Lee suggests that joint attention thus facilitates children's identification of intended referents. Clark's (2001) study of English-speaking caregivers makes the similar suggestion that adults establish joint attentional scenes to facilitate early word learning.

Note that although the other factors are typically operationalized in the same way for naturalistic and experimental studies, the factor *attention* is operationalized somewhat differently (see later section on experimental studies). In experimental conditions that are categorized as "not accessible" for *attention*, the interlocutor is either out of the room or explicitly looking away when the child initially interacts with the referent or observes the referent on video. The interlocutor in the experiment also does not attend to the referent when the target utterance is spoken, either because s/he cannot see the referent because of an obstruction or because s/he purposefully does not look at the referent. These experimentally-induced manifestations of lack of joint attention are much stronger than in a typical naturalistic interaction where the interlocutor simply does not happen to be sharing attention with the child on some referent. Therefore, the "not accessible" condition for *attention* in experiments tends to pull much more strongly for a high information form than the similar condition in naturalistic interactions.

4.10 Developmental trends

Although all of the naturalistic studies of argument realization have assessed whether sensitivity to individual accessibility features is operative at one particular age or level of linguistic ability, few studies have explored the question of how that sensitivity changes over time. Most studies have taken as their focus establishing whether children are sensitive to the effect of accessibility features on argument realization at all, and how this interacts with the typological features of the language, leaving for later research the more complex question of when and how this sensitivity develops. Further, given the constraints of naturalistic data, it is not easy to meet the criteria necessary to determine the timing of development. One would need either longitudinal data from one or more children over a sufficient time period to show developmental change or cross-sectional data from several children at each of two or more developmental stages. In addition, one would need sufficient data for each feature studied, at each time point, to do statistics or other analyses ensuring that the change from one time point to another was significantly different either quantitatively or qualitatively.

Several recent naturalistic studies are not suited to investigate development because they sample data from the target child(ren) at only one developmental point. For example, Hughes and Allen (2006) look at one child over only a 6-week period (2;0–2;1), Mishina-Mori (2007) examines four children each over only a two-month period (two older bilinguals 3;0–3;2, and two younger monolingual "controls" 2;6 and 2;9), and Narasimhan *et al.* (2005) investigate data from twelve children but at only one time point each (2;10–4;3) and not properly distributed to form groups according to age or linguistic ability. Some studies present data divided by age groups but no developmental trends are evident, either because no such trends are present or because the small number of children and/or relevant analyzable utterances obscures the trends (e.g., Cho (2004) with two Korean children aged 2;0–2;8; Clancy (1993) with two Korean children aged 1;8–2;8). Allen (2000) was originally intended to investigate development in nine months of longitudinal data from each of four children. However the author decided not to publish the developmental portion of the study because it was not clear whether there were indeed no developmental effects, whether the study did not extend long enough for development to be evident, or whether there was not sufficient data at each developmental point for unambiguous results in the domains investigated. In addition, because the four children ended up being at fairly different developmental levels and because only three data points were available for each child (months 1, 5, and 9 of the study), the developmental groups that could be formed on the basis of linguistic ability ended up being awkwardly unbalanced. The fact that one cannot determine the level of linguistic ability of participants in advance is one major drawback of naturalistic studies.

A few naturalistic studies, however, do focus on development. Serratrice *et al.* (2004) investigated subject and object realization in one English-Italian bilingual child, six Italian-speaking monolingual children, and four English-speaking monolingual children. They divided the data from each language into four developmental stages according to mean length of utterances assessed in words (rather than morphemes): I (MLUW 1.5–2.0), II (MLUW 2.0–3.0), III (MLUW 3.0–4.0), and IV (MLUW 4.0 +). Right from Stage I, a significantly higher percentage of the children's null arguments realized referents with accessible features than referents with inaccessible features, separately assessed for each of *absence*, *activation* (= *topicality*), *contrast*, *differentiation in discourse*, and *query*. The monolinguals in each of the two languages produced over 80% of their null arguments to realize accessible referents (except for *query* at Stages II and IV in English), and the bilingual child over 70% (except for *activation* at Stages II and IV in Italian and *absence* at Stage IV in English). However, the bilingual child used third person pronouns in pragmatically inappropriate contexts in 9% of instances at Stages III and IV in Italian (personal subject pronouns were not used virtually at all before this point). Pronouns in Italian normally signal contexts of focus or topic shift, whereas the bilingual child used them in fully accessible contexts where pronouns would be appropriate in English. Note that Paradis and Navarro (2003) found the same pattern of overuse of pronouns to realize accessible referents in the Spanish of their Spanish-English bilingual child, albeit at an earlier developmental stage (MLUW 1.26–2.51, equivalent to Serratrice *et al.*'s (2004) Stages I and II). However, they explained this as a result of the non-native Spanish input from the child's mother, which also contained a high proportion of pronouns used to realize accessible referents. Serratrice *et al.* did not report data from caregiver speech.

A later study of the same Italian monolingual data (Serratrice 2005) revealed a developmental shift between Stages I and II. Already at Stage I, a significantly higher proportion of the children's overt arguments realized inaccessible referents as compared to accessible referents, for each of *person*, *activation* (= *newness* + *attention* + *topicality*), and *disambiguation in discourse*. However, a significant increase was also found between Stages I and II in the proportion of overt arguments realizing inaccessible referents for each of *person* and *activation*. No change was observed for *disambiguation in discourse*, or for the other features at later stages. Serratrice (2005) hypothesizes that the proportion of overt subjects produced overall increases over time as children take more initiative in introducing topics to conversation rather than just maintaining topics linguistically introduced by caregivers.

Skarabela (2006) investigated development in children's sensitivity to the relationship between argument form and *attention*, comparing this with caregiver data from the same data set. Her data were divided into three groups according to the mean length of utterance in morphemes of all utterances containing a verb (see Allen (1996) for a justification of this grouping): I (MLUv 3.25–3.99), II (MLUv 4.0–4.74) and III (MLUv 4.75–5.49). Note that values for MLUv would be expected to be considerably higher than values for MLU taking all utterances into account, so these numbers do not represent unusual linguistic ability for children aged 2;0–3;6. Chi-square tests assessing the relationship between *attention* (accessible, inaccessible) and *argument form* (overt, null) were not significant at Stages I or II, but children at Stage III produced significantly more overt forms in the context of inaccessible referents than in the context of accessible referents ($p<.001$). When the variable *argument form* was differentiated into three categories – lexical, demonstrative, and null – the Chi-square results were significant at all three stages. As expected, children produced more null forms when *attention* was "accessible" (i.e. when the referent was jointly attended to by speaker and hearer), and more lexical forms when *attention* was "not accessible." Children at Stages I and II were equally likely to produce demonstratives for both values of *attention*. However, children at Stage III followed the adult pattern of producing more demonstratives when *attention* was accessible. Skarabela (2006) also looked at development in each child individually with data grouped according to the just-mentioned stages. Two stages were represented in the data of each child. For three of the four children, the degree of association between *attention* and *argument form* increased from the earlier to later stage. As Skarabela states, these results might be interpreted as suggestive of an increasing role of *attention* in the three different argument forms (lexical, demonstrative, null) with children's increasing MLUv.

Guerriero *et al.* (2006) is the only naturalistic study we are aware of which was explicitly designed to investigate the effect of accessibility on argument realization at predetermined developmental periods. In the first study they report (Study 1), they looked at the effect of *newness* in six English-speaking and six Japanese-speaking children at each of ages 1;9 and 3;0, as well as data from the children's mothers. MLUs for the English data were 1.09–2.25 and 2.90–4.25 respectively; MLUs for the Japanese data were 1.07–1.91 and 2.86–4.29 respectively. The English-speaking children already used more non-lexical than lexical forms to realize given referents at 1;9, and this tendency increased at 3;0. Within the non-lexical forms, null forms predominated at 1;9 but pronominal forms took over by 3;0, similar to the mothers' speech and as expected for the language typology. As for new referents, the children used slightly more non-lexical than lexical forms to realize them at 1;9, but reversed this pattern by 3;0 consistent with their mothers' performance. This suggests that it takes more time for children to learn to introduce new referents as opposed to maintaining existing referents. The Japanese-speaking children produced very few arguments at 1;9. By 3;0 these children behaved like their mothers in producing more non-lexical than lexical forms for given referents, but produced an equivalent number of lexical and non-lexical forms to realize new referents. The mothers used slightly more non-lexical than lexical forms to realize new referents at 1;9, but reversed this pattern by 3;0. Thus, it is possible that the Japanese-speaking children at 3;0 were simply following the earlier model in their input. In Study 2, Guerriero *et al.* (2006) replicated the results of Study 1 with two additional children learning each language, this time with four time points per child: I (MLU 1.0–1.99), II (MLU 2.0–2.99), III (MLU 3.0–3.99) and IV (MLU 4.0 +). The English-speaking children used primarily null forms to realize given arguments at Period I, but largely switched to pronominal forms by Period II for one child and Period III for the other consistent with language-specific patterns. Neither child introduced many new referents at Period I, but they correctly preferred to realize new referents with lexical forms from Period II where new referents started to appear in their speech. Interestingly, virtually all new referents realized with non-lexical forms in both child and mother data also co-occur with some non-linguistic indicator of the referent (e.g., gesture, touch, eye gaze). Both Japanese-speaking children correctly used non-lexical forms to realize given referents right from Period I. However, they only began to prefer lexical forms to realize new referents at Period III for one child and at Period IV for the other. As in Study 1, the Japanese-speaking children's patterns for new referents mirrored their mothers' input at the previous period. In contrast to the English speakers, the Japanese speakers used non-linguistic indicators to identify new referents expressed non-lexically only about half the time. Guerriero *et al.* (2006) suggest that the Japanese mothers are following a typical interaction style between familiar interlocutors whereby the burden is on the hearer to guess the referents from shared knowledge, rather than the English pattern of the burden being on the speaker to be as clear as possible. Children are then mirroring this pattern modelled in the input.

The developmental data taken together reveals some interesting patterns. First, children appear to be already sensitive to the relevance of accessibility to argument realization from around 2;0 or an MLU of 2.0. Second, children increase significantly in this sensitivity somewhere between MLU 2.0 and 3.0 with differences depending on the language and feature studied. Third, children seem to take somewhat longer to produce adult-like forms for inaccessible referents than for accessible referents, perhaps because the pattern in the input is often stronger for accessible referents. Fourth, children's growing sensitivity to accessibility features may be revealed more clearly by treating argument forms as having three or more levels (e.g., lexical, pronominal, null) rather than two (either overt vs. null or lexical vs. non-lexical). As noted earlier, however, it is much more difficult to study development in naturalistic data than in experimental studies; the exploration of developmental trends is one of the main contributions of experimental literature to our understanding of argument realization.

4.11 Summary

For each of the accessibility features discussed earlier, at least one study has shown a relationship between the accessibility value of a referent for that feature and the argument form with which that referent is realized in child speech. The effect of *newness* has been shown the most robustly, both with the largest effects and in the most languages. Other features such as *query* and *animacy* are less well studied and show less obvious effects across studies. Overall, however, it is clear that children show substantial sensitivity to referent accessibility in determining the form in which to realize arguments. In studies which have compared child data to caregiver data, it is also clear that children show very similar patterns of argument realization to those of their caregivers (Clancy 1993, 1997, 2003; Guerriero *et al.* 2006; Paradis and Navarro 2003; Skarabela 2006). And in studies which have investigated development, it is clear that children are sensitive to the effect of accessibility factors on argument realization from fairly early on and improve significantly in showing this sensitivity at some point between MLU 2.0 and 3.0 (roughly ages 2;0–3;0).

The preceding section has focused on the effect of the accessibility features individually to determine their unique role in argument realization. This is largely because most of the studies cited have analyzed the features individually, either using simple percentages (e.g., a higher percentage of "not accessible" than "accessible" referents is realized by a high information form), or using Chi-square to measure the statistical significance of the difference. However, there are at least three reasons to analyze the accessibility features in combination with each other. First, speakers are unlikely to consider each feature in an isolated fashion during actual discourse. The dynamics of discourse indicate that speakers rather consider each factor in light of the contribution it makes to the overall accessibility of the referent, and make decisions about argument realization based on that overall assessment. Second, we noted earlier that there is considerable overlap between some of the features – for example, *animacy* and *person*, *disambiguation* and *contrast* – so it is clear that these features should not be analyzed independently of each other.

Finally, we saw earlier that although many features have quite strong effects for one of their binary values, most do not function symmetrically and thus are very open to the influence of other features for the less strong binary value. This point is elaborated nicely by Serratrice (2005: 444–45) in her discussion of the relationship between *disambiguation* and other features. She notes that referents that are "not accessible" for *disambiguation* (i.e. that have competitor referents in the preceding discourse) should be realized with high information forms regardless of their accessibility status for other features. However, referents that are "accessible" with respect to *disambiguation* might nevertheless be realized with high information forms if they are "not accessible" for other features. In the latter case, the "not accessible" value of the other feature(s) would outrank the "accessible" value of *disambiguation* to result in the use of a high information form.

In the next section of the chapter, then, we turn to discussing the ways in which researchers have attempted to understand how accessibility features work in combination with each other.

5. Accessibility features working in combination

As just discussed, it is clear that interlocutors engaged in actual discourse attend to accessibility features in combination with one another rather than to each feature individually. However, it is not clear exactly how this happens. There are several possible ways in which speakers could be attending to the interaction between features, some of which we discuss next.

One simple possibility is a sort of threshold model. The idea here is that the crucial factor that the child attends to for purposes of argument realization is the distinction between zero and one feature coded as "not accessible," or perhaps between one and two features, and that additional features coded as "not accessible" do not add to the likelihood that a referent will be realized with a high information form. A second possibility would be that all features contribute equally to a final outcome, with all features essentially having identical "weight" with respect to one another. The effect of the features would then be incremental such that, for example, being inaccessible for two features means that a referent is twice as likely to be realized in an informative form as if it were inaccessible for only one feature. Yet a third possibility would involve features working together in a more complex way that should best be assessed by a regression model.

Possible models for attentiveness to feature interaction have not been much investigated in the domain of child argument realization. However, this is a crucial potential contribution of naturalistic corpora to this field because experimental paradigms are usually too constrained to investigate the complicated relationships of several features at once. Therefore, we outline next the attempts so far to study the ways in which accessibility features work in combination to affect argument realization in child speech.

5.1 Several features in one coding category

One possible way of acknowledging the interaction of features is to assume up front that certain features work so closely together that it makes no sense to separate them for individual analysis. Serratrice (2005) has done exactly this. She groups three of the most central features into one, labelled *activation*, which measures the degree of "identifiability and accessibility" (Serratrice 2005:440) of referring expressions in discourse. The definition of *activation* includes *newness*, *attention*, and *topicality*. Serratrice finds, as expected, that referents are more frequently realized with high information forms when they are not activated – i.e. not jointly attended to, newly introduced into discourse, and not topical. Conversely, referents are more frequently expressed with low information forms when they are activated – i.e. jointly attended to, already introduced, and topical. This approach is also followed by Clark's (2001) work on common ground and its role in word learning.

5.2 Threshold approach

A threshold approach, as noted earlier, takes as its starting point the assumption that all features have equivalent "weight" in determining argument realization, and that the child is discriminating only up to a certain threshold in his/her sensitivity to the accessibility indicated by those features. For example, the child may attend only to the distinction between zero and one feature coded as "not accessible," and any additional features coded as "not accessible" do not add to the likelihood that a referent will be realized with a high information form.

Narasimhan *et al.* (2005) follow such an approach, coding four individual features separately (*animacy, contrast, newness, query*) but analyzing them all together under the heading *pragmatic prominence*. They consider a referent pragmatically prominent if it is coded as "not accessible" for any one of the four features, and non-prominent if it is coded as "accessible" for all of them, thereby assessing in their study whether general pragmatic prominence is linked to argument form. By implication, they assume that all features contribute similarly to the speaker's overall assessment of accessibility, and that lack of accessibility for any one of the features is enough to lead to an effect on argument realization. They indeed find that lexical noun phrases are pragmatically prominent more frequently (95% of the time) than are pronominal and null arguments (64%).

Allen (2000) uses a method similar to that of Narasimhan *et al.* (2005). Recall that she coded all arguments in her data set for eight discourse-pragmatic features – *newness, absence, contrast, query, differentiation in discourse, differentiation in context, animacy*, and *person*. For the analysis assessing features together, she considered only the first six features since the final two do not tap into accessibility in the same way. She then coded each argument for whether it was "not accessible" for no features, one feature, or two or more features. This strategy essentially assumes that each feature contributes equivalently to overall accessibility. Allen then analyzed the data to find evidence for a threshold either between 0 and 1 features coded as "not accessible", or between 1 and 2 features. Through a logistic regression analysis, she found that the odds of an argument being realized with a high information form (here, overt as opposed to null form) were almost four times as large if the argument was coded as "not accessible" for one or more of the six features than if it was coded as "accessible" for all of them. A second logistic regression showed that the odds of an argument being realized with a high information form (again, overt as opposed to null form) were almost twice as large if the argument was coded as "not accessible" for two or more features than if it was coded as "not accessible" for one or fewer features. This indicates that, while being "not accessible" on the basis of one feature clearly has an effect on argument realization, being "not accessible" for two features has an additional effect. However, it is not clear evidence for a threshold at either point.

5.3 Incremental contribution

"Maxing out" at a threshold is not the only possibility if accessibility features indeed have equal "weight" in determining argument realization. Another logical possibility is that they could be added to each other, leading to an incremental effect whereby the likelihood of a referent being realized with a high information form increases with each feature for which it is "not accessible".

Allen (2007) pursued this question. She considered only the four features which were found to be significant in Allen (2000): *newness*, *absence*, *contrast*, and *differentiation in context*. As in Allen (2000), any overt form was taken to be a form of high information, in comparison with zero anaphora and verbal agreement markers which were taken to be low information forms. She found that referents which were "accessible" for all four features were realized as overt in 18% of cases, referents coded as "not accessible" for only one feature were overt in 29% of cases, referents coded as "not accessible" for two features in 57% of cases, and for three features in 86% of cases. No referents were coded as "not accessible" for all four features, at least partly because no referent could both be absent and have competitor referents in the physical context.

This result strongly suggests a cumulative effect of accessibility features in predicting argument realization. In further research, it would be interesting to investigate whether the particular features involved make a difference, or whether such an incremental effect could be obtained with any features.

5.4 Independent contribution

The most sophisticated way to determine the relative contribution of the different accessibility features is to assess them together simultaneously through a statistical model. This should allow one to determine the strength of contribution of each feature given the previous or simultaneous contribution of the others. Prediction overlap between features should thus be revealed, either rendering one feature not significant while its competitor is significant, or reducing the significance of each of the competitors.

Allen (2000) used logistic regression to assess the independent contribution of each of the eight features she assessed individually (*newness*, *absence*, *contrast*, *query*, *differentiation in discourse*, *differentiation in context*, *animacy*, and *person*). Logistic regression is the equivalent of multiple regression for categorical rather than continuous variables. It first evaluates the relationship between a particular outcome (here, argument realization as either overt or null) and the predictors taken together as a set. If a relationship is found, then one can assess the contribution to the outcome of each of the individual predictors. Allen found that the predictors as a set reliably distinguished between overt and null arguments ($p<.001$), and that the features *person*, *contrast*, *newness*, *absence*, and *differentiation in context* each contributed significantly to that prediction. Finally, she was able to determine the relative effect of each feature through the odds ratios generated by the logistic regression. For example, the odds of an argument being overt were higher for a explicitly contrasted referent ($e^B = 2.0387$) than for a new referent ($e^B = 1.7281$) or for a referent which had competitors in the physical context ($e^B = 1.3566$). Serratrice (2002) also used logistic regression in analyzing the independent contribution of each of the eight features she coded for: *newness*, *activation*, *contrast*, *absence*, *query*, *disambiguation*, *person*, and *transitivity*. She found that the predictors as a set reliably distinguished between overt and null arguments ($p<.001$), and that all features except *newness* and *query* contributed significantly.

Skarabela (2006) found similar results looking at *newness*, *contrast*, *disambiguation in physical context*, *absence*, and *attention*. The predictors as a set reliable distinguished between overt and null arguments ($p<.0001$), and all features except *absence* contributed significantly. In her analysis, *contrast* had a stronger effect than *newness* and *disambiguation*, which in turn were stronger than *attention*. This is similar to findings for caregiver data using the same procedure, except that *disambiguation* does not contribute significantly for caregivers. A multinomial logistic regression showed that the same five predictors as a set distinguished reliably between three levels of the dependent variable (lexical, demonstrative, omitted). All predictors contributed significantly to the selection of a lexical vs. omitted argument, while only four (not *disambiguation*) contributed significantly to the selection of a lexical vs. demonstrative argument (recall that Inuktitut does not allow pronouns as arguments). This is similar to findings for caregiver data using the same analysis, except that *disambiguation* contributes significantly to distinguishing between lexical and demonstrative forms in the caregiver data.

These logistic regression results are particularly interesting because other analyses of the same data using Chi-square analyses for each individual feature showed that every feature was significant (Allen (1997) assessed all features except *attention* used in Allen (2000) and Skarabela (2006); Serratrice *et al.* (2004) assessed all features in Serratrice (2005), except *newness* because it overlaps almost completely with *activation*). The comparison between features assessed individually and comparatively reveals the clear importance of more sophisticated statistical techniques in determining the effect of referent accessibility on argument realization. The more subtle and comprehensive assessment permitted through logistic regression clearly allows one to take into account that the features interact with one another and may not be significant once the effect of other features is factored out.

5.5 Case study of interaction between two features

In addition to considering all the possible accessibility features in one analysis to determine their relative strength and contribution to argument realization, it is also fruitful to more narrowly compare two features. Although this might normally be considered the domain of experimental studies, it is actually extremely difficult to set up an experimental paradigm uniquely testing two features in each of the four required conditions because the contexts come across as much too contrived given the short time period and restricted dynamics of an experimental setting. Spontaneous speech interactions allow each of these conditions to naturally occur, although some conditions are obviously much more common than others.

Skarabela and Allen (2002) pursued a narrow comparison of this sort in their study of the interaction between *newness* and *attention*. From the original data set of 3168 arguments in their Inuktitut child data, they selected only those which were "not accessible" for *person* (i.e. all third person), and which were "accessible" for *absence*, *query*, *explicit contrast*, and both linguistic and physical components of *disambiguation*. To maximize the distinction between "accessible" and "not accessible" for *newness*, they only included referents which were newly referred to (i.e. "not accessible") and those which had been referred to in the immediately preceding two utterances (i.e. "accessible"). Thus, they excluded from analysis all referents which were most recently referred to in the preceding 3 to 20 utterances. The remaining referents were categorized according to the four possible conditions: both "not accessible", both "accessible", the first "not accessible" and the second "accessible", and the reverse. Skarabela and Allen then assessed which referents were expressed using lexical forms, i.e. full noun phrases, versus null forms. Expressions using demonstratives were not considered. A total of 347 referents were included in the analysis once all the relevant criteria were controlled for.

Results showed the following. When each feature was treated separately without taking the other into account, about 21% of "not accessible" referents were realized lexically (23% for *newness*, 20% for *attention*), as compared with about 5% of "accessible" referents (7% for *newness*, 4% for *attention*). The picture changed substantially once both features were treated together. Referents which were "not accessible" for both features were lexical in 64% of cases, while referents which were "accessible" for both features were lexical in only 3% of cases. Being "not accessible" for both of these features dramatically increases the extent to which a child provides a high level of information about the referent in his or her speech. All of the situations in which a referent not accessible for both features was expressed using a low information form led to breakdown in communication between the child and his/her interlocutor; 75% of those miscommunications were repaired. Referents which were "not accessible" for *attention* but "accessible" for *newness* were lexical in 12% of cases, while the reverse situation resulted in lexical expressions in 6% of cases. This indicates that, although children may be slightly more influenced by *attention* than by *newness*, accessibility on the basis of only one of these features is generally enough for a child to use a low information form. Accessibility for both features increases the likelihood of choosing a low information form, but not drastically.

This kind of direct comparison of different features is very helpful for advancing our knowledge of which features are more important to argument realization. Spontaneous speech allows for such comparison, but experiments typically do not, or at least have not yet been successful in this regard, for the reasons mentioned earlier.

5.6 Summary

The studies just reviewed show definite evidence of children's sensitivity to accessibility features working together to determine argument realization. Both the threshold and incremental models show promise for further research, as well as constrained individual comparisons of two features and large scale statistical analyses that assess the effect of features in comparison with each other. There is clearly room for much further research in this area using much more sophisticated statistical analyses and other techniques.

6. Usefulness of extended stretches of discourse

In the previous sections we have highlighted two advantages of naturalistic over experimental studies of the effect of information flow on argument realization: identification of discourse-pragmatic factors influencing argument realization in natural settings, and understanding how the child attends to the interaction of these factors. We now turn to a third advantage of assessing argument realization in naturalistic corpora: it allows us to see how children are learning and displaying their knowledge across a series of related utterances in an extended stretch of discourse. Observing how a child realizes the same referent over various turns in conversation, for example, can show that child's understanding of how the accessibility of a referent changes over time, and how this is modelled by their caregivers. We elucidate next three ways in which the interaction between referent accessibility and argument realization over extended stretches of discourse has been investigated in the literature: Preferred Argument Structure, conversational sequences, and managing miscommunication.

6.1 Preferred argument structure

As noted earlier, Du Bois (1985, 1987) has observed a powerful pattern in discourse by which the accessibility of a referent is linked not only to the form in which that referent is realized in speech, but also to the argument role held by that referent as well as the number of referents of low accessibility which can appear in one utterance. This Preferred Argument Structure shows that new and lexical (i.e. full noun phrase) referents tend to avoid appearing in A position (subject of transitive verb), and rather appear in S (subject of intransitive verb) and/or O (object) position depending on the language at hand. Further, only one lexical and one new argument typically appear within one verbal clause. While these patterns are observed at the level of the utterance, they play out as part of the dynamics of the overall flow of discourse and thus are far less likely to be observed in isolated utterances. Only looking at extended stretches of discourse in naturalistic corpora will allow us to see these patterns.

The patterns of Preferred Argument Structure have been substantiated in a large number of adult languages (e.g., Du Bois 1985, 1987; Du Bois *et al.* 2003). In recent years, research with child data from at least six different languages – Korean (Clancy 2003), Inuktitut (Allen and Schröder 2003), Japanese, English (Guerriero *et al.* 2001; Guerriero *et al.* 2006), Hindi (Narasimhan *et al.* 2005), and Venezuelan Spanish (Bentivoglio 1996) – reveals that children are also following this pattern in their discourse. The Inuktitut-speaking children in Allen and Schröder's study, for example, produced more than one lexical or one new argument in only 0.04% of utterances in their data (only 1 out of more than 2500 utterances). Further, only 1.1% of lexical arguments and 0.7% of new arguments appear in A position in the Inuktitut child data. This shows that children are highly sensitive not only to individual links between referent accessibility and argument realization, but also to the broader discourse patterns this entails.

6.2 Conversational sequences

Clancy (1996, 1997, 2003), building on the work of Vygotsky, has long been drawing attention to the importance of the structural properties of adult-child discourse for children's acquisition of grammar. She reviews evidence from conversational sequences between children and their parents to show how structured interactions provide children with sufficient information about the relationship between discourse and grammar. In her corpus of spontaneous speech of two-year-old children learning Korean, she observes that early parent-child interactions frequently involve sequences with one predicate which occurs with the same referent, and this referent is expressed by different linguistic forms across several utterances as the referent accessibility changes. For example, a new referent is introduced with a lexical noun but subsequently the same referent is most likely expressed with a null argument. Children are thus exposed to a range of argument forms that are used with few but frequent individual predicates and, simultaneously, to a range of discourse factors associated with particular referential forms.

Similarly, Clancy argues for this iconic relationship between discourse and grammar in early stages of language acquisition in her work on Preferred Argument Structure. She shows that the nature of children's early activities is the underlying source of their early sensitivity to Preferred Argument Structure. Namely, children tend to participate in activities that involve a human agent that acts on an inanimate object. In discussing these activities they tend to produce a small number of verbs, each used frequently, that represent the human agent in A position. The inanimate object tends to be encoded in O position. While the A argument is relatively constant across different contexts, the O argument frequently changes. Clancy argues that children use the O position to direct adults' attention to new information. She finds that children also use the S position to encode new information that frequently changes, although to a lesser degree. Preferred Argument Structure therefore serves an attention-focusing function in child discourse.

Clancy's account shows that argument realization provides a powerful connection between the levels of discourse and acquisition of grammar, i.e. grammar and linguistic structures arise from discourse interactions between children and their caregivers. Clearly, however, these types of insights can be gained only from detailed analyses of long stretches of naturalistic interactions and not from experimental studies.

6.3 Managing miscommunication

Naturalistic corpora also allow us to see what happens when a speaker selects a linguistic form that does not provide enough information about the intended referent. Children may misjudge the knowledge of their hearer, or may wrongly assume that their hearer possesses the same knowledge that they do about a specific referent. As a result, they may realize a referent with a low information form when it is not in fact conceptually accessible to the listener. This leads to a situation of communication breakdown. Observing extended discourse allows us to see what a child naturally does in such a situation. Such episodes provide useful information about the specific discourse-pragmatic factors associated with these problematic referents. In addition, they also provide information about whether or not children are able to recover from these 'errors' and how.

Skarabela (2006) studied miscommunication and its effects in 780 omitted arguments from four two-year-old Inuit children. She found that although the children tended overwhelmingly to omit arguments that represented accessible referents, they also omitted arguments representing inaccessible referents. This was particularly the case in the context of children's introduction of new referents. Interestingly, however, these omitted arguments were used to realize new referents primarily in the context of joint attention. In other words, although not using the default adult form to introduce a new referent (i.e. a lexical noun), the children did show sensitivity to whether or not a referent is conceptually accessible by taking advantage of the "low cost" of contextual information rather than by linguistic means.

In a few instances, children selected omitted arguments to represent new referents in the absence of joint attention, leading to a communication breakdown. In some cases, the conversation deteriorated and led to a different topic. In others, however, children either spontaneously repaired the miscommunication with a full lexical noun phrase or, after being explicitly asked for clarification by the listener, they used verbal or non-verbal means to disambiguate the intended referent. Overall, the children were successful at identifying the sources of ambiguity and subsequent communication repair.

These instances of miscommunication can be interpreted as episodes of useful "feedback" when children are provided with explicit information about what a listener considers an accessible referent and what is the best way to realize it. In this respect, "errors" in argument realization contribute to children's developing understanding that the speaker's world is not always identical with that of the listener.

This type of information about children's abilities to realize arguments and their abilities to cope with communication breakdown is again not elicited in experimental studies. Instead, it requires naturalistic interactions between the speaker and the listener who negotiate meaning together in the flow of conversation. In addition, this method is likely to be much more useful in discovering differences in argument realization between children and adults since controlled experiments require as a prerequisite the knowledge of "the rules of the game." In this respect, using naturalistic speech data rather than experiments provides particularly insightful information about how children use different discourse-pragmatic factors.

6.4 Summary

The three areas just reviewed show how particular aspects of children's understanding of the relationship between referent accessibility and argument realization are revealed across stretches of extended discourse in ways that aren't usually visible through the isolated utterances and limited interactions characteristic of experiments in this domain. Through the lens of Preferred Argument Structure, we see that children are sensitive to the effect of discourse-pragmatic factors not only on the form in which arguments are realized but also on the syntactic role in which they appear. We see that caregivers scaffold this behaviour by realizing arguments in different forms and syntactic roles as their accessibility changes through discourse, and that children's typical early interactions also lend themselves to this patterning. Finally, we see that children are largely able to identify and correct their miscommunications resulting from speaker-hearer differences in referent accessibility.

Up to this point, we have discussed at length the values of studying argument realization in naturalistic data as opposed to experiments. However, we fully acknowledge that carefully designed experiments in this area are very helpful for triangulation of findings and can contribute important information that naturalistic data is not well suited to study. In particular, experiments allow one to assess the unique effect of one individual feature, or the relative effect of each of two features, while carefully controlling the effect of the others. Because the topic and form of interactions are controlled in experiments, they permit a better understanding of what children's intended utterances are (and thus what they are omitting) than in naturalistic studies where one must often guess what the child intended. Experiments are also ideal for illuminating the trajectory of development because they allow for testing many children at once in different groups determined by age or linguistic ability, and because the larger number of children and data points in each group permits more powerful statistical analysis and generalizability than is generally possible in naturalistic studies. Finally, experiments enable tests of comprehension effects related to argument realization, which is not possible using naturalistic studies. In the next section we review experimental literature on children's comprehension and production of arguments in different forms to illustrate the different ways in which experimental and naturalistic corpus studies contribute to our understanding of argument realization.

7. Experimental studies

Experimental studies of argument realization have focused on both comprehension and production of referential expressions. Only a small number of studies on children's comprehension of reference have been reported in the literature (e.g., Arnold, Brown-Schmidt and Trueswell 2007; Arnold, Brown-Schmidt, Trueswell and Fagnano 2005; Kayama 2003; K.S. Shin 2006; Song and Fisher 2005, 2007; Tyler 1983; Wykes 1981, 1983). They have focused on features which are known to be particularly powerful, as well as features which lend themselves well to experimental situations: *newness*, *disambiguation* in the linguistic context, and *topicality*. In a typical experiment, the child is presented with one to three sentences of a story context which exhibit one or more of the accessibility features, and then assessed to see how they determine the reference of an ambiguous form (usually a pronoun) in the final target sentence. On the basis of response times in a mispronunciation task, for example, Tyler (1983) suggested that 5-year-olds could interpret a pronoun as coreferent with the subject of a preceding story. Wykes (1983) showed that 5-year-olds could use the semantics of a preceding sentence to correctly interpret the antecedent of a later pronoun. Arnold *et al.* (2005) predicted that gender information would be a stronger cue to pronoun reference than order of mention in a preceding sentence or appearance of the antecedent in subject position, and showed the strength of gender as a cue in an off-line task with 3;5- to 4;5-year-olds. Song and Fisher (2005, 2007), in contrast, showed in a series of preferential looking studies that children aged 3;0 and 2;5, respectively, could identify referents which were made prominent by virtue of being mentioned first in the story, appearing in subject position, being mentioned more often than other referents, and being pronominalized once. Song and Fisher (2005) also succeeded in carefully comparing the effect of *disambiguation* vs. *topicality* in 3-year-olds. Use of different methodologies across studies – including act-out tasks, looking-preference paradigms and eye tracking – allows for triangulation of findings and investigations at ever-younger ages. In general, these studies have confirmed the attentiveness of children to all of these features in assessing reference.

At least five experimental production studies have recently investigated the effect of information flow in argument realization (Campbell, Brooks and Tomasello 2000; Gürcanlı, Nakipoglu and Özyürek 2007; Matthews, Lieven, Theakston and Tomasello 2006; N.L. Shin 2006; Wittek and Tomasello 2005). Most of these studies focus on either *newness* or *attention*, although a couple also investigate *disambiguation* and *absence*. In the typical methodology, a referent is presented and engaged in some action, either physically or on video. Then the participant is asked to request the referent from or recount the action to an experimenter who either did or did not observe the initial action. The linguistic form for the referent produced by the participant is assessed to determine whether it conforms to expectations based on the accessibility features present in the study. Since production (rather than comprehension) is the focus of this article, we discuss these studies in some detail next to illustrate the strengths and difficulties of experimental studies in comparison with studies based on naturalistic data.

7.1 Strengths of production studies

An excellent example of a study assessing the unique effect of one feature comes from Matthews *et al.* (2006), who studied argument realization in one hundred English-speaking children, a third each aged 2, 3 and 4 years. The first part of the study focused on the role of *attention*, holding all other features constant (all referents were "not accessible" for *newness* and *person*, and all were "accessible" for *absence*, *query*, *disambiguation*, *explicit contrast*, and *animacy*). Participants viewed 10 short video clips (e.g., clown jumping, fairy eating an apple). For one block of 5 clips, the experimenter was watching the screen with the child (i.e. "accessible" for *attention*); for the other, the experimenter was not able to view the screen (i.e. "not accessible" for *attention*). After viewing each clip, participants were asked to recount the clip to the experimenter with the request *What happened? What did you see?* Results showed that the 3- and 4-year-olds, but not the two-year-olds, chose different linguistic forms (noun vs. pronoun) to realize the referents depending on whether the interlocutor shared attention to the video or not. The second part of the study held *attention* constant (= "not accessible") and varied *newness*. The same participants narrated another block of 5 similar clips to an experimenter who could not see them, and who either mentioned or did not mention the target referent prior to asking the child what happened in the clip (e.g., *Was that the clown? Oh! What happened?* vs. *That sounds like fun! What happened?*). All three age groups differentiated their choice of referring expression depending on whether the referent had just been expressed by the experimenter or not. The authors concluded that both *attention* and *newness* influence children's argument realization, but that children are sensitive to the effect of *newness* earlier than to *attention*. Campbell *et al.* (2000) found an identical pattern of results in a study with very similar design but where the English-speaking participants viewed real-life events (rather than videos) involving inanimate (rather than animate) toys moving in different ways (e.g., being pulled on a train, sliding down a chute).

Wittek and Tomasello (2005) again found similar results in tests of *newness* and *contrast* within a similar design (both features tested but not assessed relative to each other, *attention* always "not accessible"). In their study, German-speaking children were asked to retrieve inanimate objects from a shelf where the children had placed them earlier, using the requests *What happened to the broom?* ("accessible" for both *newness* and *contrast*), *What do we need to get?* ("not accessible" for *newness*, "accessible" for *contrast*), and *Did the clown have a vacuum cleaner?* ("not accessible" for both *newness* and *contrast*). Children aged 2;5 and 3;5 used low information forms for the first question and high information forms for the other two. Children aged 2;0 produced overwhelmingly high information forms for the final question suggesting sensitivity to the effect of contrast even at this young age. However, they did not differentiate in their use of forms between the first two questions, suggesting that children become sensitive to *newness* sometime between 2;0 and 2;6.

All three of these studies are quite carefully designed for the most part, succeeding well in being as natural as possible and eliminating the effect of confounding features. They also illustrate well how age effects can be shown from experimental studies, since a large number of children within a narrow age range can be studied.

7.2 Difficulties with production studies

Other studies illustrate some of the difficulties of a less naturalistic interaction and of controlling for the effects of features other than the one under investigation. Gürcanlı *et al.* (2007) conducted a study close in design to the first part of Matthews *et al.* (2006), but with only one age group of Turkish-speaking children (3;0–4;11), as well as a group of adults, who experienced the two values of *attention* as a between-subjects rather than within-subjects condition (i.e. half the participants recounted the video clips to an experimenter who viewed the clips with them, the other half to an experimenter who was out of the room when the video was shown). Although the children produced more high information forms in the condition where the experimenter did not share attention during the video, the adults showed no difference in the two conditions. The adult participants seem to have interpreted this as a "test question" rather than as a real interaction situation because they responded using high information forms for all questions rather than following patterns that would be characteristic of a real conversation with natural dynamics of information flow. This may have happened because it is quite strange for someone to ask you to recount to them something they have just seen, and because this task was very easy for adults.

N.L. Shin (2006) study testing the sensitivity of children to *disambiguation* also suffers from unnaturalness as well as difficulty in controlling the relative effects of the other features. Participants were 181 monolingual speakers of Mexican Spanish aged 5;9 to 15;8 and 30 adults. They were told 12 two-sentence stories acted out by animate figures (e.g., *Maria and Jose sing songs. Maria sings a ranchera.*), with the third and final sentence acted out but not spoken (e.g., one of the characters sings a children's song). Under the rationale of helping the non-native researcher better understand how to speak Spanish, the participants were then asked to select from two orally-provided options which third sentence would best complete the story (e.g., *Later, she/he sings a children's song.* or *Later, Ø sings a children's song.*). In the example given, the null subject option would be preferred if Maria sings the children's song since there are no intervening competitors. In contrast, the pronoun option (here *he*) would be preferred if Jose sings the children's song because the competitor referent *Maria* intervenes between the current and previous mention of the target referent. All features other than *disambiguation* are controlled for, with a "not accessible" value for *person* and "accessible" values for all other features. The results revealed that the younger children tended to overuse null forms in situations where there was a competitor referent, indicating that they found the referent accessibility provided by the other features – probably particularly recency of mention of the referent and sharing attention with their interlocutor – far more powerful than the lack of accessibility incurred by *disambiguation*. Further, the experiment must have been somewhat repetitive and confusing since all 12 experimental items as well as 9 of 12 filler items involved the same 2 characters, Jose and Maria. In addition, a group of older children produced pronouns in many contexts where there was no competitor referent, implying that they were probably treating the questions as "test questions" rather than abstracting to natural interactional patterns.

Finally, the third study in Wittek and Tomasello (2005) illustrates the difficulty of controlling for the effect of other features. German-speaking children aged 2;6 and 3;6 again played games with an experimenter and placed the toys on the shelf after use. The features *absence* and *disambiguation* (in physical context) were manipulated, but not in comparison with one another; all other features were held constant with *newness*, *attention*, *animacy* and *person* "not accessible" and the other features "accessible". This time, each toy was placed on a shelf either out of sight in a box ("not accessible" for *absence*, not relevant for *disambiguation*), right next to another toy ("not accessible" for *disambiguation*, "accessible" for *absence*), or in a separate location on the shelf where it could be individuated by a point ("accessible" for both features). Children were instructed to ask a second experimenter (who did not witness placing of the items on the shelf) to get particular items. Although the items differed in whether they were visible and easily individuated, both groups of children typically asked for all items using noun phrases rather than pronouns, null references, or simply pointing. The authors concluded that children essentially ignored relative physical location of the objects in this task, responding much more powerfully to the lack of shared knowledge of the objects (both *newness* and *attention*) in any of the conditions.

7.3 Summary

Experimental assessments of the effect of accessibility features on argument realization have some advantages over naturalistic ones. In particular, they allow for singling out the effect of a particular feature holding all others constant, and they allow careful testing of the effect of features by age. However, no experiments have yet succeeded in comparing the effect of two features within one design, much less assessing the relative effect of all nine features taken together. This is a clear limitation in determining how argument realization works in the actual child who is attending to all of these features at once. Further, the studies cited above reveal the difficulty of assessing the effect of less powerful features such as *disambiguation* and *absence* in the face of the much more powerful features *newness* and *attention*. The latter essentially outweigh the effect of the former in the sorts of contrived situations that are the necessary setting for experiments. Even some of the authors of the experimental studies themselves point out that the experimental situations were somewhat extreme in that the information provided (or not) by the discourse was quite explicit, lacking much of the subtlety and influence from other factors that would be typical in natural interaction (e.g., Matthews *et al.* 2006). In addition, asking questions about simple events that both participant and experimenter had just witnessed is quite unnatural since these sorts of questions would be unlikely to occur in natural conversation, and clearly cannot really be asking for information. Thus, it is not clear how much the children's responses reflect their natural speech, or whether they have simply learned the expected formula to answer test questions (N.L. Shin 2006; Gürcanlı *et al.* 2007). Nevertheless, the children in most of the studies showed clearly their knowledge of the factors tested, and altered their realization of arguments accordingly. This indicates at minimum that children use the same kinds of discourse-pragmatic knowledge in answering test questions that they do in real conversation.

8. Discussion and conclusion

We have seen throughout this chapter that naturalistic studies have made an important and unique contribution to our understanding of the relationship between discourse and syntax. Naturalistic studies are essential for identifying the accessibility features that affect argument realization in every-day discourse, for investigating the ways in which children attend to those features in combination with each other, and for uncovering how children learn about the application and misapplication of those features through extended stretches of discourse with familiar interlocutors. Experiments also provide a valuable contribution to this understanding. They allow for singling out the effect of individual features, controlling the contexts of interaction to constrain the effects of competing features, systematically comparing children of different ages and linguistic ability, and amassing a large sample of participants to facilitate generalizability and powerful statistical analysis. However, the interactions are usually more contrived, and experiments are limited in the number and type of features they can investigate at once. Information from both sources – experiment and naturalistic data – clearly have their place. But without the dimensions and understanding that naturalistic data provide, we lose an essential piece of the puzzle of how children's knowledge of the principles of discourse affects their syntactic production.

Studies of argument realization from the perspective of cognitive accessibility have looked at nine main features: *newness*, *topicality*, *absence*, *query*, *disambiguation*, *explicit contrast*, *person*, *animacy*, and *attention*. Each of these has been defined slightly differently in different studies, but most have been found to be significant factors in children's argument realization. The strongest factors are likely *newness*, *explicit contrast*, *topicality*, and *absence*. These have been found significant in several studies looking at individual factors, as well as in studies using logistic regression and incremental approaches to assess the combined or comparative effect of these factors on argument realization. *Query*, *disambiguation*, and *animacy* have generally been found less consistent in effect across studies. Although *attention* has not been studied enough to be sure of its effect, it seems very promising in both naturalistic and experimental studies. *Person* is also powerful, but is less clearly a feature of accessibility than the others, and is more strongly affected by language typology (e.g., whether a language allows arguments of a certain person to appear in a particular form). These features will provide a strong base for further exploration of gaps in grammatical and performance-based claims discussed earlier. In particular, further research should use them to investigate which of the arguments shown by those perspectives to be candidates for omission – for instance, subjects of non-finite clauses, subjects of matrix clauses, subjects with long VPs – are actually omitted.

Developmental results from both naturalistic and experimental studies discussed here also bear on theoretical questions raised in the literature. The results of several studies converge to show development in children's sensitivity to several features. Experimental results suggest that *contrast* is one of the earliest features to be attended to, followed by *newness* and *attention* sometime between 2;0 and 2;6. Naturalistic data also show that *newness*, *person*, and *activation* are probably attended to early on but also are attended to more fully with age. Children's decrease in use of null arguments during the period of 2;0 to 3;0 could thus be at least partially explained by an increase in their attention to accessibility and in their sensitivity to the effect of accessibility features on argument form. The timing could also help to explain children's increase in use of strong pronouns and lexical forms towards the end of this time period. Finally, developmental data from Guerriero *et al.* (2006) can help to resolve the debate between the generative and performance perspectives concerning the continuity of null to pronominal forms. Guerriero *et al.* clearly showed that pronouns increased as null forms decreased from ages 1;9 to 3;0, while lexical forms remained fairly steady. The evidence seems to support strong continuity, consistent with the prediction of Hyams and Wexler (1993). Although the developmental results obtained to date are very useful, much research remains to be done in assessing the trajectory of development of other features not yet studied, in assessing how and when children become sensitive to the interaction of features, and in determining the mechanisms for children's learning.

As Valian (1991) first pointed out, children are quite sensitive to the typology of their language from very early on in terms of the proportion of arguments omitted in their speech. While speakers of both non-null-subject and null-subject languages over-omit arguments at the earliest stages, the proportion of omissions is much higher for speakers of null-subject languages. As mentioned in the introduction, virtually all studies of the effect of accessibility on child argument realization have been conducted in null-subject languages. Only three studies reported here investigate a non-null-subject language (English): Guerriero *et al.* (2006), Hughes and Allen (2006) and Serratrice *et al.* (2004). Each of these show that English-speaking children attend to accessibility features according to the same patterns as their counterparts speaking null-subject languages. However, no study to date has investigated particular grammatical contexts in English such as subjects of finite vs. non-finite verbs to determine how grammatical and accessibility constraints interact. This would be a very fruitful direction for future study.

A final under-researched question is how children attend to accessibility features in interaction with each other. As mentioned earlier, children clearly attend to several factors at once in evaluating the accessibility of an argument, but most studies assess the influence of factors individually. An earlier section of this chapter gives several suggestions for further exploring this issue.

Naturalistic study of the dynamics of information flow with respect to argument realization continues to be a domain with rich potential to contribute not only to our understanding of how discourse affects syntax, but also how various different factors interact in language development overall.

Integration of multiple probabilistic cues in syntax acquisition

Padraic Monaghan and Morten H. Christiansen

1. Introduction

Before the child can understand the relationship between words and referents in the world, the child must know the roles of words within the utterance. But in order to learn the roles of words, the child must know their referents. How does the child begin to solve this circular problem? One solution is that the child can learn to cluster words according to their similarities into groups, thus information about the roles and structures of the language are present within the language itself. In this chapter we focus on corpus analyses of child directed speech that have indicated various sources of information for helping the child to derive syntactic knowledge from the speech signal. We discuss studies of distributional, or contextual, information about the role of words, and studies about the effectiveness of grouping words according to phonological and prosodic properties. We discuss the information that is valuable for forming a sense of the syntactic role of words, and also consider evidence for the availability of these sources of information to the child learning the structure of their first language. Finally, we provide some future challenges for corpus analyses of language acquisition, in particular taking into account developmental trends and the potential for novel computational approaches to assimilate these constructivist processes.

2. The chicken and egg problem of syntax acquisition

To understand or produce spoken language a child must learn how sounds can be combined to form words and how words may be strung together to construct meaningful sentences. By one year of age, infants have already learned a great deal about the sound structure of their native language (for reviews see Jusczyk 1997, 1999; Kuhl 1999; Pallier, Christophe and Mehler 1997; Werker and Tees 1999). In contrast, acquiring knowledge about the grammatical structure of sentences takes several years (for reviews, see O'Grady 1997; Tomasello 1992, 2000b). When acquiring grammatical knowledge, children face a difficult "bootstrapping" problem. Discovering the syntactic constraints governing the child's native language requires being able to assign individual words to grammatical classes, such as nouns and verbs. Grammatical classes, on the other hand, are only useful for acquisition insofar as they support syntactic constraints. This interdependence of syntactic constraints and grammatical categories presents the child with a seemingly insurmountable bootstrapping problem, apparently requiring simultaneously searching through *combinations* of syntactic constraints and grammatical categories. Yet, children typically acquire grammatical knowledge with accuracy and without apparent effort.

Such a perspective on language acquisition suggests a modular view of grammar, where phonology, syntax, and semantics are seen as separate and functionally-isolated representations. In this chapter, however, we indicate ways in which phonology and syntax are likely to interact in language development which aid us to conceive how the bootstrapping problem may be solved by the child – indeed we argue that the apparent poverty of the stimulus in the child's language environment holds only if one conceives that each representational type is immune to the (helpful) influence of other representational levels. Equally, we support views of the interaction of syntax and semantics that may also assist in this process (Blackburn and Bos 2005; Croft 2001; Lakoff 1987; Pinker 1984; Tomasello 2003) in particular when these are proposed to be generated from exposure to correlations between the linguistic environment and events and objects in the world (e.g., Yu and Smith 2006).

Students learning an academic subject such as physics face a similar "bootstrapping" problem: understanding momentum or force presupposes some understanding of the physical laws in which they figure, yet these laws presuppose the concepts they interrelate. But the bootstrapping problem solved by young children seems vastly more challenging, both because the constraints governing natural language are so intricate, and because young children do not have the intellectual capacity or explicit instruction available to the academic student. Determining how children so readily solve this bootstrapping problem is crucial for understanding language acquisition and, more generally, the relation between biological and environmental factors in development.

3. Solutions to the chicken and egg problem – innate categories don't help

There are three sources of information that children could potentially bring to bear on solving the bootstrapping problem: innate knowledge in the form of linguistic universals, intra-linguistic and extra-linguistic information. The intra-linguistic information is present within the physical speech signal itself, including patterns of phonological and prosodic information within the word and distributional patterns or semantic features that have a morphological realization such as gender or number, that indicate the relation of various parts of language to each other. Extra-linguistic information concerns the observed relationships between language and objects, actions, and relations in the world. In the remainder of this article we use "semantic information" in this restricted sense: to refer to information that is not present within the language signal itself.

Although some kind of innate knowledge may play a role in language acquisition, it cannot solve the bootstrapping problem. Even with built-in abstract knowledge about grammatical categories and syntactic rules (e.g., Pinker 1984), the bootstrapping problem remains formidable: innate knowledge can only help address the bootstrapping problem by building in universal aspects of language, and relationships between words and grammatical categories clearly differ between languages (e.g., the sound /su/ is a noun in French (*sou*) but a verb in English (*sue*)). Crucially, children still have to map the right sound strings onto the right grammatical categories while determining the specific syntactic relations between these categories in their native language. Moreover, there now exists strong experimental evidence that children do not initially use abstract linguistic categories, but instead employ novel words as concrete items, thereby challenging the usefulness of hypothesized innate grammatical categories (Tomasello 2000b). Thus, independently of whether or not innate linguistic knowledge is hypothesized to play an important role in language acquisition, it seems clear that other sources of information nevertheless are necessary to solve the bootstrapping problem.

Extra-linguistic information is likely to contribute substantially to language acquisition. Correlations between environmental observations relating prior semantic categories (e.g., objects and actions) and grammatical categories (e.g., nouns and verbs) may furnish a "semantic bootstrapping" solution (Pinker 1984). However, given that children acquire linguistic distinctions with little or no semantic basis (e.g., gender in French, Karmiloff-Smith 1979), semantics cannot be the only source of information involved in solving the bootstrapping problem. Another extra-linguistic factor is cultural learning, whereby children may imitate the pairing of linguistic forms and their conventional communicative functions (Tomasello, Kruger and Ratner 1993). For example, by observing the idiom *John spilled the beans* used in the appropriate context, the child by reproducing it can discover that it means that John has revealed some sort of secret, and not that he is a messy eater. However, to break down the linguistic forms into relevant units, it appears that cultural learning must be coupled with intra-linguistic learning.

Though not the only source of information involved in language acquisition, we suggest that intra-linguistic information is fundamental to bootstrapping the child into syntax. However, although intra-linguistic input appears to be rich in potential cues to linguistic structure, there is an important caveat: the individual cues are only partially reliable, and none considered alone provides an infallible bootstrap into language. Thus, a learner could use the tendency for English nouns to be longer than verbs to determine that *elephant* is a noun, but the same strategy would fail for *investigate*. Similarly, although speakers tend to pause at linguistically meaningful places in a sentence (e.g., following a phrase or a clause, Cooper and Paccia-Cooper 1980), pauses also occur elsewhere. And although it is a good distributional bet that a determiner (e.g., *the*) will be followed by a noun, there are other possibilities (e.g., adjectives, such as *big*). To acquire language successfully, it seems that the child needs to integrate a great diversity of multiple probabilistic cues to language structure in an effective way. Fortunately, as we shall see next, there is a growing bulk of evidence showing that multiple probabilistic cues are available in intra-linguistic input, that language learners are sensitive to them, and that learning is facilitated through multiple-cue integration.

In the remainder of this chapter, we provide a review of approaches to multiple cue integration in syntax acquisition. The majority of work has concentrated on intra-linguistic cues, and so the majority of our chapter deals with these topics. We catalogue studies that have explored the richness of potential cues in the child's language environment, we indicate ways in which these sources of information may plausibly give rise to the development of syntactic categories, and we review studies that suggest these cues are actually used by the child in constraining their grammar. Though there is a multitude of potential sources of information available to the child, we limit the search for cues to linguistically-relevant material – infants, for instance, structure acoustic speech input into phoneme categories at an early stage (Kuhl, Williams, Lacerda, Stevens and Lindblom 1992) – though the generic learning mechanisms we describe could in principal be applied by the child to determine the relevance of *any* language property with respect to language structure. The search-space to grammatical structure becomes constrained by the overlap of multiple cues available in speech. We also indicate that intra-linguistic cues are just the tip of the iceberg in terms of the available environmental information to assist in bootstrapping syntax, and we discuss the potential for co-relation of intra- and extra-linguistic cues to assist in bootstrapping the syntax of the child's first language. We conclude with some future directions for studies of multiple cues in language acquisition.

4. Intra-linguistic cues in the utterance: from statistics to structure

The purpose of corpus analysis studies in language acquisition is to assess a representative sample of the child's linguistic environment and measure the information present within this environment that may assist the child in learning their language. There are two approaches for such corpus analyses. First, the aim of the analysis may be to reveal the potential information present within the child's environment. Such approaches typically employ descriptive statistics of the corpus' characteristics. Second, the aim may be to determine how such information can be used to generate or support syntactic categories within the child's language. This latter approach attempts to determine how general purpose mechanisms may give rise to a structuring of the language environment with which the child is presented. Many of the published studies have limited the assessment of grammatical category distinctions to function and content words and nouns and verbs. The former is important for the child to discover, as this enables the child to restrict their attention to link only the content words to referents in the world. Such a distinction has been shown to be a productive constraint in Cartwright and Brent's (1997) and Dominey, Hoen, and Inui's (2006) models. The noun/verb distinction has been a focus because these categories provide the largest token categories of words, and so provides a lower-bound for potential grammatical category information present in the stimulus.

4.1 Measuring potential information in the corpus

Maratsos and Chalkley (1980) proposed that grammatical categories of words could be predicted with some accuracy from certain "frames" within which those category words occurred. For instance, they suggested that only verbs could occur between a noun phrase and the *-ed* inflection. Similarly, Fries (1952) identified 19 frames within which only words of certain grammatical categories could occur, e.g., *(The)* ____ *is/was/are good.*

Using corpus analyses of small corpora of child directed speech, Mintz (2003) provided an empirical test of the idea that static frames may serve as indicators of grammatical categories. The corpora were selected as reflecting the speech directed to very young children. Furthermore, the study of speech directed toward particular children enabled an estimate of the type of information presented to an individual child. The alternative – to select a corpus of speech directed to several children – may obscure somewhat the precise usages to which a child becomes familiar in early stages of language development (e.g., Tomasello 2000b). The flip side of analyses of speech directed to multiple children, of course, is that it provides an averaged view of children's language environment, and is less prone to local fluctuations in the words that children may be exposed to on a particular recording session. Certain vagaries may be present within small samples of speech directed toward particular children. For instance, in one of the corpora studied in Mintz's (2003) study (anne01a-anne23b, Theakston, Lieven, Pine and Rowland 2001) *penguin* occurs with a frequency of 440 per million. In 5.5 million words of child directed speech from the CHILDES corpus for English (MacWhinney 2000), *penguin* has a frequency of 92 per million (see Rowland, Fletcher and Freudenthal, this volume, for further discussion of this issue).

Within each corpus, the most frequent frames were selected, and the words that occurred within these frames were classified according to their grammatical category. Mintz then measured the extent to which words of the same grammatical category occurred inside the same frames. He found that there was a high degree of accuracy for these groupings within frames – approximately 90% for each child corpus, meaning that words of the same category grouped together within the frame. The weakness of the analysis, however, was that words of the same grammatical category did not always occur in the same frame, reflected by the measure of completeness which was below 10%, meaning that the frames specified subsets of grammatical categories, and also problematic was the fact that the connection between the words occurring in the frames *you__to* and *we___to* (both verb contexts) was not determined by the analysis.

Monaghan and Christiansen (2004) explored the extent to which high accuracy but low completeness may facilitate learning the grammatical categories of the language. We contrasted the frames analysis with a grouping of words based only on the preceding word – so words that occurred after *you* were grouped together. In this latter analysis, we found overall lower accuracy – as verbs, auxiliaries, and adverbs were all likely to occur after *you* – but a much larger proportion of the words of the corpus belonging to a grouping: 69.9% compared to 14.3% in the frames analysis. A connectionist model trained to learn the grammatical categories of words based either on bigrams or frames resulted in much better learning from bigrams, suggesting that more information was present in the bigram analysis which was more conducive to learning the categories.

Pursuing this view that bigram information may be a useful indicator on its own about grammatical category, Monaghan, Chater and Christiansen (2005) assessed the extent to which combined bigrams could give information about the grammatical category of a word. This contrasts with the analyses of Mintz (2003) and Monaghan and Christiansen (2004) where contexts were considered individually for their categorization of words. In the Monaghan *et al.* (2005) analyses, the extent to which overlaps between information from bigrams could be discovered was studied. In these analyses, the strength of association between a set of high-frequency context words and the target word was assessed using a log-likelihood statistic. So, if the target word occurs after the context word more than expected by chance (e.g., the occurrence of *apple* following *the*) then this association is given a positive score, if the target word co-occurs with the context word at chance level then the value is close to zero, and if the co-occurrence is less than chance then the association is negatively scored (e.g., the co-occurrence of *you apple*).

The information contained in the associations for the 1000 most frequent words in English child directed speech was then combined using discriminant analysis. The results indicated that accuracy of classification based on these associations was up to 85.8% for distinguishing nouns from verbs, an improvement over the use of bigram cues singly, as in Monaghan and Christiansen (2004). Such a result indicates that, even within a particular type of information, integrating cues, enabling the connections between *the*___ and *a*___, for instance, increases accuracy of categorization. Similar results pertain for other languages.

Corpora of child directed speech in Dutch, French, and Japanese also indicate that combined bigram information cues provide highly accurate reflections of grammatical category distinctions between function and content words, and also between nouns and verbs (Monaghan, Christiansen and Chater 2007). In this study, the 25 most frequent words were taken from each language corpus and associations with these frequent words either preceding or succeeding each of the other words in the corpus were assessed (the 25 words contained both function and content words). Analyses taking the frequency of words into account resulted in correct classification for function and content words of 91.0% for Dutch, 78.8% for English, 85.4% for French, and 95.2% for Japanese. For nouns and verbs, classifications were also extremely accurate: 93.0% for Dutch, 93.0% for English, 84.1% for French, and 84.4% for Japanese.

However, one limitation of these studies is that the analyses are supervised – the discriminant analyses are provided with the grammatical categories and have to use the given information in the bigram cues to match the categories as closely as possible. Such an approach is extremely useful for indicating the potential information available within the child's language environment, but it does not provide an indication of how the grammatical categories may be generated by the child learning their language. An alternative approach is to combine information using unsupervised analyses, where the model's solution emerges from the structure of the information itself.

4.2 Deriving syntactic structure from the corpus

Redington, Chater and Finch (1998), in a landmark study, showed that not only was there category information present within distributional information in child directed speech, but that a cluster analysis based on this information resulted in clusters that respected the grammatical categories of the words extremely well. So, nouns tended to occur in very similar contexts to one another, as did verbs, and adjectives, and so on. The distributional information utilized in their model was based on the co-occurrence of each word with each of the 150 most frequent words in the corpus of child directed speech in one of four positions: two words before the target word, one word before the target word, one word after the target, or two words after the target. The counts were added throughout the corpus, resulting in a 600-dimensional vector for each word. Similarities between the contexts of words could then be computed by measuring the distances between the context vector for each word. The clustering procedure grouped together words that were closest in this 600-dimensional vector space.

The accuracy and completeness of this approach were spectacularly effective, resulting in high accuracy and completeness for words within the syntactic categories. Also, the clustering resulted in a structuring of words into grammatical categories with nested degrees of specificity. So, for example, adverbs were grouped at one level of the clustering tree as they were all used in similar distributional contexts, but this grouping was comprised of subordinate clusters of adverbs distinguished by more specific usage patterns. The presence of graded similarity within the clusters corresponds to constructionist grammar, whereby grammatical categories are based on patterns of usage, of varying degrees of specificity (Croft 2001, 2003). However, the plausibility of this analysis of the distributional information as a reflection of cognitive processing within the developing child is a matter of debate. One problem is that the amount of information to be tallied for each word in the child's environment is vast: maintaining counts of 600 co-occurrences for every word presumably exceeds the child's working memory. In addition, the clustering analysis performed on the assessment required distances between all words to be considered simultaneously, and there are also difficulties in deciding how many clusters there should be in the final clustering. There are two adaptations to the account that address each of these objections, without altering the principles of the approach.

First, to address the cognitive overload objection, a developmental approach can be taken for deriving the contextual co-occurrence counts, with just a few context words employed for the co-occurrence counts at early stages of language development, and counts only recorded for a small number of words within the lexicon. Then, as the child's language knowledge develops, additional context words could be iteratively introduced to refine the contextual information for words in the child's vocabulary. Furthermore, retaining all the co-occurrences between words is not necessary to determine the words' context, and may indeed be an impediment to learning distinctions between categories. Storing counts only for context words that provide variation in their co-occurrence pattern is one such way to limit storage requirements and maximize category information. For example, interjections may co-occur with all open class words (nouns, verbs, adjectives, adverbs) and as such they do not provide discrimination between these grammatical categories, and blur the distinctions that the child is required to make. In contrast, articles tend to co-occur frequently with nouns and seldom with verbs, and so such context words provide a great deal of information about grammatical categories.

To address the second objection, alternative approaches to the clustering algorithm can be used that exploit the information contained in the similarity space for a set of words Pothos and Chater's (2002, 2005) simplicity model of clustering, for instance, determines both the number of clusters *and* which items group together within those clusters by computing the optimal solution in information-theoretic terms for the similarity space. Such a clustering approach respects intuitions and experimental results in terms of the characteristics of generating categories of perceptual stimuli. The simplicity approach exploits the fact that if two similar items can be grouped together then it requires less information to store and access these two items than if they are stored separately, due to redundancies between the properties of the items (in the case of corpus analyses, similarities between the contexts in which the two words occur).

An alternative unsupervised approach to learning syntactic categories was developed by Cartwright and Brent (1997). Their model searched child directed speech for minimal pairs, where two phrases differed by only one word. When two phrases like this occurred, the differing words were grouped together, and the phrase omitting the differing words was stored as a pattern (see also Dominey *et al.* 2006). So, if the corpus comes across *the dog sat down* and *the cat sat down*, then *dog* and *cat* would be grouped together, and the frame *the* ___ *sat down* would be extracted. Similarly, if *the* ___ *sat up* also occurred with *cat* or *dog* in the gap, the frame would become *the* ___ *sat* ___, and *down* and *up* would be clustered together. The model learned to categorize words from the child directed speech corpus. In addition, the model learned the categories more accurately when semantic information about concrete nouns was also included in the simulation (see Solan, Horn, Ruppin and Edelman 2005 for a recent update on this type of approach as well as the section below on combining intra- and extra-linguistic information).

5. Intra-linguistic cues in the word: Phonology to structure

Table 1. Phonological and prosodic cues found to distinguish grammatical categories in English

Cue	Description	Grammatical category distinctions	References
Phoneme length	How long is the word in terms of phonemes?	Function < Content Noun > Verb	(Kelly 1992; Morgan, Shi and Allopenna 1996)
Syllable length	How long is the word in terms of syllables?	Function < Content Noun > Verb	(Cassidy and Kelly 1991; Kelly 1992; Morgan *et al.* 1996)
Presence of stress	Does the word receive lexical stress?	Function < Content	(Gleitman and Wanner 1982)
Position of stress	Which syllable receives lexical stress?	Noun earlier than Verb	(Kelly and Bock 1988)
Onset complexity	How many consonants in the word's onset?	Function < Content	(Shi, Morgan and Allopenna 1998)
Word complexity	How many consonants per syllable?	Function < Content	(Morgan *et al.* 1996)
Reduced syllables	What proportion of syllables contain schwa or syllabic consonant?	Function > Content	(Cutler 1993)
Reduced first syllable	Does the first syllable contain a schwa?	Function > Content	(Cutler 1993; Cutler and Carter 1987)
-*ed* inflection	Does the word end in /əd/ or /Id/?	Adjective > other categories	(Marchand 1969)
Coronals	What proportion of consonants are coronals?	Function > Content	(Morgan *et al.* 1996)
Initial /ð/	Does the word begin with /ð/?	Function > Content	(Campbell and Besner 1981)
Final voicing	Does the word finish with a voiced consonant?	Noun > Verb	(Kelly 1992)

Cue	Description	Grammatical category distinctions	References
Nasals	What proportion of consonants are nasals?	Noun > Verb	(Kelly 1992)
Stressed vowel position	Is the stressed vowel more likely to be a front vowel?	Noun < Verb	(Sereno and Jongman 1990)
Vowel position	Are the vowels more likely to be front vowels throughout the word?	Noun < Verb	(Monaghan *et al.* 2005)
Vowel height	Are the vowels more likely to be high throughout the word?	Noun < Verb	(Monaghan *et al.* 2005)
Plosives	Are plosives more likely to occur in the word?	Function < Content	(Monaghan *et al.* 2007)
Fricatives	Are fricatives more likely to occur in the word?	Function > Content	(Monaghan *et al.* 2007)
Dentals	Are dental consonants more likely to occur in the word?	Function > Content	(Monaghan *et al.* 2007)
Velars	Are velar consonants more likely to occur in the word?	Function < Content Noun < Verb	(Monaghan *et al.* 2007)
Bilabials in onset	Are bilabials more likely to occur in the word onset?	Function < Content Noun > Verb	(Monaghan *et al.* 2007)
Approximants in onset	Are approximants more likely to occur in the word onset?	Noun < Verb	(Monaghan *et al.* 2007)

Besides the potential utterance-level information indicated by distributional information in language, a similar cornucopia of cues in the speech sounds of individual words has been found to relate to different grammatical categories. Many different phonological and prosodic cues have been reported in the literature for reflecting grammatical category distinctions in English, and 22 of them are reported in Table 1, containing

16 cues reported in Monaghan *et al.* (2005), extended by 6 additional cues found to be significantly different in a study by Monaghan *et al.* (2007). Establishing that these phonological and prosodic cues are significantly distinct for grammatical categories has generally been accomplished by assessment of large corpora or subsets of the lexicon of English. However, each cue considered alone does not provide very reliable information about grammatical categories. Monaghan *et al.* (2005), for instance, demonstrated that, using the length in syllables cue, classifying all words of length two syllables or greater as nouns, and words of length one syllable or less as verbs, resulted in 54.5% correct classification of nouns and verbs from the 5000 most frequent words in English child directed speech. Though highly significant ($p<.001$), such a classification is unlikely to be useful as a sole basis for determining grammatical categories. The key question, then, is whether combined cues provide useful information for grammatical categorization, and if so, how this combination may be achieved.

5.1 Individual cues in categorization

Assessment of the use of phonological cues in language learning has also tended to be in isolation, so their combined usage is unclear. For example, Cassidy and Kelly (2001) tested children's classification of nonsense words as either nouns or verbs, based only on the number of syllables that each had. In English, as noted in Table 1, nouns tend to be longer than verbs, and children were much more likely to assign trisyllabic nonsense words to roles as nouns, whereas monosyllabic words were more likely to be assigned verb roles in describing pictorial scenes. Whereas this experiment was designed to test the single cue of syllable length, interestingly there were a number of other cues that also contributed to the noun/verb distinction for these materials. The trisyllabic words differed significantly from the monosyllabic words in terms of length in phonemes, stress position (trisyllabic words had less word-initial stress), and proportion of nasal consonants (trisyllabic words had more nasals). Monosyllabic words were also marginally significantly more likely to contain complex syllables. Each of these cues may have been integrated in affecting the child's performance.

Acoustic-level cues have also been proposed as beneficial for segregating grammatical categories. Blanc, Dodane and Dominey (2003) investigated whether the function/content word distinction could be reflected by variations in F0 peaks. They found that the F0 signal alone was sufficient for classifying over 73.1% of a small corpus of function and content words in French and 64.5% in English, with performance greater than chance levels (52% and 54% respectively). Content words were found to have higher peaks and greater variety in pitch in both languages.

5.2 Combined cues for categorization

Shi *et al.* (1998) provided an investigation of multiple cues combining to aid classification. They assessed acoustic, phonological and prosodic cues, together with distributional cues about utterance position (sentence initial, medial, or final) and frequency of occurrence in two small corpora of child directed speech in two languages – Mandarin and Turkish. In Mandarin, seven of ten cues assessed were significantly differently distributed between function and content words for both corpora. These included frequency, syllable coda (more likely to be present for content words), reduplication (repetition of a syllable), syllable nucleus (diphthongs more likely in content words), marked tone (where tonal sequence does not alternate between high and low, which is more likely in content words), and longer and louder syllables in content words. Combining these analyses into a self-organising computational model indicated that content and function words could be correctly classified to a level of 71.5%-69.9% for each mother-child corpus.

For Turkish, 8 cues were assessed, including the distributional cues of frequency and utterance position, three phonological cues, and three acoustic cues. For both corpora, 7 cues were significantly differently distributed for content and function words. Function words had higher frequency and were more likely to occur utterance medially or finally than content words. Function words tended to have fewer syllables in the morpheme, and content words were more likely to have syllable codas. Function words were more likely to exhibit vowel harmony (first vowel influences later vowels in the word in terms of vowel position, height and roundedness), and syllables were longer and louder in content words. A self-organising model based on these cues correctly classified 69.1%–63.7% of the words occurring in the corpus.

Durieux and Gillis (2001) also attempted to assess combined phonological cues for categorising words in English and Dutch in a model of instance-based learning. They employed four cues from Kelly (1996) suggested to be useful for classifying nouns and verbs: position of stress, word complexity, nasals, and vowel height. They found that, individually, cues correctly classified between 62.42% and 67.38% of words from the English CELEX database into a broad set of categories, and combined cues performed slightly better, with 67.68% correctly classified. In the same study, Durieux and Gillis (2001) also tested the extent to which these cues generalized to Dutch. They found that the individual cues classified between 57.9% and 66.8% of Dutch words from CELEX, with stress position being the poorest, and word complexity being the best. Combined cues produced much better accuracy than any cue alone, classifying correctly 75.2% of the words. The same set of cues was also found to be useful for forming further individuations among the content word categories in English and Dutch, correctly classifying 66.6% of English nouns, verbs, adjectives, and adverbs, and 71.0% of these categories in Dutch.

In an assessment of Dutch, English, French, and Japanese, Monaghan *et al.* (2007) used discriminant analyses to find the extent to which distributions of phonological properties, principally in terms of manner and place features of consonants within the words, distinguished function from content words, and nouns from verbs. They assessed child directed speech in each of the four languages and used combined cues to ascertain the extent to which these cues could potentially operate in concert for categorization. For token-based analyses, where the frequency of lexical items was taken into account in the classifications, they found extremely high accuracy for classification. For function and content words, correct classification reached 82.9% for Dutch, 68.7% for English, 85.2% for French, and 93.4% for Japanese. For nouns and verbs, the results were also extremely high, with 89.6% of Dutch words correctly classified, 67.5% for English, 82.0% for French, and 82.2% for Japanese. Combined cues, then, for these four languages, resulted in very impressive classifications, all well above chance levels ($p<.0001$). Similarly, Onnis and Christiansen (2005) found that the beginning and ending phonemes of words in the same four languages provide sufficient information for reliably distinguishing between nouns and verbs. The discrimination of words based on the intra-linguistic cues we have reported results in some words being misclassified according to the benchmark categories. However, achieving accuracy approaching 90% is a persuasive demonstration that there is a high degree of useful information available within these cue types, that can be employed to constrain grammatical categories in the child's developing language and be utilized to begin the process of bootstrapping categories. Yet, the benchmark categories ignore the graded nature of grammatical categories (e.g., Croft 2003; Labov 1973), and a more graded system of grammatical categories may well result in greater accuracy of classification based on these cues.

6. Combining intra-linguistic cues

The intra-linguistic cues we have discussed in the previous two sections – both at the utterance and the word level – have been revealed by corpus analysis studies to provide a large amount of information about a word's grammatical category. Combined distributional cues provide greater reliability and accuracy of information about categories, and the same applies for the combined analyses of phonological and prosodic cues. Furthermore, these patterns of benefit have been shown to be language-general, extending across Germanic, Romance, and Japonic language families in Durieux and Gillis (2001) and Monaghan *et al.*'s (2007) studies, and Sino-Tibetan and Turkic language families in Shi *et al.*'s (1998) study.

Considered separately, each set of cues can provide impressive classification, demonstrating that the language environment is extremely rich in supporting the development of grammatical categories in the child learning her first language. But what benefit would accrue from connecting utterance-level and word-level intra-linguistic information for classification? Shi *et al.* (1998) have already pointed to the potential accumulative benefits of integrating distributional, phonological, and acoustic cues to reflect the function/content word distinction. However, our multiple cue integration analyses have revealed that not only does accuracy increase based on converging cues, but that cues from different modalities interact in surprising ways for categorization.

Monaghan *et al.* (2005) used discriminant analyses of combined bigram distributional cues and phonological cues for categorising function and content words and nouns and verbs in English. They found that combined cues provided more accurate classification than just distributional or phonological cues alone. However, the relative benefit of these types of cues varied for different frequency groupings. For higher-frequency words, distributional cues were more reliable than phonological cues, whereas for lower-frequency words, the effectiveness of phonological cues overtook the contribution of distributional cues. For these low-frequency words, there were few occurrences of them in the child's environment, and so the certainty with which the language learner can form associations between words is limited. Fortunately, under these circumstances basing grammatical category judgement solely on the phonological cues is, in terms of the information present in the language, an effective approach (see also Durieux and Gillis 2001).

Christiansen and Monaghan (2006) focused on the classification of nouns and verbs and the contribution of distributional and phonological information for classifying words of each category. They found that distributional cues tended to be more reliable for classifying verbs than nouns, whereas verbs were more accurately classified by phonological cues. Verbs tend to occur in a wider variety of contexts (McDonald and Shillcock 2001), and so associations formed for verbs with the set of high-frequency context words is less likely to be reliable, due to being less constrained. Nouns, in contrast, tend to occur in more prescribed contexts. Yet, once again, serendipitously for the language learner, phonological information is more effective for classifying verbs than nouns and so can compensate for the lower accuracy in distributional information.

In a set of crosslinguistic analyses, Monaghan *et al.* (2007) found that the pattern of effects reported in Christiansen and Monaghan (2006) for the interaction of different modalities of cue with the noun/verb distinction were also found for Dutch, French, and Japanese. In addition, a similar interaction of reliability of cue types was found for categorising function and content words. Classification of function words was less accurate using distributional cues – despite their higher mean frequency, they tended not to co-occur reliably with other high-frequency words as they tended to occur immediately before or after content words, and could occur in a wide variety of contexts. Yet again, phonological information was more reliable for these words. Morgan *et al.* (1996) discuss the pressures on function words, due to their high-frequency and predictability, to be produced with minimal effort in speech, hence vowel-reductions and consonant-voicing are common in this category of words. A consequence of this is that such function words may be easily identified as such given minimal, but coherent phonological information in the speech signal (see also Shi, Werker and Morgan 1999).

7. Converging evidence for the use of multiple cues

The corpus analyses we have thus far discussed have indicated the potential benefits from drawing together multiple cues in order to determine the extent to which grammatical categories may be learned from the environment during language acquisition. However, experimental approaches provide converging evidence for the *use* of these cues in acquiring language structure. There are two paradigms in the literature for such experimental investigation of cues for language acquisition. The first we discuss are artificial language learning (ALL) studies of segmentation, the second are word categorization studies.

7.1 Learning to segment artificial language with multiple cues

ALL tasks involve training human participants on artificial miniature languages with particular structural constraints, and then testing their knowledge of the language. Importantly, the ability to acquire linguistic structure can be studied independently of semantic influences. Because ALL permits researchers to investigate the language learning abilities of infants and children in a highly controlled environment, the paradigm is becoming increasingly popular as a method for studying language acquisition (for reviews, see e.g., Gómez and Gerken 2000; Saffran 2003). We suggest that ALL can be applied to the investigation of issues pertaining to the usefulness of cues in language acquisition in much the same way as computational modelling is currently being used. One advantage of ALL over computational modelling is that it is possible to show that hypothesized cues actually *affect* human learning and processing and are not only potentially useful for language acquisition.

The role of distributional cues in ALL has been extensively investigated, both in terms of the extent to which this information can be exploited to learn the structure in terms of word boundaries within speech, and also the relationships between words within sentences. Saffran, Aslin, and Newport (1996) in an influential study on language acquisition in infants devised a nonsense language composed of words of three syllables each. Words were concatenated into continuous speech, such that transitions for syllables between words were of low probability and transitions for syllables within words were of high probability. Infants were found to be sensitive to such distributional information in determining their preference for sequences of syllables that respected the word structure over those that crossed word boundaries.

This approach to cues available to language learners for learning the structure of words within the language has been extended to test the benefit of including cues from other modalities for revealing language structure. In English, final syllables of words tend to be slightly longer than initial or medial word syllables in articulation. Adding this cue into an ALL segmentation task resulted in better performance for adult participants than when the first syllable was lengthened (Saffran *et al.* 1996). In English, also, words tend to be stressed on the first syllable and infants can use this to segment artificial languages even in the absence of distributional information (Curtin, Mintz and Christiansen 2005). Moreover, Johnson and Jusczyk (2001) found that the distributional information was more accurately discovered when the first syllable was stressed, and that performance appeared to be worse than chance when the final syllable was stressed. These results indicate that multiple cues are beneficial for aiding speech segmentation, but only when the cues are consistent with the patterns found in the hearer's language environment. In the case of stress, the misplacement appeared to over-ride the use of distributional information in language processing.

ALL studies have also been used to reveal the extent to which more complex distributional information can be used for learning language structure. Peña, Bonatti, Nespor and Mehler (2002) devised a language composed of trisyllabic words, where the transitional probabilities between all adjacent syllables in the speech were identical, but where syllables within the same word (*Ai* and *Bi*), but separated by an intervening syllable (*X*), had a dependency of 1. Hence, the language was of the form *AiXBiAjXBj*… where *Ai* and *Bi* always co-occurred in the speech. Peña *et al.* found that participants could use these non-adjacencies to discover word structure, demonstrating a preference for words over sequences composed of part-words from the speech. However, Onnis, Monaghan, Richmond and Chater (2005) demonstrated that such structure could only be discovered when it was supported by similarities in terms of the phonemes from which the non-adjacent syllables were composed. In Peña *et al.*'s (2002) studies, the non-adjacent syllables were stop consonants, whereas the intervening syllables were always continuants. If this phonology was removed then learning was not observed, but learning did take place if the non-adjacent dependent syllables were both continuants and the intervening syllable was a stop. Such a view of multiple cues conspiring to support learning is consistent with the pattern of effects found in Newport and Aslin (2004) for supporting learning non-adjacencies – learning was only found to occur when there was phonological similarity between distributionally dependent syllables.

The innovation in Peña *et al.*'s (2002) study, however, was that not only could discovery of the structure of the words in the language occur, but also that the ability of participants to generalize the structure of the language could be measured. The language was identical to before, but participants were this time tested on their preference for rule-words compared to part-words. Rule-words were composed of *Ai* and *Bi* pairs with another *Aj* or *Bj* syllable intervening between them, so they respected the non-adjacent structure but had not been encountered during training. Participants were found to prefer the rule-words over the part-words only when an additional cue of a short gap was placed before the first syllable in each word during training on the speech. Such a cue was sufficient to enable realization of the generalizable structure of the language to participants.

7.2 Learning to categorize artificial language with multiple cues

Multiple, converging cues have also been used for investigating learning categories of words in ALL studies. Valian and Coulson (1988) investigated the extent to which two categories of words could be learned from simple sentences containing reliable bigram information about category membership. Sentences were of the form *aAibBj* or *bBiaAj* where *a* and *b* were invariant marker words and *Ai* and *Bj* were category words, drawn from a set of 8 words each. Valian and Coulson (1988) found that adult participants could learn to accept valid sentences that did not occur during training on the language and correctly reject sentences where there was a mismatch between the marker words and the category words (e.g., *aBibAj*). Monaghan *et al.* (2005) extended this experimental paradigm to incorporate phonological information within the *Ai* and *Bi* category words. Words in each category had distinct phonological properties according to those found to be useful for distinguishing different grammatical categories in English. Monaghan *et al.* (2005) found that when the category words were supported by phonological information then learning of the categories was much more accurate than when phonological information was not present.

Learning the categorical distinction between different genders has been of particular interest in language learning studies. This is because extra-linguistic information provides few cues about how many genders a language may have and about gender membership for particular lexical items. However, Corbett (1991) noted that there are various potential sources of information to grammatical gender. Certain semantic groupings may have the same gender, for instance in German superordinate terms are neuter (Köpcke 1982). In addition, there is correspondence between phonological and morphological cues and gender. For example, in French the endings *-age* and *-ble* tend to indicate masculine nouns. However, there remains the difficulty of how these gender categories are developed, and the question of how and when the correspondence between particular semantic groups and gender may be exploited by the learner.

In learning to categorize words, Braine, Brody, Brooks, Sudhalter, Ross, Catalano and Fisch (1990) found that categories could be learned in their study only when there was a consistent morphological marker that applied only to that category. However, Brooks, Braine, Catalano, Brody and Sudhalter (1993), in a related study, trained participants on word categories some of which had a consistent morphological marker. They found that the category of words that were marked with the consistent morphology was judged accurately, but also performance was good on words that were of the same category but did not have the morphological marker. Generalization to phrases that had not occurred in the training but were consistent with the structure was also seen to occur, but only under the conditions of consistent marking of the categories (see also Frigo and McDonald 1998).

8. How are multiple cues integrated?

In sum, the ALL experiments indicate that multiple, multimodal cues to language structure assist language learners in developing a sense of their language, both to be able to respond to what is an accurate form in the language and also in order to generalize from this structure. Taken together with the corpus analysis studies, there are two possibilities for the benefit of multiple cues for learning. One possibility is that, as Braine (1987) contends, phonological cues that are consistent with language structure are necessary in order for that structure to be learned, in other words without the phonological correspondence the structure is unlearnable. Hence, the distributional information is emphasized by its reflection in differences in the phonology of words belonging to different categories (whether this information is in the word root or in morphosyntactic marking). Under such a view, the learner benefits from the alignment of structures in these different modalities. Monaghan *et al.* (2007) discuss a possible mechanism for this alignment, based on the Redington *et al.* (1998) corpus analyses. Redington *et al.* (1998) suggested that words are clustered according to their similarity in terms of the contexts in which they occur – words that have the same distribution in the language that the child is exposed to will be grouped together. A similar clustering could take place based on the phonological properties of words. Indeed, Farmer, Christiansen and Monaghan (2006) illustrate the fact that nouns cluster more closely to other nouns than they do to verbs in terms of their phonological properties, and similarly verbs cluster with other verbs, and furthermore the closeness of the word to the centre of its cluster in terms of phonology has an influence on accuracy and speed of its processing in sentence contexts. The two clusters – one based on distributional information, and the other based on phonological information – can then be combined to provide a more refined clustering that more accurately reflects the objective grammatical categories in the language.

The alternative is that the importance of multiple cues is due to their redundancy. Learning a language where there is only just enough information to be able to transmit the structure would be extremely difficult, and inattention to a crucial feature of the language to reveal its structure would be catastrophic. It may be that multiple cues provide a safety-net for learning. This latter perspective is consistent with the use of multiple cues in modalities other than language. In determining depth perception, for instance, viewers are sensitive to a multitude of cues (Cutting and Vishton 1995), however each cue alone is unreliable and consistent with a range of depths under different viewing conditions (for a review see Jacobs 2002). In each viewing situation, the viewer must determine which cues are valid for the current environment. For instance, distant objects tend to appear bluer, but in some scenes blue-coloured objects may be closer than yellow objects, say. The literature on multiple-cue use in depth perception has principally attended to the issue of how the viewer decides on the reliability of particular cues in the environment. There are two views for how this may proceed. Either reliability is determined according to the ambiguity of the cue, or cues that correlate well with other cues are processed as more reliable. Once the reliability of cues has been determined, then viewers tend to place more weight in their decision about depth from cues with greater reliability. Given the quirks and variations of the visual environment, selecting from a large set of cues is doubtless a useful process in maintaining accuracy of judgement. The same reasoning applies to the noisy language environment through which the child navigates, and Christiansen and Dale (2001) provided an indication for how this may apply in a simulation of multiple-cue integration in language learning. They found that when the model was presented with four syntactically relevant cues and four distractor cues, the model learned to take advantage of the informative cues while ignoring the irrelevant cues.

Our view is that the advantage of multiple cues is some combination of the benefits of both the redundancy of overlapping information and the safety-net of being able to draw on several cues for the categorization decision. The corpus analyses, for instance, indicate that for some words (high frequency, content words, nouns) distributional information is extremely useful, whereas for other word types (lower frequency, function words, verbs) phonological information is more reliable for determining grammatical categories. Hence, reliability of different cue types varies, and placing more weight on the more reliable distributional cues for these words is likely to be a useful procedure. Yet, phonological information is still present for high-frequency words, content words, and nouns, and so this weaker but potentially useful information is still contributing toward the child's ability to learn these grammatical categories.

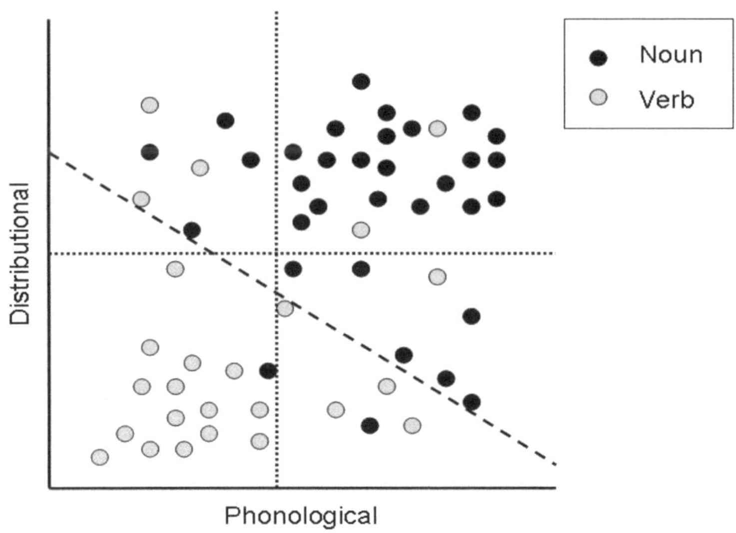

Figure 1. Classifications of nouns and verbs based on distributional cues alone (horizontal dotted line), phonological cues alone (vertical dotted line), and combined cues (oblique dashed line)

Figure 1 illustrates an idealized view of the benefit of combined cues. Words can be conceived as points in space defined by their distributional features and phonological/prosodic properties, and in the Figure we represent idealized nouns and verbs. Phonological properties are illustrated by the x-axis, where words that are close together share phonological cues. Similarly, distributional cues are illustrated by the y-axis. Using just distributional information to classify nouns and verbs results in a distinction around the horizontal dotted line – points above this line are classified as nouns according to their distributional properties, and points below are classified as verbs. A classification based only on phonological cues is shown by the vertical dotted line. In this case, points to the right of the line have phonological cues in line with the majority of nouns, and points to the left are more verb-like. In each of these single-modality classifications, several words are misclassified. However, when both cue types are combined, a line can be drawn in two-dimensional space, illustrated by the oblique dashed line, resulting in greater accuracy of classification. In this case, nouns are above right of the line, verbs below left of the line, and there are many fewer misclassifications than using a single modality of cue alone.

9. Extra-linguistic cues and language learning

In this chapter, so far, we have focused our discussion on the integration of phonological, prosodic (such as stress presence and position), and distributional cues as potential contributors to grammatical categorization in the language learner. Yet, there is certainly a vast array of other potential cues available in the child's environment.

One such source of information is contextual information from the child's environment. Language is not spoken in a vacuum, as it is in certain laboratory experimental conditions, and the surroundings – objects and actions – in the child's environment and their parallels in the spoken language may contribute enormously to language structure. Such information is likely to be extremely valuable in constraining language learning, though empirical investigations of this correlation of environment and language have not been explored until only recently. Yu (2006) investigated corpora of parents narrating a picture book with children aged between 1 and 3 years. The study correlated the words spoken with the objects present on that page of the book. The corpus analysis revealed that there was a great deal of ambiguity for the referents of words spoken at a particular page in the picture book, with a mean of more than 8 words and 3 objects for each learning situation (situations were individuated by speech pauses).

Given this input, a computational model was trained to learn grammatical categories of words, based on a system similar to that of Cartwright and Brent (1997), where words were extracted from common sentence patterns. This "syntactic" system learned in collaboration with a "semantic" system, which learned the associations between particular words and objects in the environment. Words that occurred in similar sentence contexts *and* had strong associations with objects in the visual world provided a high degree of confidence that those words belonged to the same category (though "semantic" categories were given to the model in this case). This assisted both nouns by accentuating nodes representing nouns, as well as other grammatical categories which were boosted in activation when no objects were present in the environment. A computational model that had both syntactic and semantic learning performed better than a semantic learning model alone in learning the associations between words and objects.

In related work, Yu and Smith (2006) provided a laboratory-based paradigm for assessing learning of the co-occurrences of words and objects in the environment. Undergraduate participants were exposed to a set of words spoken in the presence of a set of pictures of uncommon objects. The number of words spoken and the number of different objects occurring within each picture was altered between conditions, varying between 2 and 4. The participants' task was to learn what the names of objects were in the language, and this was only possible if the associations between particular objects and names were learned across learning situations. In all cases, participants learned the names of objects better than chance, indicating that the correlations with environmental objects were available to learners of the language.

In computational modelling of learning mappings between words and meanings, Monaghan and Christiansen (2006) explored the potential benefit of contextual information that limits the possible assignations of words to objects in the environment. We found that, when contextual information was present, mappings between phonological and meaning forms for words was accomplished effectively. Furthermore, when phonological similarity within a syntactic category was available then words of the same category were more easily grouped together.

These studies point toward future research in analysing multiple cues that assist in language learning. Yu and Smith's (2006) research indicates that visual contextual information can be effectively combined with syntactic information in human language learning, and Monaghan and Christiansen (2006) show that there are potential benefits from integrating distributional and phonological information. There is clearly potency in studies that combine all three information sources (see e.g., Tomasello 2003 for a similar view of the future of multiple cue integration). In the case of each of these new sources of cues for grammatical category, an additional dimension can be added to Figure 1 to enable greater accuracy of classification. The more dimensions there are in designing a plane through the space, the greater the accuracy of distinguishing different grammatical categories.

10. Future directions for multiple cue research

The past decade has seen a growing bulk of corpus-based analyses that provide support for the multiple-cue integration perspective on language acquisition. Many different types of cues have been found to be potentially helpful for learning about syntactic structure, often attested to across a variety of different languages. However, several challenges remain for multiple-cue integration research, including finding ways of quantifying new cues and incorporating cues to phrasal structure, integrating and utilising cues across different levels of linguistic analyses (such as speech segmentation and lexical category discovery, and relationships between discourse and syntax, e.g., Allen, Skarabela and Hughes this volume), and the development of more comprehensive models to explain when and how children use various cues across development. In this final section, we discuss some of these outstanding challenges for future research in multiple-cue integration.

10.1 Quantifying new cues

We noted earlier that recent work had begun to look at how extra-linguistic cues might be integrated with intra-linguistic information (e.g., Monaghan and Christiansen 2006; Yu 2006). Although this work has yielded promising results, integration of extra-linguistic cues is complicated by the difficulties involved in describing and quantifying this type of information. For example, extra-linguistic cues not only include the visual environment in which the language learner is situated but also the social context within which the interactions take place as well as the internal mental states of the learner. Each of these information sources are very hard to capture adequately in a way that facilitates the kind of computational analyses that now have become typical of corpus-based research. Nonetheless, progress is under way in the context of the CHILDES database, which now includes digital video that can be linked to corpus transcripts (see Behrens this volume; MacWhinney this volume for further discussion). However, more technical innovations are likely to be needed before most extra-linguistic cues can be incorporated into multiple-cue integration research at the same level and amount of detail as is currently the case for phonological and distributional information.

One type of cue that may be more readily amenable to corpus-based analyses is information about sentential prosody. Whereas most multiple-cue integration research so far has focused on cues relevant for lexical category discovery, intonational sentence prosody provide potential cues for phrasal structure (for reviews, see Gerken (1996); Gleitman and Wanner (1982); Jusczyk and Kemler-Nelson (1996); Morgan (1996), though see Fernald and McRoberts (1996) for cautionary remarks). Infants seem highly sensitive to language-specific prosodic patterns (Gerken, Jusczyk and Mandel 1994; Kemler-Nelson, Hirsh-Pasek, Jusczyk and Wright Cassidy 1989) – a sensitivity that may start *in utero* (Mehler, Jusczyk, Lambertz, Halsted, Bertoncini and Amiel-Tison 1988). Prosodic information also improves sentence comprehension in two-year-olds (Shady and Gerken 1999). Results from artificial language learning experiments with adults furthermore show that prosodic marking of syntactic phrase boundaries facilitates learning (Morgan, Meier and Newport 1987; Valian and Levitt 1996). Yet, few corpus-based efforts have tried to quantify just how useful such prosodic information may be. One notable exception is the acoustic analyses by Fisher and Tokura (1996), suggesting that differences in pause length, vowel duration, and pitch provide probabilistic cues to phrase boundaries in both English and Japanese child directed speech. Although this study was on a relatively small scale due to the labor intensiveness of acoustic analyses, progress in automated acoustic analyses may provide a way in which large-scale future quantitative studies can be carried out across different languages.

10.2 Cues for different levels of language learning

Another important challenge for future work on multiple-cue integration is when and how cues might be utilized to facilitate learning at different levels of linguistic analyses. For example, as discussed above, phonology provides useful cues for distinguishing between words from different lexical categories, such as nouns and verbs. However, phonological information is also crucial for discovering words in fluent speech. Christiansen, Hockema and Onnis (2006) conducted a two-stage analysis of a large corpus of child-directed speech to determine whether information about phoneme distributions could be used first to segment speech and then as a cue to lexical categories. They found that the distribution of biphones essentially is bimodal with the phonemes either being inside a word or straddling a word boundary (see also Hockema 2006). Using these biphone distributions more than 70% of the corpus could be correctly segmented. When initial and final phonemes then were used to distinguish nouns and verbs from other words from the segmented corpus, 62% of the words were correctly classified. This indicates that the same type of information may function as a probabilistic cue at different levels of linguistic analyses. Developing a comprehensive model that allows for such cue use and integration across various levels of linguistic representation is an important nontrivial challenge for future multiple-cue integration research.

Given that different languages employ different constellations of cues to signal different syntactic distinctions, an important question for further research is exactly how children (or rather, their learning mechanisms) determine which cues are relevant for which aspect of syntax and which are just noise. This problem is even further compounded by the fact that the same cue may work in different directions across different languages. A case in point is that nouns tend to contain more vowels and fewer consonants than verbs in English, whereas nouns and verbs in French show the opposite pattern (Monaghan *et al.* 2007). So how can the child learn which cues are relevant and in which direction?

One method may be that the child exploits the correlations between cues in the environment, as discussed above. This view is further underscored by mathematical analyses couched in terms of the Vapnik-Chervonenkis (VC) dimension (Abu-Mostafa 1993), showing that the integration of multiple sources of correlated information is likely to reduce the number of hypotheses a learning system has to entertain. The VC dimension establishes an upper bound for the number of examples needed by a learning process that starts with a set of hypotheses about the task solution. Cue information may lead to a reduction in the VC dimension by weeding out bad hypotheses and thereby lowering the number of examples needed to learn the solution. In other words, the integration of multiple cues may reduce learning time by reducing the number of steps necessary to find an appropriate implementation of the target function as well as decrease the number of candidate functions for the target function being learned, thus potentially ensuring better generalization.

10.3 Computational and developmental approaches to multiple cues

More generally, the development of computational multiple-cue integration models is still in its infancy. By now there are many studies indicating the usefulness of a variety of different cues for language acquisition, and although theoretical models abound (e.g., Gleitman and Wanner (1982); and contributions in Morgan and Demuth (1996); Weissenborn and Höhle (2001)), only a few psychologically plausible computational models for multiple-cue integration currently exists (e.g., Cartwright and Brent 1997; Christiansen and Dale 2001; Reali, Christiansen and Monaghan 2003). The existing models, however, tend to model the end-state of learning rather the developmental process itself. This ignores the different time-scales at which different cues may become important for acquisition. For example, the ability to use visually-based contextual information to constrain the interpretation of a syntactically ambiguous sentence does not appear until about eight years of age, considerably later than sensitivity to constraints on the possible kinds of constructions that may follow specific verbs (Snedeker and Trueswell 2004). To fully understand multiple-cue integration and how it develops, models must be devised that capture the developmental trajectory of cue use across different stages of language acquisition. We anticipate that the availability of so-called "dense" corpora (e.g., Behrens 2006; Maslen, Theakston, Lieven and Tomasello 2004) will facilitate the development of this kind of more constructivist-oriented computational models of language acquisition.

A further issue that remains underdeveloped is attention to the *development* of language. The studies of cue availability in the child's environment and the computational treatments of this information consider all information simultaneously. This is an over-simplification: children's productions indicate that the whole language is not acquired in one step, but that multiple stages are observed, where learning progresses based on what has already been learned. Attempts to explain and exploit these learning stages in computational models have met with considerable success for simulating early processing constraints that facilitate later learning of complex syntactic structures (Elman 1993), phrasal productions and errors in young children (Freudenthal, Pine and Gobet 2006), and the development of the lexicon (Steyvers and Tenenbaum 2005). Such approaches could equally be applied to the searches for cues we have presented in this chapter: the reliability of phonological, prosodic, or distributional cues could be based on the most frequent, or earliest-learned words, and constructed incrementally, and such a constructionist approach would enhance the cognitive plausibility of the availability and process of use of such cues by the developing child.

11. Conclusion

The analyses of multiple cues for syntax acquisition reviewed in this chapter indicate the inherent richness of the language environment for the child. The child's first tentative cognitive steps are supported by a wealth of information to help in bootstrapping the structure of their first language. This "wealth of the stimulus" argument indicates that assumptions that the child's linguistic environment is inadequate for constraining the language should be reformulated. Principles of parsimony in scientific research require that the vast array of interacting cues that correlate with syntactic distinctions should not be under-estimated in terms of their contribution to constructing syntactic categories. This chapter has indicated that the cues we know about – that we have begun to measure in the child's environment – provide coherent and reliable information when considered in concert. This chapter also catalogues some potential cues that we know about but haven't yet taken into consideration in large-scale studies of the child's linguistic environment. In the words of Donald Rumsfeld (US Secretary of Defense under President George W. Bush), we've covered the known knowns, the known unknowns, but that still leaves the unknown unknowns – the cues we don't know we don't know – within the empiricist fold.

Enriching CHILDES for morphosyntactic analysis

Brian MacWhinney

1. Introduction

The modern study of child language development owes much to the methodological and conceptual advances introduced by Brown (1973). In his study of the language development of Adam, Eve, and Sarah, Roger Brown focused on a variety of core measurement issues, such as acquisition sequence, growth curves, morpheme inventories, productivity analysis, grammar formulation, and sampling methodology. The basic question that Brown was trying to answer was how one could use transcripts of interactions between children and adults to test theoretical claims regarding the child's learning of grammar. Like many other child language researchers, Brown considered the utterances produced by children to be a remarkably rich data source for testing theoretical claims. At the same time, Brown realized that one needed to specify a highly systematic methodology for collecting and analyzing these spontaneous productions.

Language acquisition theory has advanced in many ways since Brown (1973), but we are still dealing with many of the same basic methodological issues he confronted. Elaborating on Brown's approach, researchers have formulated increasingly reliable methods for measuring the growth of grammar, or morphosyntax, in the child. These new approaches serve to extend Brown's vision into the modern world of computers and computational linguistics. New methods for tagging parts of speech and grammatical relations now open up new and more powerful ways of testing hypotheses and models regarding children's language learning.

The current paper examines a particular approach to morphosyntactic analysis that has been elaborated in the context of the CHILDES (Child Language Data Exchange System) database. Readers unfamiliar with this database and its role in child language acquisition research may find it useful to download and study the materials (manuals, programs, and database) that are available for free over the web at http://childes.psy.cmu.edu. However, before doing this, users should read the "Ground Rules" for proper usage of the system. This database now contains over 44 million spoken words from 28 different languages. In fact, CHILDES is the largest corpus of conversational spoken language data currently in existence. In terms of size, the next largest collection of conversational data are the Spoken Dutch Corpus with 9 million words and the British National Corpus with 5 million words. What makes CHILDES a single corpus is the fact that all of the data in the system are consistently coded using a single transcript format called CHAT. Moreover, for several languages, all of the corpora have been tagged for part of speech using an automatic tagging program called MOR.

When Catherine Snow and I proposed the formation of the CHILDES database in 1984, we envisioned the construction of a large corpus base would allow child language researchers to improve the empirical grounding of their analyses. In fact, the overwhelming majority of new studies of the development of grammatical production rely on the programs and data in the CHILDES database. In 2002, we conducted a review of articles based on the use of the database and found that more than 2000 articles had used the data and/or programs. The fact that CHILDES has had this effect on the field is enormously gratifying to all of us who have worked to build the database. At the same time, the quality and size of the database constitutes a testimony to the collegiality of the many researchers in child language who have contributed their data for the use of future generations.

For the future, our goal is to build on these successful uses of the database to promote even more high quality transcription, analysis, and research. In order to move in this direction, it is important for the research community to understand why we have devoted so much attention to the improvement of morphosyntactic coding in CHILDES. To communicate effectively regarding this new morphosyntactic coding, we need to address the interests of three very different types of readers. Some readers are already very familiar with CHILDES and have perhaps already worked with the development and use of tools like MOR and POST. For these readers, this chapter is designed to highlight problematic areas in morphosyntactic coding and areas of new activity. It is perhaps a good idea to warn this group of readers that there have been major improvements in the programs and database over the last ten years. As a result, commands that worked with an earlier version of the programs will no longer work in the same way. It is a good idea for all active researchers to use this chapter as a way of refreshing their understanding of the CHILDES and TalkBank tools

A second group of readers will have extensive background in computational methods, but little familiarity with the CHILDES corpus. For these readers, this chapter is an introduction to the possibilities that CHILDES offers for the development of new computational approaches and analyses. Finally, for child language researchers who are not yet familiar with the use of CHILDES for studying grammatical development, this chapter should be approached as an introduction to the possibilities that are now available. Readers in this last group will find some of the sections rather technical. Beginning users do not need to master all of these technical details at once. Instead, they should just approach the chapter as an introduction to possible modes of analysis that they may wish to use some time in the future.

Before embarking on our review of computational tools in CHILDES, it is helpful to review briefly the ways in which researchers have come to use transcripts to study morphosyntactic development. When Brown collected his corpora back in the 1960s, the application of generative grammar to language development was in its infancy. However, throughout the 1980s and 1990s (Chomsky and Lasnik 1993), linguistic theory developed increasingly specific proposals about how the facts of child language learning could illuminate the shape of Universal Grammar. At the same time, learning theorists were developing increasingly powerful methods for extracting linguistic patterns from input data. Some of these new methods relied on distributed neural networks (Rumelhart and McClelland 1986), but others focused more on the ways in which children can pick up a wide variety of patterns in terms of relative cue validity (MacWhinney 1987b).

These two very different research traditions have each assigned a pivotal role to the acquisition of morphosyntax in illuminating core issues in learning and development. Generativist theories have emphasized issues such as: the role of triggers in the early setting of a parameter for subject omission (Hyams and Wexler 1993), evidence for advanced early syntactic competence (Wexler 1998), evidence for early absence of functional categories that attach to the IP node (Radford 1990), the role of optional infinitives in normal and disordered acquisition (Rice 1997), and the child's ability to process syntax without any exposure to relevant data (Crain 1991). Generativists have sometimes been criticized for paying inadequate attention to the empirical patterns of distribution in children's productions. However, work by researchers, such as Stromswold (1994), van Kampen (1998), and Meisel (1986), demonstrates the important role that transcript data can play in evaluating alternative generative accounts.

Learning theorists have placed an even greater emphasis on the use of transcripts for understanding morphosyntactic development. Neural network models have shown how cue validities can determine the sequence of acquisition for both morphological (MacWhinney, Leinbach, Taraban and McDonald 1989; MacWhinney and Leinbach 1991; Plunkett and Marchman 1991) and syntactic (Elman 1993; Mintz, Newport and Bever 2002; Siskind 1999) development. This work derives further support from a broad movement within linguistics toward a focus on data-driven models (Bybee and Hopper 2001) for understanding language learning and structure. These accounts formulate accounts that view constructions (Tomasello 2003) and item-based patterns (MacWhinney 1975) as the loci for statistical learning.

2. Analysis by transcript scanning

Although the CHILDES Project has succeeded in many ways, it has not yet provided a complete set of computational linguistic tools for the study of morphosyntactic development. In order to conduct serious corpus-based research on the development of morphosyntax, users will want to supplement corpora with tags that identify the morphological and syntactic status of every morpheme in the corpus. Without these tags, researchers who want to track the development of specific word forms or syntactic structures are forced to work with a methodology that is not much more advanced than that used by Brown in the 1960s. In those days, researchers looking for the occurrence of a particular morphosyntactic structure, such as auxiliary fronting in *yes/no* questions, would have to simply scan through entire transcripts and mark occurrences in the margins of the paper copy using a red pencil. With the advent of the personal computer in the 1980s, the marks in the margins were replaced by codes entered on a %syn (syntactic structure) or %mor (morphological analysis with parts of speech) coding tier. However, it was still necessary to pour over the full transcripts line by line to locate occurrences of the relevant target forms.

3. Analysis by lexical tracking

If a researcher is clever, there are ways to convince the computer to help out in this exhausting process of transcript scanning. An easy first step is to download the CLAN programs from the CHILDES website at http://childes.psy.cmu.edu. These programs provide several methods for tracing patterns within and between words. For example, if you are interested in studying the learning of English verb morphology, you can create a file containing all the irregular past tense verbs of English, as listed in the CHILDES manual. After typing all of these words into a file and then naming that file something like irreg.cut, you can use the CLAN program called KWAL with the +s@ irreg.cut switch to locate all the occurrences of irregular past tense forms. Or, if you only want a frequency count, you can run FREQ with the same switch to get a frequency count of the various forms and the overall frequency of irregulars. Although this type of search is very helpful, you will also want to be able to search for overregularizations and overmarkings such as **ranned*, **runned*, **goed*, or **jumpeded*. Unless these are already specially marked in the transcripts, the only way to locate these forms is to create an even bigger list with all possible overmarkings. This is possible for the common irregular overmarkings, but doing this for all overmarked regulars, such as **playeded*, is not really possible. Finally, you also want to locate all correctly marked regular verbs. Here, again, making the search list is a difficult matter. You can search for all words ending in *-ed*, but you will have to cull out from this list forms like *bed*, *moped*, and *sled*. A good illustration of research based on generalized lexical searches of this type can be found in the study of English verb learning by Marcus, Pinker, Ullman, Hollander, Rosen and Xu (1992).

Or, to take another example, suppose you would like to trace the learning of auxiliary fronting in *yes/no*-questions. For this, you would need to create a list of possible English auxiliaries to be included in a file called aux.cut. Using this, you could easily find all sentences with auxiliaries and then write out these sentences to a file for further analysis. However, only a minority of these sentences will involve *yes/no*-questions. Thus, to further sharpen your analysis, you would want to further limit the search to sentences in which the auxiliary begins the utterance. To do this, you would need to dig carefully through the electronic version of the CHILDES manual to find the ways in which to use the COMBO program to compose search strings that include markers for the beginnings and ends of sentences. Also, you may wish to separate out sentences in which the auxiliary is moved to follow a *wh*-word. Here, again, you can compose a complicated COMBO search string that looks for a list of possible initial interrogative or *wh*-words, followed by a list of possible auxiliaries. Although such searches are possible, they tend to be difficult, slow, and prone to error. Clearly, it would be better if the searches could examine not strings of words, but rather strings of morphosyntactic categories. For example, we would be able to trace sentences with initial *wh*-words followed by auxiliaries by just looking for the pattern of "int + aux". However, in order to perform such searches, we must first tag our corpora for the relevant morphosyntactic features. The current article explains how this is done.

4. Measures of morphosyntactic development

The tagging of corpora is crucial not only for research on morphosyntactic development, but also for the development of automatic ways of evaluating children's level of grammatical development. Let us consider four common measures of grammatical development: MLU, VOCD, DSS, and IPSyn.

MLU. The computation of the mean length of utterance (MLU) is usually governed by a set of nine detailed criteria specified by Brown (1973). These nine criteria are discussed in detail in the CLAN manual (http://childes.psy.cmu.edu/manuals/clan.pdf) under the heading for the MLU program. When Brown applied these criteria to his typewritten corpora in the 1960s, he and his assistants actually looked at every word in the transcript and applied each of the nine criteria to each word in each sentence in order to compute MLU. Of course, they figured out how to do this very quickly, since they all had important dissertations to write. Four decades later, relying on computerized corpora and search algorithms, we can compute MLU automatically in seconds. However, to do this accurately, we must first code the data in ways that allow the computer to apply the criteria correctly. The SALT program (Miller and Chapman 1983) achieves this effect by dividing words directly into their component morphemes on the main line, as in *boot-s* or *boot-3S* for *boots*. Earlier versions of CHILDES followed this same method, but we soon discovered that transcribers were not applying these codes consistently. Instead, they were producing high levels of error that impacted not only the computation of MLU, but also the overall value of the database. Beginning in 1998, we removed all main line segmentations from the database and began instead to rely on the computation of MLU from the %mor line, as we will discuss in detail later. To further control accurate computation of MLU, we rely on symbols like *&text*, *xxx*, and certain postcodes to exclude material from the count. Researchers wishing to compute MLU in words, rather than morphemes, can perform this computation from either the main line or the %mor line.

VOCD. Beginning in 1997 (Malvern and Richards 1997) and culminating with a book-length publication in 2004 (Malvern, Richards, Chipere and Purán 2004), Malvern and colleagues introduced a new measure called VOCD (VOCabulary Diversity) as a replacement for the earlier concept of a type/token ratio (TTR). The TTR is a simple ratio of the types of words user by a speaker in a transcript over the total number of words in the transcript. For example, if the child uses 30 different words and produces a total output of 120 words, then the TTR is 30/120 or 25. The problem with the TTR is that it is too sensitive to sample size. Small transcripts often have inaccurately high TTR ratios, simply because they are not big enough to allow for word repetitions. VOCD corrects this problem statistically for all but the smallest samples (for details, see the CLAN manual). Like MLU, one can compute VOCD either from the main line or the %mor line. However, the goal of both TTR and VOCD is to measure lexical diversity. For such analyses, it is not appropriate to treat variant inflected forms of the same base as different. To avoid this problem, one can now compute VOCD from the %mor line using the +m switch to control the filtering of affixes.

DSS. A third common measure of morphosyntactic development is the DSS (Developmental Sentence Score) from Lee (1974). This score is computed through a checklist system for tracking children's acquisition of a variety of syntactic structures, ranging from tag questions to auxiliary placement. By summing scores across a wide range of structures by hand, researchers can compute an overall developmental sentence score or DSS. However, using the %mor line in CHAT files and the CLAN DSS program, it is now possible to compute DSS automatically. After automatic running of DSS, there may be a few remaining codes that will have to be judged by eye. This requires a second "interactive" pass where these remaining issues are resolved. The DSS measure has also been adapted for use in Japanese, where it forms an important part of the Kokusai project, organized by Susanne Miyata.

IPSyn. Scarborough (1990) introduced another checklist measure of syntactic growth called IPSyn (Index of Productive Syntax). Although IPSyn overlaps with DSS in many dimensions, it is easier for human coders to compute and it places a bit more emphasis on syntactic, rather than morphological structures. IPSyn has gained much popularity in recent years, being used in at least 70 published studies. Unlike the DSS, correct coding of IPSyn requires attention to not only the parts of speech of lexical items, but also the grammatical relation between words. In order to automate the computation of IPSyn, Sagae, Lavie and MacWhinney (2005) built a program that uses information on the %syn and %mor lines in a CHAT file or a collection of CHAT files. Sagae *et al.* were able to show that the accuracy rate for this automatic IPSyn is very close to the 95% accuracy level achieved by the best human coders and significantly better than the lexically-based method developed used in the Computerized Profiling system (Long and Channell 2001).

5. Generative frameworks

We have discussed the ways in which researchers have used CHILDES corpora to study the acquisition of particular constructions and the ways in which they use corpora to compute measures of morphosyntactic development. There is a third approach to morphosyntactic analysis that is important to the field, but currently unsupported by the CLAN programs. This is the use of the database to construct and validate full generative grammars. Here, the term "generative" refers not just to grammars in the tradition of Chomsky (1957, 1965, 1995), but rather to any computational system that manages to generate all the sentences that would be accepted by the child and none that would be outside the child's range of production. A generative grammar of this type can function as both a generator and a recognizer or parser. As a generator, it would produce sentences of the types found in the CHILDES database. As a recognizer, it would assign grammatical relations to the words in the actual utterances produced by children in the CHILDES database. A generative grammar could be implemented through a variety of formalisms, including rewrite rules (Culicover and Jackendoff 2005), item-based patterns (MacWhinney 2005), constraint hierarchies (Sells 2001), neural networks (Miikkulainen and Mayberry 1999), or parser-generators (Hausser 1999). In each case, the goal would be to use the grammar to generate or parse all of the sentences in the transcripts without producing or recognizing sentences that would not be possible in the child's idiolect.

In the typical case, we would want to construct these grammars on the basis of induction from samples of the data. For grammars based on minimalist theory, the induction could be based on parameter setting, either discrete (Hyams 1986) or driven by statistical analysis (Buttery 2004; Pearl 2005). For grammars based on statistical learning, the induction might involve unsupervised linking of words without tags (Edelman, Solan, Horn and Ruppin 2004; Stolcke and Omohundro 1994). For item-based grammar learning systems (Gobet and Pine 1997; Pine and Lieven 1997), learning involves tracking local binary pair combinations. For all of these systems, it would be "cheating" to rely on the categories and grammatical relations found in the %mor and %syn lines. However, once the induction is completed, it is crucial to use this information as the "gold standard" for evaluation. For example, the most recent CoNNL (Computational Natural Language Learning) Shared Task competition includes a component that focuses on the construction of parsers for the English corpora in the CHILDES database. In this shared task, parsing systems compete both in terms of their ability to learn on labelled (tagged) and unlabelled (untagged) data.

In summary, then, we have seen that a wide range of approaches to morphosyntactic development, measurement, and grammar induction all depend heavily on annotated information regarding part of speech and grammatical relations. Because of the centrality of these codes to the research community, we have devoted years of work to building up systems for automatic coding of morphosyntax. This paper explains the current state of this work and reviews the many detailed coding decisions that are needed to achieve accurate tagging of child language corpora.

6. Analysis based on automatic morphosyntactic coding

So far, our analysis has examined how researchers can use the database through transcript scanning and lexical scanning. However, often these methods are inadequate for addressing broader and more complex issues such as detailed syntactic analysis or the comparisons and evaluations of full generative frameworks. To address these more complex issues, the CHILDES system now provides full support for analysis based on automatic morphosyntactic coding. The core programs used in this work are MOR, POST, and GRASP.

The initial morphological tagging of the CHILDES database relies on the application of the MOR program. Running MOR on a CHAT file is easy. In the simplest case, it involves nothing much more than a one-line command. However, before discussing the mechanics of MOR, let us take a look at what it produces. To give an example of the results of a MOR analysis for English, consider this sentence from eve15.cha in Roger Brown's corpus for Eve.

*CHI: oop I spilled it.
%mor: int|oop pro|I v|spill-PAST pro|it.

Here, the main line gives the child's production and the %mor line gives the part of speech for each word, along with the morphological analysis of affixes, such as the past tense mark (-PAST) on the verb. The %mor lines in these files were not created by hand. To produce them, we ran the MOR program, using the MOR grammar for English, which can be downloaded from http://childes.psy.cmu.edu/morgrams/.

The command for running MOR, which is described in detail in the CLAN manual, is nothing more in this case than "mor *.cha". After running MOR, the file looks like this:

*CHI: oop I spilled it.
%mor: int|oop pro|I part|spill-PERF^v|spill-PAST pro|it.

Notice that the word *spilled* is initially ambiguous between the past tense and participle readings. To resolve such ambiguities, we run a program called POST. Running POST for English is also simple. The command is just "post *.cha" After POST has been run, the sentence is then "disambiguated." Using this disambiguated form, we can then run the GRASP program, which is currently a separate program available from the CHILDES website, to create the representation given in the %xsyn line below:

*CHI: oop I spilled it.
%mor: int|oop pro|I v|spill-PAST pro|it.

%xsyn: 1|3|JCT 2|3|SUBJ 3|0|ROOT 4|3|OBJ 5|3|PUNCT

In this %xsyn line, we see that the second word *I* is related to the verb (*spilled*) through the grammatical relation of Subject. The fourth word *it* is related to the verb through the grammatical relation of Object.

Using GRASP, we have recently inserted dependency grammar tags for all of these grammatical relations in the Eve corpus. In tests run on the Eve corpus, 94% of the tags were assigned accurately (Sagae, Davis, Lavie, MacWhinney and Wintner 2007). A further test of GRASP on the Adam corpus also yielded an accuracy level of 94%. For both of these corpora, grammatical relations were mistagged 6% of the time. It is likely that, over time, this level of accuracy will improve, although we would never expect 100% accuracy for any tagging program. In fact, only a few human taggers can achieve 94% accuracy in their first pass tagging of a corpus.

The work of building MOR, POST, and GRASP has been supported by a number of people. Mitzi Morris built MOR in 1997, using design specifications from Roland Hausser. Since 2000, Leonid Spektor has extended MOR in many ways. Christophe Parisse built POST and POSTTRAIN (Parisse and Le Normand 2000) and continues to maintain and refine them. Kenji Sagae built GRASP as a part of his dissertation work for the Language Technologies Institute at Carnegie Mellon University (Sagae, MacWhinney and Lavie 2004a,b). GRASP was then applied in detail to the Eve and Adam corpus by Eric Davis and Shuly Wintner.

These initial experiments with GRASP and computational modelling of grammatical development in the CHILDES corpora underscore the increasing importance of methods from computational linguistics for the analysis of child language data. Together with statistical computational analyses (Edelman *et al.* 2004) and neural network analyses (Li, Zhao and MacWhinney 2007), we should expect to see increasing input from computational linguistics, as the morphosyntactic tagging of the CHILDES database becomes increasingly refined and accurate.

6.1. MOR and FST

We have now constructed MOR grammars for 10 languages, including Cantonese, Dutch, English, French, German, Hebrew, Japanese, Italian, Putonghua, and Spanish. These grammars can be downloaded from http://childes.psy.cmu.edu/morgrams/ The grammars for Dutch and German are still in the development phase and have not yet been applied systematically to CHILDES corpora. However, the grammars for the other seven languages are all well advanced and have been used to process all or most of the transcripts for the relevant languages. In this section, we will focus on the construction of the MOR grammar for English, taking up the issue of MOR for other languages in the next section.

Before looking closely at MOR, it may be a good idea to situate the status of this program within the larger framework of computational approaches to morphological tagging. This is an area where there has been serious computational and linguistic work for several decades, much of it culminating in the formulation of an approach based on the use of finite state transition (FST) networks based on the two-level morphology of Koskenniemi (1983), but later modified to fit into the general framework of finite state automata. Software called XFST for building and running FSM (finite state morphology) taggers has been made available from Xerox-Parc (http://www.fsmbook.com) and a detailed description of this work was published by Beasley and Karttunen (2003). Although this framework is extremely solid in computational terms, it has several limitations for use in the context of the CHILDES Project.

1. Although XFST has been used to develop taggers for many languages, nearly all of this work is unavailable for general academic use, either because it is based on commercial applications or because it is subject to various licensing restrictions.
2. The FSM framework does not have facilities that allow it to take into consideration the various special codings needed for spoken language transcription in CHAT.
3. XFST systems tend to overgenerate and it is not always easy to see how to constrain this overgeneration.
4. Learning to build taggers in XFST requires good training in programming. Building MOR taggers requires careful attention to linguistic theory, feeding-bleeding relations, and categories, but no special ability in programming.
5. As Wintner (2007) argues, the greater memory capacity and speed of modern computers makes it feasible to approach morphological analysis through generation (the approach taken in MOR), rather than being limited to recognition (the approach taken in XFST).
6. MOR invokes a clearer separation of the lexical resources from the analysis programs than does XFST. This is quite important for maintenance and extension of the analyzer.
7. XFST does not provide as clear debugging information as does MOR.

For these various reasons, we have decided to continue our development of MOR grammars for the languages in CHILDES, rather than shifting to work with the more prominent and better-documented XFST system.

6.2. Understanding MOR

When MOR runs, it breaks up morphemes into their component parts. In a relatively analytic language like English, many words require no analysis at all. However, even in English, a word like *coworkers* can be seen to contain four component morphemes, including the prefix *co*, the stem, the agential suffix, and the plural. For this form, MOR will produce the analysis: co#n:v|work-AGT-PL. This representation uses the symbols # and – to separate the four different morphemes. Here, the prefix stands at the beginning of the analysis, followed by the stem (*n|work*), and the two suffixes. In general, stems always have the form of a part of speech category, such as *n* for noun, followed by the vertical bar and then a statement of the stem's lexical form.

In order to understand the functioning of the MOR grammar for English, the best place to begin is with a tour of the files inside the /English folder that you can download from the server. At the top level, you will see these files:

1. ar.cut – These are the rules that generate allomorphic variants from stems.
2. cr.cut – These are the rules that specify the possible combinations of morphemes going from left to right in an English word.
3. debug.cdc – This file holds the complete trace of an analysis of a given word by MOR. It always holds the results of the most recent analysis. It is mostly useful for people who are developing new ar.cut or cr.cut files as a way of tracing out or debugging problems with these rules.
4. docs – This is a folder containing a file of instructions on how to train POST and a list of tags and categories used in the English grammar.
5. eng.db – This is a file used by POST and should be left untouched.
6. ex.cut – This file includes analyses that are being "overgenerated" by MOR and should simply be filtered out or excluded whenever they occur.
7. lex – This is the heart of the MOR grammar. We will examine it in greater detail below.
8. posttags.cut – This is a list of the grammatical tags of English that should be included whenever running POST.
9. sf.cut – This file tells MOR how to deal with words that end with certain special form markers such as *@b* for babbling.
10. traintags.cut – This is a list of the tags that are used by POSTTRAIN when it creates the eng.db database.

Please note: When examining these files and others, please note that the exact shapes of the files, the word listings, and the rules are sure to change over time. We recommend that users open up these various files to understand their contents. However, over time, the contents will diverge more and more from the names and examples given here. Still, it should be possible to trace through the same basic principles, even given these inevitable changes.

We will study the ar.cut, cr.cut, and sf.cut files in more detail later. For now, let us take a look at the many files contained inside the /lex folder. Here, we find 72 files that break out the possible words of English into different files for each specific part of speech or compound structure. Because these distinctions are so important to the correct transcription of child language and the correct running of MOR, it is worthwhile to consider the contents of each of these various files. As the following table shows, about half of these word types involve different part of speech configurations within compounds. This analysis of compounds into their part of speech components is intended to support the study of the child's learning of compounds, as well as to provide good information regarding the part of speech of the whole. The name of the compound files indicates their composition. For example the name adj+n+adj.cut indicates compounds with a noun followed by an adjective (n+adj) whose overall function is that of an adjective. In English, the part of speech of a compound is usually the same as that of the last component of the compound.

File	Function	Example
0affix.cut	prefixes and suffixes	see expanded list below
0uk.cut	terms local to the UK	fave, doofer, sixpence
adj-dup.cut	baby talk doubles	nice+nice, pink+pink
adj-ir.cut	irregular adjectives	better, furthest
adj-kidy.cut	adjectives with babytalk –y	bunchy, eaty, crawly
adj.cut	regular adjectives	tall, redundant
adj+adj+adj.cut	compounds	half+hearted, hot+crossed
adj+adj+adj(on).cut	compounds	super+duper, easy+peasy
adj+n+adj.cut	compounds	dog+eared, stir+crazy
adj+v+prep+n.cut	compounds	pay+per+view
adj+v+v.cut	compounds	make+believe, see+through
adv-int.cut	intensifying adverbs	really, plumb, quite
adv-loc.cut	locative adverbs	north, upstairs
adv-tem.cut	temporal adverbs	tomorrow, tonight, anytime
adv.cut	regular adverbs	ajar, fast, mostly
adv+adj+adv.cut	compounds	half+off, slant+wise
adv+adj+n.cut	compounds	half+way, off+shore
adv+n+prep+n.cut	compounds	face+to+face
auxil.cut	auxiliaries and modals	should, can, are
co-cant.cut	cantonese bilngual forms	wo, wai, la
co-voc.cut	vocative communicators	honey, dear, sir
co.cut	regular communicators	blah, bybye, gah, no
conj.cut	conjunctions	and, although, because
det.cut	deictic determiners	this, that, the,
fil.cut	fillers	um, uh, er
int-rhymes.cut	rhymes as interjections	fee_figh_foe_fum
int.cut	interjections	farewell, boohoo, hubba
int+int+int.cut	compounds	good+afternoon
int+int+int+int.cut	compounds	ready+set+go
n-abbrev.cut	abbreviations	c_d, t_v, w_c
n-baby.cut	babytalk forms	passie, wawa, booboo
n-dashed.cut	non-compound combinations	cul_de_sac, seven_up
n-dup.cut	duplicate nouns	cow+cow, chick_chick
n-ir.cut	irregular nouns	children, cacti, teeth
n-loan.cut	loan words	goyim, amigo, smuck

File	Function	Example
n-pluraletant.cut	nouns with no singular	golashes, kinesics, scissors
n.cut	regular nouns	dog, corner, window
n+adj+n.cut	compounds	big+shot, cutie+pie
n+adj+v+adj.cut	compounds	merry+go+round
n+n+conj+n.cut	compounds	four+by+four, dot+to+dot
n+n+n-on.cut	compounds	quack+duck, moo+cow
n+n+n.cut	compounds	candy+bar, foot+race
n+n+novel.cut	compounds	children+bed, dog+fish
n+n+prep+det+n.cut	compounds	corn+on+the+cob
n+on+on-baby.cut	compounds	wee+wee, meow+meow
n+v+x+n.cut	compounds	jump+over+hand
n+v+n.cut	compounds	squirm+worm, snap+bead
n+v+ptl.cut	compounds	chin+up, hide+out
num-ord.cut	ordinals	fourth, thirteenth
num.cut	cardinals	five, twenty
on.cut	onomatopoeia	boom, choo_choo
on+on+on.cut	compounds	cluck+cluck, knock+knock
prep.cut	prepositions	under, minus
pro.cut	pronouns	he, nobody, himself
ptl.cut	verbal particle	up, about, on
quan.cut	quantifier	some, all, only, most
small.cut	assorted forms	not, to, xxx, yyy
v-baby.cut	baby verbs	wee, poo
v-clit.cut	cliticized forms	gonna, looka
v-dup.cut	verb duplications	eat+eat, drip+drip
v-ir.cut	irregular verbs	came, beset, slept
v.cut	regular verbs	run, take, remember
v+adj+v.cut	compounds	deep+fry, tippy+toe
v+n+v.cut	compounds	bunny+hop, sleep+walk
v+v+conj+v.cut	compounds	hide+and+seek
wh.cut	interrogatives	which, how, why
zero.cut	omitted words	0know, 0conj, 0is

The construction of these lexicon files involves a variety of decisions. Here are some of the most important issues to consider.

1. Words may often appear in several files. For example, virtually every noun in English can also function as a verb. However, when this function is indicated by a suffix, as in *milking* the noun can be recognized as a verb through a process of morphological derivation contained in a rule in the cr.cut file. In such cases, it is

not necessary to list the word as a verb. Of course, this process fails for unmarked verbs. However, it is generally not a good idea to represent all nouns as verbs, since this tends to overgenerate ambiguity. Instead, it is possible to use the POSTMORTEM program to detect cases where nouns are functioning as bare verbs.

2. If a word can be analyzed morphologically, it should not be given a full listing. For example, since *coworker* can be analyzed by MOR into three morphemes as *co#n:v|work-AGT*, it should not be separately listed in the n.cut file. If it is, then POST will not be able to distinguish *co#n:v|work-AGT* from *n|coworker*.
3. In the zero.cut file, possible omitted words are listed without the preceding 0. For example, there is an entry for *conj* and *the*. However, in the transcript, these would be represented as *0conj* and *0the*.
4. It is always best to use spaces to break up word sequences that are really just combinations of words. For example, instead of transcribing 1964 as *nineteen +sixty+four*, *nineteen-sixty-four*, or *nineteen_sixty_four*, it is best to transcribe simply as *nineteen sixty four*. This principle is particularly important for Chinese, where there is a tendency to underutilize spaces, since Chinese itself is written without spaces.
5. For most languages that use Roman characters, you can rely on capitalization to force MOR to treat words as proper nouns. To understand this, take a look at the forms in the sf.cut file at the top of the MOR directory. These various entries tell MOR how to process forms like *k@l* for the letter *k* or *John_Paul_Jones* for the famous admiral. The symbol \c indicates that a form is capitalized and the symbol \l indicates that it is lowercase.
6. Deciding how to represent compounds is a difficult matter. See the discussion in the next section.

6.3 Compounds and complex forms

The initial formulations of CHAT that were published in MacWhinney (1991, 1995, 2000) specified no guidelines for the annotation of compounds. They only stipulated that compounds should be represented with a plus. When MOR saw a word with a plus, it simply tagged it as a noun compound. This was a big mistake, since many of the compounds tagged in this way were not common nouns. Instead, they included verbs, adjectives, proper nouns, idioms, greetings, onomatopoeia, and many other nonstandard forms. Unfortunately, once this genie had been let out of the bottle, it was very difficult to convince it to go back in. To solve this problem, we had to shift from blanket recognition of compounds to an exhaustive listing of the actual forms of possible compounds. The result of this shift is that we have now created many special compound files such as n+n+n.cut or v+n+v.cut. Fixing the forms in the database to correspond to this new, tighter standard was a huge job, perhaps even more tedious than that involved in removing main line morphemicization from the corpus. However, now that we have a full analysis of compounds, there is a much more accurate analysis of children's learning of these forms.

In the current system, compounds are listed in the lexical files according to both their overall part of speech (X-bar) and the parts of speech of their components. However, there are seven types of complex word combinations that should not be treated as compounds.

1. **Underscored words**. The n-dashed.cut file includes 40 forms that resemble compounds, but are best viewed as units with non-morphemic components. For example, *kool_aid* and *band_aid* are not really combinations of morphemes, although they clearly have two components. The same is true for *hi_fi* and *coca_cola*. In general, MOR and CLAN pay little attention to the underscore character, so it can be used as needed when a plus for compounding is not appropriate. The underscore mark is particularly useful for representing the combinations of words found in proper nouns such as *John_Paul_Jones*, *Columbia_University*, or *The_Beauty_and_the_Beast*. As long as these words are capitalized, they do not need to be included in the MOR lexicon, since all capitalized words are taken as proper nouns in English. However, these forms cannot contain pluses, since compounds are not proper nouns. And please be careful not to overuse this form.
2. **Separate words**. Many noun-noun combinations in English should just be written out as separate words. An example would be "faucet stem assembly rubber gasket holder". We don't want to write this as *Faucet_stem_assembly_rubber_gasket_holder* or *faucet_stem_assembly_rubber_gasket_holder* or even *faucet+stem+assembly+rubber+gasket+holder*. It is worth noting here that German treats all such forms as single words. This means that different conventions have to be adopted for German in order to avoid the need for exhaustive listing of the infinite number of German compound nouns.
3. **Spelling sequences**. Sequences of letter names such as *O-U-T* for the spelling of *out* are transcribed with the suffix @k, as in *out@k*.
4. **Acronyms**. Forms such as FBI are transcribed with underscores, as in *F_B_I*. Presence of the initial capital letter tells MOR to treat *F_B_I* as a proper noun. This same format is used for non-proper abbreviations such as *c_d* or *d_v_d*.
5. **Products**. Coming up with good forms for commercial products such as *Coca-Cola* is tricky. Because of the need to ban the use of the dash on the main line, we have avoided the use of the dash in these names. It is clear that they should not be compounds, as in *coca+cola*, and compounds cannot be capitalized, so *Coca+Cola* is not possible. This leaves us with the option of either *coca_cola* or *Coca_Cola*. The option *coca_cola* seems best, since this is not really a proper noun.
6. **Interjections**. The choice between underscoring, compounding, and writing as single words is particularly tricky for interjections and set phrases. A careful study of files such as co-voc.cut, co.cut, n-dashed.cut, n-abbrev.cut, int-rhymes.cut, int.cut, inti+int+int.cut, and int+int+int.cut will show how difficult it is to apply these distinctions consistently. We continue to sharpen these distinctions, so the best

way to trace these categories is to scan through the relevant files to see the principles that are being used to separate forms into these various types.
7. **Babbling and word play**. In earlier versions of CHAT and MOR, transcribers often represent sequences of babbling or word play syllables as compounds. This was done mostly because the plus provides a nice way of separating out the separate syllables in these productions. In order to make it clear that these separations are simply marked for purposes of syllabification, we now ask transcribers to use forms such as *ba^ba^ga^ga@wp* or *choo^bung^choo^bung@o* to represent these patterns.

The introduction of this more precise system for transcription of complex forms opens up additional options for programs like MLU, KWAL, FREQ, and GRASP. For MLU, compounds will be counted as single words, unless the plus sign is added to the morpheme delimiter set using the +b+ option switch. For GRASP, processing of compounds only needs to look at the part of speech of the compound as a whole, since the internal composition of the compound is not relevant to the syntax. Additionally, forms such as *faucet handle valve washer assembly* do not need to be treated as compounds, since GRASP can learn to treat sequences of nouns as complex phrases header by the final noun.

6.4 Lemmatization

Researchers are often interested in computing frequency profiles that are computed using lemmas or root forms, rather inflected forms. For example, they may want to treat *dropped* as an instance of the use of the lemma *drop*. In order to perform these types of computations, the KWAL and FREQ programs provide a series of options that allow users to refer to various parts of complex structures in the %mor line. This system recognizes the following structures on the %mor line:

Element	**Symbol**	**Example**	**Representation**	**Part**
prefix	#	unwinding	un#v|wind-PROG	un#
stem	r	unwinding	un#v|wind-PROG	wind
suffix	–	unwinding	un#v|wind-PROG	PROG
fusion	&	unwound	un#v|wind&PAST	PAST
translation	=	gato	n|gato=cat	cat
other	o	–	–	–

To illustrate the use of these symbols, let us look at several possible commands. All of these commands take the form: freq +t%mor -t* filename.cha. However, in addition, they add the +s switches that are given in the second column. In these commands, the asterisk is used to distinguish across forms in the frequency count and the % sign is used to combine across forms.

Function	String
All stems with their parts of speech, merge the rest	+s@"r+*,|+*,o+%"
Only verbs	+s@"|+v"
All forms of the stem *go*	+s@"r+go"
The different parts of speech of the stem *go*	+s@"r+go,|+*,o+%"
The stem *go* only when it is a verb	+s@"r+go,|+v,o+%"
All stems, merge the rest	+s@"r+*,o+%"

Of these various forms, the last one given above would be the one required for conducting a frequency count based on lemmas or stems alone. Essentially CLAN breaks every element on %mor tier into its individual components and then matches either literal strings or wild cards provided by the user to each component.

6.5 Errors and replacements

Transcriptions on the main line have to serve two, sometimes conflicting, functions (Edwards 1992). On the one hand, they need to represent the form of the speech as actually produced. On the other hand, they need to provide input that can be used for morphosyntactic analysis. When words are pronounced in their standard form, these two functions are in alignment. However, when words are pronounced with phonological or morphological errors, it is important to separate out the actual production from the morphological target. This can be done through a system of main line tagging of errors. This system largely replaces the coding of errors on a separate %err line, although that form is still available, if needed. The form of the newer system is illustrated here:

CHI: him [case] ated [: ate] [* +ed-sup] a f(l)ower and a pun [: bun].

For the first error, there is no need to provide a replacement, since MOR can process *him* as a pronoun. However, since the second error is not a real word form, the replacement is necessary in order to tell MOR how to process the form. The third error is just an omission of *l* from the cluster and the final error is a mispronunciation of the initial consonant. Phonological errors are not coded here, since that level of analysis is best conducted inside the Phon program (Rose, MacWhinney, Byrne, Hedlund, Maddocks and O'Brien 2005).

7. Using MOR with a new corpus

Because the English MOR grammar is stable and robust, the work of analyzing a new corpus seldom involves changes to the rules in the ar.cut or cr.cut files. However, a new

English corpus is still likely to need extensive lexical clean up before it is fully recognized by MOR. The unrecognized words can be identified quickly by running this command:

mor +xl *.cha

This command will go through a collection of files and output a single file "mini lexicon" of unrecognized words. The output is given the name of the first file in the collection. After this command finishes, open up the file and you will see all the words not recognized by MOR. There are several typical reasons for a word not being recognized:

1. The word is misspelled.
2. The word should be preceded by an ampersand (&) to block look up through MOR. Specifically, incomplete words should be transcribed as &text so that the ampersand character can block MOR look up. Similarly, sounds like laughing can be transcribed as *&=laughs* to achieve the same effect.
3. The word should have been transcribed with a special form marker, as in bobo@o or *bo^bo@o* for onomatopoeia. It is impossible to list all possible onomatopoeic forms in the MOR lexicon, so the *@o* marker solves this problem by telling MOR how to treat the form. This approach will be needed for other special forms, such as babbling, word play, and so on.
4. The word was transcribed in "eye-dialect" to represent phonological reductions. When this is done, there are two basic ways to allow MOR to achieve correct lookup. If the word can be transcribed with parentheses for the missing material, as in *(be)cause*, then MOR will be happy. This method is particularly useful in Spanish and German. Alternatively, if there is a sound substitution, then you can transcribe using the [: text] replacement method, as in *pittie [: kittie]*.
5. You should treat the word as a proper noun by capitalizing the first letter. This method works for many languages, but not in German where all nouns are capitalized and not in Asian languages, since those languages do not have systems for capitalization.
6. The word should be treated as a compound, as discussed in the previous section.
7. The stem is in MOR, but the inflected form is not recognized. In this case, it is possible that one of the analytic rules of MOR is not working. These problems can be reported to me at macw@cmu.edu.
8. The stem or word is missing from MOR. In that case, you can create a file called something like 0add.cut in the /lex folder of the MOR grammar. Once you have accumulated a collection of such words, you can email them to me for permanent addition to the lexicon.

Some of these forms can be corrected during the initial process of transcription by running CHECK. However, others will not be evident until you run the mor +xl command and get a list of unrecognized words. In order to correct these forms, there are basically two possible tools. The first is the KWAL program built in to CLAN. Let us say that your filename.ulx.cex list of unrecognized words has the form *cuaght* as a misspelling of *caught*. Let us further imagine that you have a single collection of 80 files in one folder. To correct this error, just type this command into the Commands window:

kwal *.cha +scuaght

KWAL will then send input to your screen as it goes through the 80 files. There may be no more than one case of this misspelling in the whole collection. You will see this as the output scrolls by. If necessary, just scroll back in the CLAN Output window to find the error and then triple click to go to the spot of the error and then retype the word correctly.

For errors that are not too frequent, this method works fairly well. However, if you have made some error consistently and frequently, you may need stronger methods. Perhaps you transcribed *byebye* as *bye+bye* as many as 60 times. In this case, you could use the CHSTRING program to fix this, but a better method would involve the use of a powerful Programmer's Editor system such as BBEdit for the Mac or Epsilon for Windows. Any system you use must include an ability to process Regular Expressions (RegExp) and to operate smoothly across whole directories at a time. However, let me give a word of warning about the use of more powerful editors. When using these systems, particularly at first, you may make some mistakes. Always make sure that you keep a backup copy of your entire folder before each major replacement command that you issue.

Once you have succeeded in reducing the context of the minilex to zero, you are ready to run a final pass of MOR. After that, if there is a .db file in the MOR grammar for your language, you can run POST to disambiguate your file. After disambiguation, you should run CHECK again. There may be some errors if POST was not able to disambiguate everything. In that case, you would either need to fix MOR or else just use CLAN's disambiguate tier function (escape-2) to finish the final stages of disambiguation.

8. Affixes and control features

At this point, it is probably a good idea to warn beginning users of CLAN and MOR that the remaining sections in this paper deal with a variety of increasingly difficult technical aspects of programs, coding, and analysis. As a result, beginning users will probably want to just scan these remaining sections and return to them when they have become more thoroughly acquainted with the use of CLAN.

To complete our tour of the MOR lexicon for English, we will take a brief look at the 0affix.cut file, as well some additional control features in the other lexical files. The responsibility of processing inflectional and derivational morphology is divided across these three files. Let us first look at a few entries in the 0affix.cut file.

1. This file begins with a list of prefixes such as *mis* and *semi* that attach either to nouns or verbs. Each prefix also has a permission feature, such as [allow mis]. This feature only comes into play when a noun or verb in n.cut or v.cut also has the fea-

ture [pre no]. For example, the verb *test* has the feature [pre no] included in order to block prefixing with *de-* to produce *detest* which is not a derivational form of *test*. At the same time, we want to permit prefixing with *re-*, the entry for *test* has [pre no][allow re]. Then, when the relevant rule in cr.cut sees a verb following *re-* it checks for a match in the [allow] feature and allows the attachment in this case.

2. Next we see some derivational suffixes such as diminutive *–ie* or agential *–er*. Unlike the prefixes, these suffixes often change the spelling of the stem by dropping silent *e* or doubling final consonants. The ar.cut file controls this process, and the [allo x] features listed there control the selection of the correct form of the suffix.
3. Each suffix is represented by a grammatical category in parentheses. These categories are taken from a typologically valid list given in the CHAT Manual.
4. Each suffix specifies the grammatical category of the form that will result after its attachment. For suffixes that change the part of speech, this is given in the scat, as in [scat adj:n]. Prefixes do not change parts of speech, so they are simply listed as [scat pfx] and use the [pcat x] feature to specify the shape of the forms to which they can attach.
5. The long list of suffixes concludes with a list of cliticized auxiliaries and reduced main verbs. These forms are represented in English as contractions. Many of these forms are multiply ambiguous and it will be the job of POST to choose the correct reading from among the various alternatives.

Outside of the 0affix.cut file, in the various other *.cut lexical files, there are several control features that specify how stems should be treated. One important set includes the [comp x+x] features for compounds. These features control how compounds will be unpacked for formatting on the %mor line. Irregular adjectives in adj-ir.cut have features specifying their degree as comparative or superlative. Irregular nouns have features controlling the use of the plural. Irregular verbs have features controlling consonant doubling [gg +] and the formation of the perfect tense.

9. MOR for bilingual corpora

It is now possible to use MOR and POST to process bilingual corpora. The first application of this method has been to the transcripts collected by Virginia Yip and Stephen Matthews from Cantonese-English bilingual children in Hong Kong. In these corpora, parents, caretakers, and children often switch back and forth between the two languages. In order to tell MOR which grammar to use for which utterances, each sentence must be clearly identified for language. It turns out that this is not too difficult to do. First, by the nature of the goals of the study and the people conversing with the child, certain files are typically biased toward one language or the other. In the YipMatthews corpus, English is the default language in folders such as SophieEng or TimEng and Cantonese is the default in folders such as SophieCan and TimCan. Within the

English files, the postcode [+ can] is placed at the end of utterances that are primarily in Cantonese. If single Cantonese words are used inside English utterances, they are marked with the special form marker *@s:c*. For the files that are primarily in Cantonese, the opposite pattern is used. In those files, English sentences are marked as [+ eng] and English words inside Cantonese are marked by *@s:e*.

To minimize cross-language listing, it was also helpful to create easy ways of representing words that were shared between languages. This was particularly important for the names of family members or relation names. For example, the Cantonese form 姐姐 for *big sister* can be written in English as *Zeze*, so that this form can be processed correctly as a proper noun address term. Similarly, Cantonese has borrowed a set of English salutations such as *byebye* and *sorry* which are simply added directly to the Cantonese grammar in the co-eng.cut file.

Once these various adaptations and markings are completed, it is then possible to run MOR in two passes on the corpus. For the English corpora, the steps are:

1. Set the MOR library to English and run: mor -s"<+ can>" *.cha +1
2. Disambiguate the results with: post *.cha +1
3. Run CHECK to check for problems.
4. Set the MOR library to Cantonese and run: mor +s"<+ can>" *.cha +1
5. Disambiguate the results with: post +dcant.db *.cha +1
6. Run CHECK to check for problems.

To illustrate the result of this process, here is a representative snippet from the te951130.cha file in the /TimEng folder. Note that the default language here is English and that sentences in Cantonese are explicitly marked as [+ can].

*LIN:	where is grandma first, tell me?
%mor:	adv:wh|where v|be n|grandma adv|first v|tell pro|me?
*LIN:	well, what's this?
%mor:	co|well pro:wh|what~v|be pro:dem|this?
*CHI:	xxx 呢 個 唔 夠 架. [+ can]
%mor:	unk|xxx det|ni1=this cl|go3=cl neg|m4=not adv|gau3=enough sfp|gaa3=sfp. [+ can]
*LIN:	呢 個 唔 夠. [+ can]
%mor:	det|ni1=this cl|go3=cl neg|m4=not adv|gau3=enough. [+ can]
*LIN:	<what does it mean> [>]?
%mor:	pro:wh|what v:aux|do pro|it v|mean?

Currently, this type of analysis is possible whenever MOR grammars exist for both languages, as would be the case for Japanese-English, Spanish-French, Putonghua-Cantonese, or Italian-Chinese bilinguals.

10. Training POST

The English POST disambiguator currently achieves over 95% correct disambiguation. We have not yet computed the levels of accuracy for the other disambiguators. However, the levels may be a bit better for inflectional languages like Spanish or Italian. In order to train the POST disambiguator, we first had to create a hand-annotated training set for each language. We created this corpus through a process of bootstrapping. Here is the sequence of basic steps in training.

1. First run MOR on a small corpus and used the escape-2 hand disambiguation process to disambiguate.
2. Then rename the %mor line in the corpus to %trn.
3. Run MOR again to create a separate %mor line.
4. Run POSTTRAIN with this command: posttrain +ttraintags.cut +c +o0errors.cut +x *.cha
5. This will create a new eng.db database.
6. You then need to go through the 0errors.cut file line by line to eliminate each mismatch between your %trn line and the codes of the %mor line. Mismatches arise primarily from changes made to the MOR codes in between runs of MOR.
7. Disambiguate the MOR line with: post +deng.db +tposttags.cut *.cha +1
8. Compare the results of POST with your hand disambiguation using: trnfix *.cha

In order to perform careful comparison using trnfix, you can set your *.trn.cex files into CA font and run longtier *.cha +1. This will show clearly the differences between the %trn and %mor lines. Sometimes the %trn will be at fault and sometimes %mor will be at fault. You can only fix the %trn line. To fix the %mor results, you just have to keep on compiling more training data by iterating the above process. As a rule of thumb, you eventually want to have at least 5000 utterances in your training corpus. However, a corpus with 1000 utterances will be useful initially.

11. Difficult decisions

During work in constructing the training corpus for POSTTRAIN, you will eventually bump into some areas of English grammar where the distinction between parts of speech is difficult to make without careful specification of detailed criteria. We can identify three areas that are particularly problematic in terms of their subsequent effects on GR (grammatical relation) identification:

1. **Adverb vs. preposition vs. particle**. The words *about, across, after, away, back, down, in, off, on, out, over,* and *up* belong to three categories: ADVerb, PREPosition and ParTicLe. To annotate them correctly, we apply the following criteria. First, a preposition must have a prepositional object. Second, a preposition forms a constituent with its noun phrase object, and hence is more closely bound to its

object than an adverb or a particle. Third, prepositional phrases can be fronted, whereas the noun phrases that happen to follow adverbs or particles cannot. Fourth, a manner adverb can be placed between the verb and a preposition, but not between a verb and a particle. To distinguish between an adverb and a particle, the meaning of the head verb is considered. If the meaning of the verb and the target word, taken together, cannot be predicted from the meanings of the verb and the target word separately, then the target word is a particle. In all other cases it is an adverb.

2. **Verb vs. auxiliary**. Distinguishing between Verb and AUXiliary is especially tricky for the verbs *be, do* and *have*. The following tests can be applied. First, if the target word is accompanied by a nonfinite verb in the same clause, it is an auxiliary, as in *I have had enough* or *I do not like eggs*. Another test that works for these examples is fronting. In interrogative sentences, the auxiliary is moved to the beginning of the clause, as in *Have I had enough?* and *Do I like eggs?* whereas main verbs do not move. In verb-participle constructions headed by the verb *be*, if the participle is in the progressive tense (*John is smiling*), then the head verb is labeled as an AUXiliary, otherwise it is a Verb (*John is happy*).
3. **Communicator vs. Interjection vs. Locative adverbs**. COmmunicators can be hard to distinguish from interjections, and locative adverbs, especially at the beginning of a sentence. Consider a sentence such as *There you are* where *there* could be interpreted as either specifying a location or as providing an attentional focus, much like French voilà. The convention we have adopted is that CO must modify an entire sentence, so if a word appears by itself, it cannot be a CO. For example, utterances that begin with *here* or *there* without a following break are labelled as ADVerb. However, if these words appear at the beginning of a sentence and are followed by a break or pause, then they are labelled CO. Additionally, for lack of a better label, in *here/there you are/go*, here or there are labelled CO. Interjections, such as *oh+my+goodness* are often transcribed at the beginning of sentences as if they behaved like communicators. However, they might better be considered as sentence fragments in their own right.

12. Building MOR grammars

So far, this discussion of the MOR grammar for English has avoided an examination of the ar.cut and cr.cut files. It is true that users of English MOR will seldom need to tinker with these files. However, serious students of morphosyntax need to understand how MOR and POST operate. In order to do this, they have to understand how the ar.cut and cr.cut files work. Fortunately, for English at least, these rule files are not too complex. The relative simplicity of English morphology is reflected in the fact that the ar.cut file for English has only 391 lines, whereas the same file for Spanish has 3172 lines. In English, the main patterns involve consonant doubling, silent *–e*, changes of *y* to *i*, and irregulars like *knives* or *leaves*. The rules use the spelling of final consonants and vowels to predict these various allomorphic variations. Variables such as *$V* or *$C* are set up at the beginning of the file to refer to vowels and consonants and then the rules use these variables to describe alternative lexical patterns and the shapes of allomorphs. For example the rule for consonant doubling takes this shape:

```
LEX-ENTRY:
LEXSURF = $O$V$C
LEXCAT = [scat v],![tense OR past perf],![gem no] % to block putting
ALLO:
ALLOSURF = $O$V$C$C
ALLOCAT = LEXCAT, ADD [allo vHb]
ALLO:
ALLOSURF = LEXSURF
ALLOCAT = LEXCAT, ADD [allo vHa]
```

Here, the string OV$C characterizes verbs like *bat* that end with vowels followed by consonants. The first allo will produce words like *batting* or *batter* and the second will give a stem for *bats* or *bat*. A complete list of allomorphy types for English is given in the file engcats.cdc in the /docs folder in the MOR grammar.

When a user types the "mor" command to CLAN, the program loads up all the *.cut files in the lexicon and then passes each lexical form past the rules of the ar.cut file. The rules in the ar.cut file are strictly ordered. If a form matches a rule, that rule fires and the allomorphs it produces are encoded into a lexical tree based on a "trie" structure. Then MOR moves on to the next lexical form, without considering any additional rules. This means that it is important to place more specific cases before more general cases in a standard bleeding relation. There is no "feeding" relation in the ar.cut file, since each form is shipped over to the tree structure after matching.

The other "core" file in a MOR grammar is the cr.cut file that contains the rules that specify pathways through possible words. The basic idea of crules or concatenation or continuation rules is taken from Hausser's (1999) left-associative grammar which specifies the shape of possible "continuations" as a parser moves from left to right through a word. Unlike the rules of the ar.cut file, the rules in the cr.cut file are not ordered. Instead, they work through a "feeding" relation. MOR goes through a candidate word from left to right to match up the current sequence with forms in the lexical trie structure. When a match is made, the categories of the current form become a part of the STARTCAT. If the STARTCAT matches up with the STARTCAT of one of the rules in cr.cut, as well as satisfying some additional matching conditions specified in the rule, then that rule fires. The result of this firing is to change the shape of the STARTCAT and to then thread processing into some additional rules. For example, let us consider the processing of the verb *reconsidering*. Here, the first rule to fire is the specific-vpfx-start rule which matches the fact that *re-* has the feature [scat pfx] and [pcat v]. This initial recognition of the prefix then threads into the specific-vpfx-verb rule that requires the next item have the feature [scat v]. This rule has the feature CTYPE # which serves to introduce the # sign into the final tagging to produce *re#part|consider-PROG*. After the verb *consider* is accepted, the RULEPACKAGE tells MOR to move on to three other rules: v-conj, n:v-deriv, and adj:v-deriv. Each of these rules can be viewed as a separate thread out of the specific-vpfx-verb rule. At this point in processing the word, the remaining orthographic material is *-ing*. Looking at the 0affix.cut file, we see that *ing* has three entries: [scat part], [scat v:n], and [scat n:gerund]. One of the pathways at this point leads through the v-conj rule. Within v-conj, only the fourth clause fires, since that clause matches [scat part]. This clause can lead on to three further threads, but, since there is no further orthographic material, there is no NEXTCAT for these rules. Therefore, this thread then goes on to the end rules and outputs the first successful parse of *reconsidering*. The second thread from the specific-vpfx-verb rule leads to the n:v-deriv rule. This rule accepts the reading of *ing* as [scat n:gerund] to produce the second reading of *reconsidering*. Finally, MOR traces the third thread from the specific-vpfx-verb rule which leads to adj:v-deriv. This route produces no matches, so processing terminates with this result:

Result: re#part|consider-PROG^re#n:gerund|consider-GERUND

Later, POST will work to choose between these two possible readings of *reconsidering* on the basis of the syntactic context. As we noted earlier, when *reconsidering* follows an auxiliary (*is eating*) or when it functions adjectivally (*an eating binge*), it is treated as a participle. However, when it appears as the head of an NP (*eating is good for you*), it is treated as a gerund. Categories and processes of this type can be modified to match up with the requirements of the GRASP program to be discussed below.

The process of building ar.cut and cr.cut files for a new language involves a slow iteration of lexicon building with rule building. During this process, and throughout work with development of MOR, it is often helpful to use MOR in its interactive mode by typing: mor +xi. When using MOR in this mode, there are several additional options that become available in the CLAN Output window. They are:

word – analyze this word
:q quit- exit program
:c print out current set of crules
:d display application of a rules.
:l re-load rules and lexicon files
:h help – print this message

If you type in a word, such as *dog* or *perro*. MOR will try to analyze it and give you its component morphemes. If all is well, you can move on the next word. If it is not, you need to change your rules or the lexicon. You can stay within CLAN and just open these using the Editor. After you save your changes, use :l to reload and retest the word again.

The problem with building up a MOR grammar one word at a time like this is that changes that favour the analysis of one word can break the analysis of other words. To make sure that this is not happening, it is important to have a collection of test words that you continually monitor using mor *+xl*. One approach to this is just to have a growing set of transcripts or utterances that can be analyzed. Another approach is to have a systematic target set configured not as sentences but as transcripts with one word in each sentence. An example of this approach can be found in the /verbi folder in the Italian MOR grammar. This folder has one file for each of the 106 verbal paradigms of the Berlitz Italian Verb Handbook (2005). That handbook gives the full paradigm of one "leading" verb for each conjugational type. We then typed all of the relevant forms into CHAT files. Then, as we built up the ar.cut file for Italian, we designed allo types using features that matched the numbers in the Handbook. In the end, things become a bit more complex in Spanish, Italian, and French.

1. The initial rules of the ar.cut file for these languages specify the most limited and lexically-bound patterns by listing almost the full stem, as in $Xdice for verbs like *dicere*, *predicere* or *benedicere* which all behave similarly, or *nuoce* which is the only verb of its type.
2. Further in the rule list, verbs are listed through a general phonology, but often limited to the presence of a lexical tag such as [type 16] that indicates verb membership in a conjugational class.
3. Within the rule for each verb type, the grammar specifies up to 12 stem allomorph types. Some of these have the same surface phonology. However, to match up properly across the paradigm, it is important to generate this full set. Once this basic grid is determined, it is easy to add new rules for each additional conjugational type by a process of cut-and-paste followed by local modifications.
4. Where possible, the rules are left in an order that corresponds to the order of the conjugational numbers of the Berlitz Handbook. However, when this order interferes with rule bleeding, it is changed.
5. Perhaps the biggest conceptual challenge is the formulation of a good set of [allo x] tags for the paradigm. The current Italian grammar mixes together tags like [allo vv] that are defined on phonological grounds and tags like [allo vpart] that are defined on paradigmatic grounds. A more systematic analysis would probably use a somewhat larger set of tags to cover all tense-aspect-mood slots and use the phonological tags as a secondary overlay on the basic semantic tags.
6. Although verbs are the major challenge in Romance languages, it is also important to manage verbal clitics and noun and adjectives plurals. In the end, all nouns must be listed with gender information. Nouns that have both masculine and feminine forms are listed with the feature [anim yes] that allows the ar.cut file to generate both sets of allomorphs.
7. Spanish has additional complexities involving the placement of stress marks for infinitives and imperatives with suffixed clitics, such as dámelo. Italian has additional complications for forms such as *nello* and the various pronominal and clitic forms.

To begin the process, start working with the sample "minMOR" grammars available from the net. These files should allow you to build up a lexicon of uninflected stems.

Try to build up separate files for each of the parts of speech in your language. As you start to feel comfortable with this, you should begin to add affixes. To do this, you need to create a lexicon file for affixes, such as affix.cut. Using the technique found in unification grammars, you want to set up categories and allos for these affixes that will allow them to match up with the right stems when the crules fire. For example, you might want to assign [scat nsfx] to the noun plural suffix in order to emphasize the fact that it should attach to nouns. And you could give the designation [allo mdim] to the masculine diminutive suffix -ito in Spanish in order to make sure that it only attaches to masculine stems and produces a masculine output.

As you progress with your work, continually check each new rule change by entering :l (colon followed by *l* for load) into the CLAN Output window and then testing some crucial words. If you have changed something in a way that produces a syntactic violation, you will learn this immediately and be able to change it back. If you find that a method fails, you should first rethink your logic. Consider these factors:

1. Arules are strictly ordered. Maybe you have placed a general case before a specific case.
2. Crules depend on direction from the RULEPACKAGES statement. Perhaps you are not reaching the rule that needs to fire.
3. There has to be a START and END rule for each part of speech. If you are getting too many entries for a word, maybe you have started it twice. Alternatively, you may have created too many allomorphs with the arules.
4. Possibly, your form is not satisfying the requirements of the end rules. If it doesn't these rules will not "let it out."
5. If you have a MATCHCAT allos statement, all allos must match. The operation DEL [allo] deletes all allos and you must add back any you want to keep.
6. Make sure that you understand the use of variable notation and pattern matching symbols for specifying the surface form in the arules.

However, sometimes it is not clear why a method is not working. In this case, you will want to check the application of the crules using the :c option in the CLAN Output window. You then need to trace through the firing of the rules. The most important information is often at the end of this output.

If the stem itself is not being recognized, you will need to also trace the operation of the arules. To do this, you should either use the +e option in standard MOR or else the :d option in interactive MOR. The latter is probably the most useful. To use this option, you should create a directory called testlex with a single file with the words you are working with. Then run: mor +xi +ltestlex

Once this runs, type :d and then :l and the output of the arules for this test lexicon will go to debug.cdc. Use your editor to open that file and try to trace what is happening there.

As you progress with the construction of rules and the enlargement of the lexicon, you can tackle whole corpora. At this point you will occasionally run the +xl analysis. Then you take the problems noted by +xl and use them as the basis for repeated testing using the +xi switch and repeated reloading of the rules as you improve them. As you build up your rule sets, you will want to annotate them fully using comments preceded by the % symbol.

13. Chinese MOR

In comparison to the morphologies of languages like Italian or Japanese, the development of MOR grammars for Putonghua or Cantonese is much simpler. This is because these languages have essentially no affixes. The few exceptions to this are the four forms listed in the 0affix.cut file for Putonghua. There are no suffixes for Cantonese at all. In addition, both Cantonese and Putonghua have a single rule that produces diminutive reduplications for nouns and verbs. For adjectives, the pattern is more complex and is listed for each possible lexical form.

Although Putonghua and Cantonese have few suffixes, they have very productive systems of compounding. However, because Chinese characters are written with spaces to separate words, there is no systematic tradition for lemmatization of Chinese compounds. One current trend tends to include adjectives with nouns as compounds, forming single words from combinations such as *good boy* or *train station*. Of course, Chinese has many true compounds, such as 图书馆 "tu2shu1guan3" for *library* or 椭圆形"tuo3yuan2xing2" for *oval*. Within the verbs, there is a tendency to treat combination of serial verbs such as 上去 "shang4qu4" *up go* as units, perhaps under the influence of translations from English. However, the meanings in such cases are fully combinatorial. Figuring out how to list true compounds without adding superfluous compounds remains a major task for work on Chinese. The basic criteria here should be the same as in other languages. Word sequences should not be listed as single words if the meaning is fully predicted from the combination of the separate pieces and if there are no processes of allomorphy triggered by the combination.

The other major challenge in Chinese is the specification of part of speech tags. Currently available lexicons use a wide variety of tags deriving from different grammatical analyses. Often adjectives are treated as verbs. It is likely that this is done because Chinese deletes the copula. Without a copula to serve as the predicate, the adjective is then promoted to the status of a full verb. However, a clearer treatment of the relevant syntax would treat sentences with missing copulas as representing topic + comment structures. In that analysis, adjectives would simply function as adjectives. Similar issues arise with the listing of adjectives as adverbs. Here again, part of speech categorization is being driven by the selection of a particular syntactic analysis. Despite these various problems with part of speech categorization, we have managed to construct Chinese lexicons and training corpora that can be successfully used to achieve automatic disambiguation with POST at a high level of accuracy.

14. GRASP

After finishing tagging with MOR and POST, researchers will want to run the GRASP program (also called MEGRASP in the version on the web) to create a %xsyn line with tagged grammatical relations. GRASP produces labelled dependency structures for CHILDES transcript data. The system uses the 29 relations summarized in this table:

GR	Definition	Example
SUBJ	nonclausal subj	Mary saw a movie.
CSUBJ	finite clausal subject	That Mary screamed scared John.
XSUBJ	nonfinite clausal subject	Eating vegetables is important.
OBJ	direct object	Mary saw a movie.
OBJ2	indirect object	Mary gave John a book.
IOBJ	required prepositional phrase	Mary gave a book to John.
COMP	finite clausal verb complement	I think that Mary saw a movie.
XCOMP	nonfinite clausal verb complement	Mary likes watching movies.
PRED	predicate nominal or adjective	Mary is a student.
CPRED	predicate finite clausal complement	The problem is that Mary sings.
XPRED	predicate nonfinite clausal comp.	My goal is to win the race.
JCT	PP or adv as adjunct Head is v, adj, or adv	Mary spoke clearly. Mary spoke at the meeting Mary spoke very clearly.
CJCT	finite clause as adjunct	Mary left after she heard the news.
XJCT	nonfinite clause as adjunct	Mary left after hearing the news.
MOD	nonclausal modifier	Mary saw a red car.
CMOD	finite clausal modifier	The car that bumped me was red.
XMOD	nonfinite clausal modifier	The car driving by is red.
AUX	auxiliary of a verb or modal	Mary has seen many movies.
NEG	verbal negation	I am not eating cake.
DET	determiner of a noun (art, poss pro)	The students ate that cake.
POBJ	object of a preposition	Mary saw the book on her desk.
PTL	verb particle	Mary put off the meeting.
CPZR	complementizer	I think that Mary left.
COM	communicator	Okay, you can go.
INF	infinitival	Mary wants to go.
VOC	vocative	Mary, you look lovely.
TAG	tag questions	That is good, isn't it?
COORD	coordination, conj is the head	Mary likes cats and dogs.
ROOT	relation between verb and left wall	Mary saw Jim last week.

When these GRs are applied to a string of words in files, they yield a labeled dependency structure. Here is an example from the Eve corpus.

*COL: do we have everything?
%mor: v:aux|do pro|we v|have pro:indef|everything?
%xsyn: 1|3|AUX 2|3|SUBJ 3|0|ROOT 4|3|OBJ 5|3|PUNCT

The relations given on the %xsyn line can be reformatted into a graph structure in which all of the elements depend on the verb (item #3) and the verb itself is attached to the root (item #0). Or to take a slightly more complex example:

*MOT: well it's already out # isn't it?
%mor: co|well pro|it~v|be&3S adv|already adv|out v|be&3S~neg|not pro|it?
%xsyn: 1|3|COM 2|3|SUBJ 3|0|ROOT 4|5|JCT 5|3|PRED 6|3|TAG 7|6|NEG 8|6|SUBJ 9|3|PUNCT

Here, the word *out* is treated as a predicate modifying the verb and *already* is a daughter of *out*. This seems correct semantically. The final words are processed as a tag question.

Currently, GRASP processing is limited to English. However, it can be extended to other languages, and we would be happy to work with colleagues on such extensions. Ongoing progress in the development of the GRASP system has been described in three recent papers (Sagae *et al.* 2004a, 2005, 2007). The following discussion of the current state of GRASP is taken from Sagae *et al.* (2007).

Our most recent work began with the completion of hand-annotations for 15 of the 20 files in the Eve section of Roger Brown's corpus. These files included 18,863 fully hand-annotated utterances with 10,280 from adults and 8,563 from Eve. The utterances contained 84,226 grammatical relations and 65,363 words. The parser is highly efficient. Training on the Eve corpus takes 20 minutes and, once trained, the corpus can be parsed in 20 seconds. The parser produces correct dependency relations for 96% of the relations in the gold standard. In addition, the dependency relations are labelled with the correct GR 94% of the time. Performance was slightly better on the adult utterances with 95% correct labelling for adult GRs and 93% correct labelling for child GRs.

The parser relies on a best-first probabilistic shift-reduce algorithm, working left-to-right to find labelled dependencies one at a time. The two main data structures in the algorithm are a stack and a queue. The stack holds subtrees, and the queue holds the words in an input sentence that have not yet been assigned to subtrees. At the beginning of processing, the stack is empty and the queue holds all the words in the sentence with the first word of the sentence in the front of the queue. The parser performs two main types of actions: shift and reduce. When a shift action is taken, a word is shifted from the front of the queue, and placed on the top of the stack. When a reduce action is taken, the two top items on the top of the stack are popped, and a new item is pushed onto the stack. Depending on whether the head of the new tree is to the left or to the right of its new dependent, we call the action either shift-left or shift-right. Each tree fragment built in this way must also be given a grammatical relation label.

To extend this deterministic model to a probabilistic model, we use a best-first strategy. This involves an extension of the deterministic shift-reduce into a best-first shift-reduce algorithm based on selection of a parser action from a heap of parser actions ordered by their relative probabilities. The parser uses maximum entropy modelling (Berger, Della Pietra and Pietra 1996) to determine the actions and their probabilities. Features used in classification at any point during parsing are derived from the parser's current configuration (contents of the stack and queue) at that point. The specific features fed into the classifier include: the word and its POS tag, the shape of related dependencies, and the shape of recently applied rules.

15. Research using the new infrastructure

The goal of all this tagging work is to support easier analysis of morphosyntactic development and more accurate computation of automatic indices such as MLU, VOCD, DSS, and IPSyn. Currently, researchers will find that the easiest way to make use of these new tags is to use the basic CLAN search programs of KWAL, COMBO, and MODREP. For example, if you want to study the acquisition of auxiliary verbs, you can simply search the %mor line using a command like this:

```
kwal +t%mor +s"v:aux|*" *.cha
```

If you want to study the development of compounds, you could use commands like these:

```
kwal +t%mor +s"n|+n*" *.cha
```

If you want to trace combinations of parts of speech, you can use the COMBO command. For example, this command would search for auxiliaries followed by nouns in *yes/no*-questions:

```
combo +t%mor +s"v:aux|*^n|*" *.cha
```

You can also use a combination of the MODREP and COMBO commands to search for cases when something has a particularly part of speech role on the %mor line and a grammatical relation role on the %xsyn line. For example, you could search in this way for pronouns that are objects of prepositions.

The %mor and %xsyn lines open up a wide variety of possibilities for increasing precision in the study of morphosyntactic development. The range of topics that can be investigated in this area is limited only by the imagination of researchers and the scopes of the relevant theories. Consider some of the following possibilities:

1. Optional infinitival errors – tags on the %mor and %xsyn line will allow you to identify both correct and incorrect uses of infinitives.

2. Case errors – working from the %xsyn structure, one can identify pronouns with and without correct case marking.
3. Fronted auxiliaries – these forms can be readily identified from the %mor line.
4. Grammatical role identification – roles can be read off the %xsyn line.
5. Distinguishing particular argument structures – using the %xsyn line, one can distinguish between *to* phrases used to mark datives and those used to mark location.
6. Locating double object constructions. The %xsyn line will identify structures with double objects.

Searches within the %xsyn tier have a similar logic. One can use KWAL to find basic GR types, such as complements or relative clauses. Thus, these tags would fully automate an analysis of the type found in Diessel and Tomasello (2001). For linear combinations of types, you can use COMBO. In the future, we hope to provide more powerful methods for searching syntactic structures on the %xsyn line.

16. Next steps

Once our work with the tagging and parsing of the CHILDES database is largely completed, we need to provide tools that will allow researchers to take full advantage of this new tagged infrastructure. First, we need to construct methods for searching effectively through the dependency graphs constructed by GRASP. Consider the example of the structures examined in MacWhinney (2005). These involve sentences such as these:

1. The man who is running is coming.
2. *Is the man who running is coming?
3. Is the man who is running coming?

In his debate with Jean Piaget (Piattelli-Palmarini 1980), Chomsky argued that children would know immediately that (2) is ungrammatical, despite the fact that they never hear sentences like (3). According to Chomsky, this means that the child's acquisition of grammar is "hopelessly underdetermined by the fragmentary evidence available." A study by Crain and Nakayama (1987) supports the idea that children are sensitive to the ungrammaticality of (2) and a corpus search in MacWhinney (2005) for sentences such as (3) in CHILDES supports Chomsky's belief that such sentences are virtually absent in the input. However, MacWhinney also found extensive evidence for slightly different, but related sentences that provide clear positive evidence for learning regarding the acceptability of (3). In searching for the relevant contexts, MacWhinney was forced to rely on searches based on the %mor tier. To do this, it was necessary to compose search strings involving AUX, WH, and other categories. Although these search patterns are effective in catching most relevant patterns, there is always a possibility that they are missing some cases. Moreover, they do not provide good categorizations of the relevant structures by grammatical relations. And that is, after all, what is involved in this debate.

By constructing search methods that can look at relative clauses in different structural conditions, we will be able to understand such issues more explicitly.

Work with these tagged corpora is not limited to processing of specific constructions. It is also possible to use these new tags to explore ways of inducing grammars from corpora. As we complete the GR tagging of the database, it will be possible to evaluate alternative learning systems in terms of their ability to move through longitudinal data and match the tags at each stage computed by GRASP. As we noted earlier, these systems could utilize perspectives from Minimalism with parameters (Buttery 2004), HPSG (Wintner, MacWhinney and Lavie 2007), item-based grammars (Gobet and Pine 1997), or statistical learning (Edelman *et al.* 2004). In each case, we will be providing a level playing field for the evaluation of the abilities of these contrasting systems.

17. Conclusion

This paper has surveyed a wide variety of issues in the automatic construction of morphosyntactic tags for the CHILDES database. This discussion was targeted to three audiences: experienced CHILDES users, researchers new to CHILDES, and computational linguists. Experienced researchers doing work on morphosyntactic analysis need to understand all of these issues in great detail. Researchers who are new to the use of CHILDES data need to be aware of the various options open for analysis as they learn to use transcripts to address theoretical questions. Computational linguists can use the CHILDES database as a test bed for evaluating new methods for tagging and analyzing corpus material. Much of the material discussed in this chapter has involved issues that could be dismissed as "messy" coding details. However, in reality, making systematic decisions about the treatment of interjections, adverbs, or specific grammatical relations involves fundamental theoretical thinking about the shape of human language and the ways in which language presents itself to the child.

Exploiting corpora for language acquisition research

Katherine Demuth

1. Introduction

Language corpora have long provided a rich source of information about children's language development. Many of these first appeared in the form of diary studies (Darwin 1877; Deville 1891), and this continues to be a rich source of information still exploited today (e.g., Bowerman 1974). However, the increasing affordability of audio/video recording equipment, computers and memory, plus the creation of a central public storage venue for child language corpora (CHILDES, MacWhinney 2000), has led to a recent surge in language acquisition corpora (see MacWhinney this volume). The further development of tools useful for exploiting these computerized corpora (e.g., CLAN (MacWhinney 2000), PHON (Rose, MacWhinney, Byrne, Hedlund, Maddocks and O'Brien 2005)) has enhanced the usability of these corpora for addressing research questions at multiple levels of linguistic structure (e.g., phonology, morphology, the lexicon), and in children as well as adults. This growth in the use of large datasets follows a larger trend that is now common in fields such as computational linguistics, speech research, sociolinguistics, and historical linguistics.

Although technological developments have facilitated the ability to collect and analyze these large corpora, the primary motivation for corpus construction (which is still tedious and labour intensive to transcribe) has been to provide the data needed to address certain theoretical issues. In particular, corpora have been useful for examining the course of language acquisition over time, as well as characteristics of the input language learners typically hear. The amount of data collected, how it is collected, and how it is prepared and transcribed, all influence the utility of a particular corpus. This chapter reviews some of the issues that are important to the creation and use of corpora, and their potential for assessing children's knowledge of language.

2. Corpus creation

Ideally, any corpus should be collected with specific theoretical issues in mind. This will guide decisions about the corpus design. This involves decisions regarding the number of children to be included in the study, the setting for recording (home, lab, school), the interlocutors (parent, siblings, experimenter), the activities ('natural', prompted with a specific set of toys/tasks), the amount of data recorded (how long recordings should be), the number of sessions/ages recorded per child (i.e., longitudinal or not, how frequently sampled), the placement and type of microphones used (critical for conducting acoustic analysis), and the use of video. Similar decisions arise at the level of transcription and coding (orthographic, phonetic, situational information, etc.).

3. Corpus size

The quantity of data available in a particular corpus is an issue of critical importance. As Rowland, Fletcher and Hughes (this volume) discuss, estimating both errors and productivity present different problems depending on corpus size. Various statistical procedures can be used to estimate the probability of both. However, to some extent, corpus construction can also be designed to address some of these issues. For example, the examination of certain relatively high-frequency phonological phenomena (e.g., segmental acquisition, the acquisition of coda consonants in Germanic languages) can more easily be addressed with fewer hours of data than can the acquisition of lower-frequency syntactic phenomena (e.g., the acquisition of passive constructions in English). Since many researchers are interested in aspects of syntax acquisition, this has led to the collection of dense corpora (several hours per week) for more effectively examining morphological and syntactic development (e.g., the Leipzig Corpora – Lieven, Behrens, Speares and Tomasello 2003). However, the context of recording (location, activating, interlocutors, time of day) may also be critical in terms of encouraging more utterances on the part of the child.

4. Longitudinal case studies

Much of the field of language acquisition has been conducted using cross-sectional experiments, where several children are tested at a given age to determine if they have mastered a certain grammatical structure. Thus, much of the field of acquisition provides us with a snap shot of children's grammatical competence at a particular point in time. This type of information is extremely valuable for providing norms of typical development that can be used by theoreticians and clinicians alike. However, it less clearly addresses one of the primary goals of the field, which is to understand how a given child's knowledge of language develops over time. Given enough data, longitudinal case studies can provide exactly the type of detailed, fine-grained information need to examine how children's grammars move from one stage of generalization to the next, providing a much-needed window into the language learning process. Such studies can also expose individual differences in the learning process (cf. Lieven this volume), providing critical information about the types of generalizations different language learners make. This in turn can inform our theories about how language is learned.

5. Early production data (ages 1–2)

The field of infant speech perception has pioneered several different methods for examining children's sensitivities to various types of phonetic, phonological, morphological, lexical and distributional information before the age of two. However, it is not yet clear what the relationship is between perception and production. Recent research on early comprehension, and children's ability to process lexical and morphosyntactic information, begins to provide a better understanding of what children 'know' about language, and how they can begin to put this to use in language processing (e.g., Lew-Williams and Fernald 2007). However, it is extremely difficult to conduct elicited production studies with children much below the age of 2 (though see Kehoe and Stoel Gammon (2001) for success at 1;6 years). For those children who begin to produce their first words by 11 months, the second year of life provides an extremely rich arena for exploring aspects of both phonological and morphological development. Longitudinal spontaneous production corpora during this time provide a rich source of information regarding language development during this period (Demuth, Culbertson and Alter 2006; Demuth and Tremblay 2008; Fikkert 1994; Levelt, Schiller and Levelt 2000).

6. Nature of the input and learnability issues

Much of the research on language acquisition has been conducted in a context that is oblivious to what language learners actually hear. This has often proved problematic for language learning theories, which assume that the target grammar for the child is the full adult model. However, recent research suggests that the model to be learned is actually quite close to that of everyday speech directed toward the child. If so, this means that we need a much more complete model/description of child directed speech at all levels of structure. Only then can we more effectively begin to understand the nature of the learning problem. Information about the frequency of occurrence and distribution of different phonological, lexical, morphological and syntactic phenomena is therefore needed to inform the design of our experiments and the interpretation of the behavioural results. For example, Ravid, Dressler, Nir-Sagev, Korecky-Kröll,

Soumann, Rehfeldt, Laaha, Bertl, Basbøll and Gillis (this volume) show that, across languages, plurals account for a small percentage of the total nouns children hear, and that the frequency distribution of morphological marking of plurals is the same as that found in early child speech. This is consistent with other findings in the field. For example Demuth (1989) suggests that the early acquisition of passives in Sesotho (as compared to English) is due to the much higher use of passives in Sesotho everyday speech. Once again, corpora provide a means for evaluating these issues, and help to explain the behavioural results found.

Information about the nature of the input learners hear is also important for designing models of how language learning might proceed. Monaghan and Christensen (this volume) explore what types of distributional information and phonological properties might be useful for clustering together certain natural classes of words. Other models take a more probabilistic, Bayesian approach to morphological segmentation, exploring the contributions of learning across types versus tokens (e.g., Goldwater 2006). Corpora of child directed speech therefore play an important role in helping to explore not only the nature of the input, but also how learners can use this input in constructing their earlier grammars.

7. Discourse context and the structure of language

Information about the input also provides the context needed for exploring the acquisition of discourse-dependent aspects of language. For example, Allen, Skarabela and Hughes (this volume) use both video and audio information to examine the role of discourse context in licensing null objects. Thus, although much acquisition research often focuses on words or sentences, learners must be aware of the larger discourse context to be able to use and interpret both overt and null pronouns/objects in an appropriate fashion. This is critical for our understanding of how children learn the argument structure of verbs.

Recent corpus research on the argument structure of Sesotho verbs discovered that null objects are permitted in that language as well, even though this was not mentioned in any grammars (Demuth, Machobane, Moloi and Odato 2005). Since linguists often elicit grammaticality judgements at the level of the sentence, such discourse related issues are often overlooked. Thus, corpora may be especially useful for exploring discourse-related aspects of the syntax of lesser-studied languages, again providing the background needed for a full assessment of language learning issues.

8. Interactions between corpus and experimental studies

Corpora can also provide a wealth of pilot and subsequent data for designing and interpreting experimental results. For example, corpus analysis revealed that certain double object applicative constructions never occurred in 98 hours of adult and child speech in the Demuth Sesotho Corpus (Demuth 1992). Experiments were then needed to determine when Sesotho-speaking children learned that the animate object must be immediately ordered after the verb, rather than the benefactive argument, as in other Bantu languages (Demuth *et al.* 2005). Since there is no MacArthur CDI for Sesotho, the corpus analysis was extremely useful for identifying the high-frequency verbs which Sesotho-speaking 2-year-olds should know. Further analysis showed that the worst experimental performance occurred on the highest-frequency verbs. This suggested that children expected these verbs to occur in their high-frequency syntactic frame (i.e., with one of the objects realized as a preverbal clitic rather than a lexical object). This suggests that certain high-frequency verbs may 'prime' high-frequency frames (Bock and Loebell 1990).

In another corpus study, Song and Demuth (2005) found that some children exhibit phonotactic complexity effects on the production of 3rd person singular morphemes. This provided the impetus for further cross-sectional experimental study, where an interaction was found between phonotactic complexity and position within the utterance. This in turn is prompting a return to the corpus to examine possible positional effects. Thus, information from experiments and corpora can often exist in a symbiotic relationship, each providing a piece of the evidence needed for understanding the factors that influence how language is acquired.

9. Areas ripe for further corpus research

Many early corpora contain data from children who are productively using language, often from the age of 2 onwards (e.g., Brown 1973). The focus of such studies has typically been morphological and syntactic development, where the data were 'orthographically' transcribed. As a result, most of the language acquisition studies that have used corpora have explored (morpho)syntactic issues. Less corpus research has focused on earlier aspects of phonological and morpho-phonological development. However, this is beginning to change with the increasing availability of longitudinal, phonetically transcribed corpora and the tools needed to exploit them (see Demuth (in press) for review). Many of these corpora are also linked to acoustic files, providing the means for conducting acoustic analysis of children's early speech productions (Song and Demuth in press). In addition, many of these corpora contain data on child directed speech, providing much-needed information about the early input children hear. Importantly, many of these new corpora come from a variety of languages, providing a critically-needed crosslinguistic perspective on the input children hear, and how this influences the realization of their early speech productions (see Demuth (2006) for review). Ultimately, this type of investigation should lead to developing a model of early language production, which may help account for some of the variability in children's early speech.

10. Limitations of corpus research

As discussed above, longitudinal language acquisition corpora provide a rich source of information for examining phonological, morphological, lexical and syntactic development over time. As with any method, however, there are limitations on what it can tell us about the development of linguistic representations. For example, many of the corpora gathered to date contain information on only a few children. Given that there is also a large amount of individual variation, data from more children are needed in order to provide a robust picture of how language develops over time, even for English, and for the adult input as well. In addition, there is a need for denser corpora than that usually collected, with several hours of speech collected at certain points in time. Even with optimally dense data, with several children, it is difficult to know what the frequency of certain lexical items is for a given child. Furthermore, the contexts in which these appear may be highly variable, making it difficult to control for possible context effects (e.g., position within the sentence, prosodic factors). Even with ideal corpora, it may be necessary to complement these studies with experiments, where novel words and/or carefully controlled contexts can be used.

Finally, corpus studies may overestimate or under-estimate children's grammatical knowledge of a certain form. It has long been observed that children's perceptual abilities are often in advance of production abilities, and this is typically the case with comprehension as well. However, full comprehension and/or knowledge of a particular morphological or syntactic construction may take years to reach adult-like competence. For example, Demuth *et al.* (2005) found that, although 4-year-olds were above chance in placing the animate object immediately after the verb in double object applicative constructions, 8-year-olds still performed significantly worse than adults. Only by 12 years did Sesotho-speaking children show adult-like word-order performance in experiments. Since these constructions are relatively rare in everyday speech, such findings would have been almost impossible to find in corpus analysis.

11. Converging evidence from corpus and experimental studies

As discussed above, the use of corpora for addressing questions of how language is learned has certain limitations. However, experiments are also limited in what they can tell us, and experimental artefacts abound – especially when experiments are designed with little understanding of what children actually hear, and the frequency/ priming biases they may have. Thus, the field can greatly benefit from a research paradigm that draws on converging evidence from multiple sources of information, including both corpora studies and experimental results. Several laboratories are now beginning to take this approach, with students trained in both corpus analysis and experimental techniques. With the growing availability of new corpora, and the tools needed to exploit them, the field of language acquisition is now prepared to probe the processes of language acquisition more effectively than every before.

References

Abbot-Smith, K. and Behrens, H. 2006. "How Known Constructions Influence the Acquisition of New Constructions: The German Periphrastic Passive and Future Constructions." *Cognitive Science* 30:995–1026.

Abu-Mostafa, Y. S. 1993. "Hints and the VC Dimension." *Neural Computation* 5:278–88.

Aguado-Orea, J. 2004. The Acquisition of Morpho-Syntax in Spanish: Implications for Current Theories of Development. University of Nottingham: Doctoral Dissertation.

Aguado-Orea, J. and Pine, J. 2002. "Assessing the Productivity of Verb Morphology in Early Child Spanish." Paper presented at the *9th International Conference of the Association for the Study of Child Language*, Madison, WI, USA.

Aguado-Orea, J. and Pine, J. 2005. "What Kind of Knowledge Underlies the Early Use of Inflectional Morphology in Spanish? Effects of Frequency and Lexical Specificity on Accuracy." Paper presented at the *10th International Congress for the Study of Child Language*, Berlin, Germany.

Akhtar, N. 1999. "Acquiring Basic Word Order: Evidence for Data-Driven Learning of Syntactic Structure." *Journal of Child Language* 26:339–56.

Akmajian, A., Steele, S. and Wasow, T. 1979. "The Category AUX in Universal Grammar." *Linguistic Inquiry* 10:1–64.

Allan, R., Holmes, P. and Lundskær-Nielsen, T. 1995. *Danish: A Comprehensive Grammar.* London: Routledge.

Allen, S. 1996. *Aspects of Argument Structure Acquisition in Inuktitut.* Amsterdam: John Benjamins.

—. 1997. "A Discourse-Pragmatic Explanation for the Subject-Object Asymmetry in Early Null Arguments: The Principle of Informativeness Revisited." In *Proceedings of the Gala '97 Conference on Language Acquisition*, A. Sorace, C. Heycock and R. Shillcock (eds.), 10–15. Edinburgh: University of Edinburgh.

—. 2000. "A Discourse-Pragmatic Explanation for Argument Representation in Child Inuktitut." *Linguistics* 38:483–521.

—. 2006. "Formalism and Functionalism Working Together? Exploring Roles for Complementary Contributions in the Domain of Child Null Arguments." In *Inquiries on Linguistic Development: In Honor of Lydia White*, R. Slabakova, S. Montrul and P. Prévost (eds.), 233–55. Amsterdam: John Benjamins.

—. 2007. "Interacting Pragmatic Influences on Children's Argument Realization." In *Crosslinguistic Perspectives on Argument Structure: Implications for Learnability*, M. Bowerman and P. Brown (eds.), 119–212. Mahwah: Lawrence Erlbaum Associates.

Allen, S. and Crago, M. 1996. "Early Passive Acquisition in Inuktitut." *Journal of Child Language* 23:129–55.

Allen, S. and Schröder, H. 2003. "Preferred Argument Structure in Early Inuktitut Spontaneous Speech Data." In *Preferred Argument Structure: Grammar as Architecture for Function*, J. Du Bois, L. Kumpf and W. Ashby (eds.), 301–38. Amsterdam: John Benjamins.

Altmann, J. 1974. "Observational Study of Behaviour: Sampling Methods." *Behaviour* 49:227–67.

Ambridge, B. & Rowland C.F (submitted). Predicting Children's Errors with Negative Questions: Testing a Schema-Combination Account. University of Liverpool: Unpublished manuscript.

Ambridge, B., Rowland, C., Theakston, A. and Tomasello, M. 2006. "Comparing Different Accounts of Inversion Error in Children's Non Subject Wh-Questions: 'What Experimental Data Can Tell Us?'." *Journal of Child Language* 33:519–57.

Ariel, M. 1988. "Referring and Accessibility." *Journal of Linguistics* 24:65–87.

—. 1990. *Accessing Noun-Phrase Antecedents.* London: Routledge.

—. 1994. "Interpreting Anaphoric Expressions: A Cognitive Versus a Pragmatic Approach." *Journal of Linguistics* 30:3–42.

—. 2001. "Accessibility Theory: An Overview." In *Text Representation: Linguistic and Psycholinguistic Aspects*, T. Sanders, J. Schilperoord and W. Spooren (eds.), 29–87. Amsterdam: John Benjamins.

Arnold, J. 1998. *Reference Form and Discourse Patterns.* Stanford University: Doctoral Dissertation.

Arnold, J., Brown-Schmidt, S. and Trueswell, J. 2007. "Children's Use of Gender and Order-of-Mention During Pronoun Comprehension." *Language and Cognitive Processes* 22:527–65.

Arnold, J., Brown-Schmidt, S., Trueswell, J. and Fagnano, M. 2005. "Children's Use of Gender and Order of Mention During Pronoun Comprehension." In *Processing World-Situated Language: Bridging the Language-as-Product and Language-as-Action Traditions*, J. Trueswell and M. Tanenhaus (eds.), 261–81. Cambridge MA: The MIT Press.

Arnold, J. and Griffin, Z. 2007. "The Effect of Additional Characters on Choice of Referring Expressions: Everyone Competes." *Journal of Memory and Language* 56:521–36.

Baayen, H., Dijkstra, T. and Schreuder, R. 1997. "Singulars and Plurals in Dutch: Evidence for a Parallel Dual-Route Model." *Journal of Memory and Language* 37:94–117.

Baayen, H., Schreuder, R., De Jong, N. and Krott, A. 2002. "Dutch Inflection: The Rules That Prove the Exception." In *Storage and Computation in the Language Faculty*, S. Nooteboom, F. Weerman and F. Wijnen (eds.), 61–92. Dordrecht: Kluwer.

Bar-Adon, A. and Leopold, W.F. 1971. *Child Language: A Book of Readings.* Englewood Cliffs: Prentice-Hall.

Bartke, S., Marcus, G. and Clahsen, H. 1995. "Acquiring German Noun Plurals." In *Proceedings of the 19th Annual Boston University Conference on Language Development*, D. MacLaughlin and S. McEwen (eds.), 60–69. Somerville MA: Cascadilla Press.

Basbøll, H. 2005. *The Phonology of Danish.* Oxford: Oxford University Press.

Bauer, L. 2003. "Review of *The Morphology of Dutch*." *Language* 79:626–28.

Beasley, K. and Karttunen, L. 2003. *Finite State Morphology.* Stanford CA: CSLI Publications.

Behrens, H. 2006. "The Input-Output Relationship in First Language Acquisition." *Language and Cognitive Processes* 21:2–24.

Behrens, H. and Deutsch, W. 1991. "Die Tagebücher von Clara und William Stern." In *Theorien und Methoden psychologiegeschichtlicher Forschung*, H. Lück and R. Miller (eds.), 66–76. Göttingen: Hogrefe.

Bellugi, U. 1967. The Acquisition of Negation. Harvard University: Doctoral Dissertation.

Bentivoglio, P. 1996. "Acquisition of Preferred Argument Structure in Venezuelan Spanish." Paper presented at the *Seventh International Congress for the Study of Child Language*, Istanbul, Turkey.

Berent, I., Pinker, S. and Shimron, J. 1999. "Default Nominal Inflection in Hebrew: Evidence for Mental Variables." *Cognition* 72:1–44.

—. 2002. "The Nature of Regularity and Irregularity: Evidence from Hebrew Nominal Inflection." *Journal of Psycholinguistic Research* 31:459–502.

Berger, A., Della Pietra, S.A. and Pietra, Della V.J. 1996. "A Maximum Entropy Approach to Natural Language Processing." *Computational Linguistics* 22:39–71.

Berlitz. 2005. *Berlitz Italian Verbs Handbook.* New York: Berlitz.

Berman, R. 1981. "Children's Regularizations of Plural Forms." *Papers and Reports on Child Language Development* 20:34–44.

—. 1985. *Acquisition of Hebrew.* Hillsdale NJ: Lawrence Erlbaum Associates.

Berman, R.A. and Slobin, D. I. (eds.) 1994. *Relating Events in Narrative: A Crosslinguistic Developmental Study.* Hillsdale NJ: Lawrence Erlbaum Associates.

Bertinetto, P. M. 2003. "Centro' e 'Periferia' del Linguaggio: Una Mappa per Orientarsi." In *Modelli Recenti in Linguistica*, D. Maggi and D. Poli (eds.), 157–211. Roma: Il Calamo.

Blackburn, P. and Bos, J. 2005. *Representation and Inference for Natural Language: A First Course in Computational Semantics.* Chicago IL: CSLI Publications.

Blanc, J. M., Dodane, C. and Dominey, P. F. 2003. "Temporal Processing for Syntax Acquisition: A Simulation Study." In *Proceedings of the 25th Conference of the Cognitive Science Society*, R. Alterman and D. Kirsch (eds.), 145–50. London: Routledge.

Bloom, L. 1970. *Language Development: Form and Function in Emerging Grammars.* Cambridge: MIT Press.

Bloom, L., Lightbown, P. and Hood, L. 1975. "Structure and Variation in Child Language." *Monographs of the Society for Research in Child Development* 40:1–78.

Bloom, P. 1990. "Subjectless Sentences in Child Language." *Linguistic Inquiry* 21:491–504.

—. 1993. "Grammatical Continuity in Language Development: The Case of Subjectless Sentences." *Linguistic Inquiry* 24:721–34.

Bock, J.K. and Loebell, H. 1990. "Framing Sentences." *Cognition* 35:1–39.

Bock, J.K. and Warren, R.K. 1985. "Conceptual Accessibility and Syntactic Structure in Sentence Formulation." *Cognition* 21:47–67.

Boersma, P. and Weenink, D. 2007. Praat: Doing Phonetics by Computer (Version 4.6.38) [Computer program]. Retrieved November 19, 2007, from http://www.praat.org/

Bonin, P., Barry, C., Méot, A. and Chalard, M. 2004. "The Influence of Age of Acquisition in Word Reading and Other Tasks: A Never Ending Story?" *Journal of Memory and Language* 50:456–76.

Booij, G. 2001. *The Morphology of Dutch.* Oxford: Oxford University Press.

Bowerman, M. 1973. *Early Syntactic Development.* Cambridge: Cambridge University Press.

—. 1974. "Learning the Structure of Causative Verbs: A Study in the Relationship of Cognitive, Semantic and Syntactic Development." *Papers and Reports on Child Language Development* 8:142–78.

—. 1982. "Evaluating Competing Linguistic Models with Language Acquisition Data: Implications of Developmental Errors with Causative Verbs." *Quaderni di Semantica* 3:5–66.

Braine, M. 1976. "Children's First Word Combinations." *Monographs of the Society for Research in Child Development* 41:1–104.

—. 1987. "What Is Learned in Acquiring Word Classes: A Step toward an Acquisition Theory." In *Mechanisms of Language Acquisition*, B. MacWhinney (ed.), 65–87. Hillsdale NJ: Lawrence Erlbaum Associates.

Braine, M., Brody, R., Brooks, P., Sudhalter, V., Ross, J., Catalano, L. and Fisch, S. 1990. "Exploring Language Acquisition in Children with a Miniature Artificial Language: Effects of Item and Pattern Frequency, Arbitrary Subclasses, and Correction." *Journal of Memory and Language* 29:591–610.

Braunwald, S.R. and Brislin, R.W. 1979. "The Diary Method Updated." In *Developmental Pragmatics*, E. Ochs and B. Schieffelin (eds.), 21–41. New York NY: Academic Press.

Brennan, S. 1995. "Centering Attention in Discourse." *Language and Cognitive Processes* 102:137–67.

Brink, L., Lund, J., Heger, S. and Jørgensen, J. 1991. *Den Store Danske Udtaleordbog*. Copenhagen: Munksgaard.

Brooks, P., Braine, M., Catalano, L., Brody, R. and Sudhalter, V. 1993. "Acquisition of Gender-Like Noun Subclasses in an Artificial Language: The Contribution of Phonological Markers to Learning." *Journal of Memory and Language* 32:79–95.

Brown, R. 1973. *A First Language: The Early Stages*. Cambridge MA: Harvard University Press.

Budwig, N. and Chaudhary, N. 1996. "Hindi-speaking Caregivers' Input: Towards an Integration of Typological and Language Socialization Approaches." In *Proceedings of the 20th Annual Boston University Conference on Language Development*, A. Stringfellow, D. Cahana-Amitay, E. Hughes, & A. Zukowski (eds.), 135–145. Somerville MA: Cascadilla Press.

Burani, C., Barca, L. and Arduino, L. 2001. "Una basa di dati sui valori di età di acquisizione, frequenza, familiarità, immaginabilità, concretezza, e altri variabili lessicali e sublessecali per 626 nomi dell'italiano." *Giornale italiano di psicologia* 28:839–54.

Buttery, P. 2004. "A Quantitative Evaluation of Naturalistic Models of Language Acquisition: The Efficiency of the Triggering Learning Algorithm Compared to a Categorial Grammar Learner." In *Proceedings of the 20th International Conference on Computational Linguistics*, 1–8. Geneva: COLING.

Bybee, J. 1985. *Morphology: A Study of the Relation between Meaning and Form*. Amsterdam: John Benjamins.

—. 1995. "Regular Morphology and the Lexicon." *Language and Cognitive Processes* 10:425–55.

—. 2006. "From Usage to Grammar: The Mind's Response to Repetition." *Language* 82:711–33.

Bybee, J. and Hopper, P. 2001. *Frequency and the Emergence of Linguistic Structure*. Amsterdam: John Benjamins.

Cameron-Faulkner, T., Lieven, E. and Tomasello, M. 2003. "A Construction Based Analysis of Child Directed Speech." *Cognitive Science* 27:843–73.

Campbell, A., Brooks, P. and Tomasello, M. 2000. "Factors Affecting Young Children's Use of Pronouns as Referring Expressions." *Journal of Speech, Language, and Hearing Research* 43:1337–49.

Campbell, R. and Besner, D. 1981. "This and Thap – Constraints on the Pronunciation of New Written Words." *Quarterly Journal of Experimental Psychology* 33:375–96.

Cartwright, T. and Brent, M. 1997. "Syntactic Categorization in Early Language Acquisition: Formalizing the Role of Distributional Analysis." *Cognition* 63:121–70.

Cassidy, K. and Kelly, M. 1991. "Phonological Information for Grammatical Category Assignments." *Journal of Memory and Language* 30:348–69.

—. 2001. "Children's Use of Phonology to Infer Grammatical Class in Vocabulary Learning." *Psychonomic Bulletin and Review* 8:519–23.

Chafe, W. 1976. "Givenness, Contrastiveness, Definiteness, Subjects, Topics, and Point of View." In *Subject and Topic*, C. Li (ed.), 25–56. New York NY: Academic Press.

—. 1987. "Cognitive Constraints on Information Flow." In *Coherence and Grounding in Discourse*, R. Tomlin (ed.), 21–51. Amsterdam: John Benjamins.

—. 1994. *Discourse, Consciousness and Time: The Flow and Displacement of Conscious Experience in Speaking and Writing.* Chicago: The University of Chicago Press.

—. 1996. "Inferring Identifiably and Accessibility." In *Reference and Referent Accessibility*, T. Fretheim and J. Gundel (eds.), 37–46. Amsterdam: John Benjamins.

Cho, S. 2004. *Argument Ellipsis in Korean-Speaking Children's Early Speech.* Harvard University: Doctoral Dissertation.

Chomsky, C. 1969. *The Acquisition of Syntax in Children from 5 to 10.* Cambridge MA: The MIT Press.

Chomsky, N. 1957. *Syntactic Structures.* The Hague: Mouton.

—. 1965. *Aspects of the Theory of Syntax.* Cambridge MA: The MIT Press.

—. 1980. *Rules and Representations.* New York NY: Columbia University Press.

—. 1995. *The Minimalist Program.* Cambridge MA: The MIT Press.

Chomsky, N. and Lasnik, H. 1993. "The Theory of Principles and Parameters" In *Syntax: An International Handbook of Contemporary Research*, J. Jacobs (ed.), 1–32. Berlin: Walter de Gruyter.

Chouinard, M. and Clark, E. 2003. "Adult Reformulations of Child Errors as Negative Evidence." *Journal of Child Language* 30:637–69.

Christiansen, M. and Dale, R. 2001. "Integrating Distributional, Prosodic and Phonological Information in a Connectionist Model of Language Acquisition." In *Proceedings of the 23rd Annual Conference of the Cognitive Science Society*, J. Moore and K. Stenning (eds.), 220–25. Mahwah NJ: Lawrence Erlbaum Associates.

Christiansen, M. and Monaghan, P. 2006. "Discovering Verbs through Multiple-Cue Integration." In *Action Meets Word: How Children Learn Verbs*, K. Hirsh-Pasek and R. Golinkoff (eds.), 88–107. Oxford: Oxford University Press.

Christiansen, M. H., Hockema, S. A. and Onnis, L. 2006. "Using Phoneme Distributions to Discover Words and Lexical Categories in Unsegmented Speech." In *Proceedings of the 28th Annual Conference of the Cognitive Science Society*, R. Sun and N. Miyake (eds.), 172–77. Mahwah NJ: Lawrence Erlbaum Associates.

Cipriani, P., Pfanner, P., Chilosi, A., Cittadoni, L., Ciuti, A., Maccari, A., Pantano, N., Pfanner, L., Poli, P., Sarno, S., Bottari, P., Cappelli, G., Colombo, C. and Veneziano, E. 1989. *Protocolli diagnostici e terapeutici nello sviluppo e nella patologia del linguaggio. (Italian Ministry of Health 1/84).* Pisa: Stella Maris Foundation.

Clahsen, H. 1999. "Lexical Entries and Rules of Language: A Multidisciplinary Study of German Inflection." *Behavioral and Brain Sciences* 22:991–1060.

Clahsen, H., Rothweiler, M., Woest, A. and Marcus, G. 1992. "Regular and Irregular Inflection in the Acquisition of German Noun Plurals." *Cognition* 45:225–55.

Clancy, P. 1980. "Referential Choice in English and Japanese Narrative Discourse." In *The Pear Stories: Cognitive, Cultural, and Linguistic Aspects of Narrative Production*, W.L. Chafe (ed.), 127–202. Norwood NJ: Ablex.

—. 1992. "Referential Strategies in the Narratives of Japanese Children." *Discourse Processes* 15:441–67.

—. 1993. "Preferred Argument Structure in Korean Acquisition." In *Proceedings of the 25th Annual Child Language Research Forum*, E. Clark (ed.), 307–14. Stanford CA: CSLI Publications.

—. 1997. "Discourse Motivations for Referential Choice in Korean Acquisition." In *Japanese/Korean Linguistics Vi*, H.-M. Sohn and J. Haig (eds.), 639–59. Stanford CA: CSLI Publications.

—. 2003. "The Lexicon in Interaction: Developmental Origins of Preferred Argument Structure in Korean." In *Preferred Argument Structure: Grammar as Architecture for Function*, J. Du Bois, L. Kumpf and W. Ashby (eds.), 81–108. Amsterdam: John Benjamins.

Clark, E. 2001. "Grounding and Attention in Language Acquisition." In *Proceedings from the Main Session of the 37th Meeting of the Chicago Linguistic Society*, M. Andronis, C. Ball, H. Elston and S. Neuvel (eds.), 95–116. Chicago IL: Chicago Linguistic Society.

—. 2003. *First Language Acquisition.* Cambridge: Cambridge University Press.

Clark, H. 1996. *Using Language.* Cambridge: Cambridge University Press.

Clark, H. and Haviland, S. 1977. "Comprehension and the Given-New Contract." In *Discourse Processes: Advances in Research and Theory*, R. Freedle (ed.), 1–40. Norwood NJ: Ablex.

Clark, H. and Marshall, C. 1981. "Definite Reference and Mutual Knowledge." In *Elements of Discourse Understanding*, A. Joshi, B. Webber and I. Sag (eds.), 10–63. Cambridge: Cambridge University Press.

Comrie, B. 1989. *Language Universals and Linguistic Typology.* Chicago IL: The University of Chicago Press.

Cooper, W. and Paccia-Cooper, J. 1980. *Syntax and Speech.* Cambridge: Harvard University Press.

Corbett, G. 1991. *Gender.* Cambridge: Cambridge University Press.

—. 2000. *Number.* Cambridge: Cambridge University Press.

Crain, S. 1991. "Language Acquisition in the Absence of Experience." *Behavioral and Brain Sciences* 14:597–611.

Crain, S. and Nakayama, M. 1987. "Structure Dependence in Grammar Formation." *Language* 63:522–43.

Croft, W. A. 2001. *Radical Construction Grammar: Syntactic Theory in Typological Perspective.* Oxford: Oxford University Press.

—. 2003. *Typology and Universals.* Cambridge: Cambridge University Press.

Crystal, D. 1979. *Working with LARSP.* London: Edward Arnold.

Culicover, P. and Jackendoff, R. 2005. *Simpler Syntax.* Oxford: Oxford University Press.

Curtin, S., Mintz, T. and Christiansen, M. 2005. "Stress Changes the Representational Landscape: Evidence from Word Segmentation." *Cognition* 96:233–62.

Cutler, A. 1993. "Phonological Cues to Open- and Closed-Class Words in the Processing of Spoken Sentences." *Journal of Psycholinguistic Research* 22:109–31.

Cutler, A. and Carter, D. 1987. "The predominance of strong initial syllables in the English vocabulary." *Computer Speech and Language* 2:133–42

Cutting, J. and Vishton, P. 1995. "Perceiving Layout and Knowing Distances: The Integration, Relative Potency, and Contextual Use of Different Information About Depth." In *Perception of Space and Motion*, W. Epstein and S. Rogers (eds.), 69–117. San Diego CA: Academic Press.

Dąbrowska, E. 2000. "From Formula to Schema: The Acquisition of English Questions." *Cognitive Linguistics* 1:83–102.

Dąbrowska, E. and Lieven, E. 2005. "Towards a Lexically Specific Grammar of Children's Question Constructions." *Cognitive Linguistics* 16:437–74.
Daneš, F. 1966. "Centre and Periphery as a Language Universal." *Travaux linguistiques de Prague* 2:9–21.
Darwin, C. 1877. "A Biographical Sketch of an Infant." *Mind* 2:285–94.
—. 1886. *The Autobiography of Charles Darwin: 1809–1882: With Original Omissions Restored / Ed. Appendix and Notes by His Granddaughter Nora Barlow.* New York NY: Norton 1958.
Daugherty, K. and Seidenberg, M. 1994. "Beyond Rules and Exceptions: A Connectionist Approach to Inflectional Morphology." In *The Reality of Linguistic Rules*, S. Lima, R. Corrigan and G. Iverson (eds.), 353–88. Amsterdam: John Benjamins.
De Haas, W. and Trommelen, M. 1993. *Morfologisch Handboek van het Nederlands.* 's-Gravenhage: SDU.
Demuth, K. 1989. "Maturation and the Acquisition of Sesotho Passive." *Language* 65:56–80.
—. 1992. "Acquisition of Sesotho." In *The Cross-Linguistic Study of Language Acquisition*, D.I. Slobin (ed.), 557–638. Hillsdale: Lawrence Erlbaum Associates.
—. 2006. "Crosslinguistic Perspectives on the Development of Prosodic Words." *Language and Speech (Special Issue)* 49:129–297.
—. in press. "The Acquisition of Phonology." In *The Handbook of Phonological Theory*, J. Goldsmith, J. Riggle and A. Yu (eds.). Malden MA: Blackwell.
Demuth, K., Culbertson, J. and Alter, J. 2006. "Word-Minimality, Epenthesis, and Coda Licensing in the Acquisition of English." *Language and Speech* 49:137–74.
Demuth, K., Machobane, M., Moloi, F. and Odato, C. 2005. "Learning Animacy Hierarchy Effects in Sesotho Double Object Applicatives." *Language* 81:421–47.
Demuth, K. and Tremblay, A. 2008. "Prosodically-Conditioned Variability in Children's Production of French Determiners." *Journal of Child Language* 35:99–127.
Deuchar, M. and Quay, S. 2000. *Bilingual Acquisition: Theoretical Implications of a Case Study.* Oxford: Oxford University Press.
Deville, G. 1891. "Notes sur le développement du langage II." *Revue de linguistique et de philology comparée* 24:10–42, 128–43, 242–57, 300–20.
DeVilliers, J. 1991. "Why Questions?" In *Papers in the Acquisition of Wh*, T. Maxfield and B. Plunkett (eds.), 155–71. Amherst MA: University of Massachusetts Occasional Papers.
DeVilliers, J. and DeVilliers, P. 1973. "A Cross Sectional Study of the Acquisition of Grammatical Morphemes in Child Speech." *Journal of Psycholinguistic Research* 2:267–78.
—. 1974. "Competence and Performance in Child Language: Are Children Really Competent to Judge?" *Journal of Child Language* 1:11–22.
Diessel, H. and Tomasello, M. 2001. "The Acquisition of Finite Complement Clauses in English: A Corpus-Based Analysis." *Cognitive Linguistics* 12:97–141.
Dominey, P., Hoen, M. and Inui, T. 2006. "A Neurolinguistic Model of Grammatical Construction Processing." *Journal of Cognitive Neuroscience* 18:2088–107.
Dressler, W. 1989. "Prototypical Differences between Inflection and Derivation." *Zeitschrift für Phonetik, Sprachwissenschaft und Kommunikationsforschung* 42:3–10.
—. 2003. "Degrees of Grammatical Productivity in Inflectional Morphology." *Italian Journal of Linguistics* 15:31–62.
Du Bois, J. 1985. "Competing Motivations." In *Iconicity in Syntax*, J. Haiman (ed.), 343–65. Amsterdam: John Benjamins.
—. 1987. "The Discourse Basis of Ergativity." *Language* 63:805–55.

Du Bois, J., Kumpf, L. and Ashby, W. (eds.) 2003. *Preferred Argument Structure: Grammar as Architecture for Function.* Amsterdam: John Benjamins.

Dunn, J. 1988. *The Beginnings of Social Understanding.* Cambridge MA: Harvard University Press.

Durieux, G. and Gillis, S. 2001. "Predicting Grammatical Classes from Phonological Cues: An Empirical Test." In *Approaches to Bootstrapping: Phonological, Lexical, Syntactic and Neurophysiological Aspects of Early Language Acquisition*, J. Weissenborn and B. Höhle (eds.), 189–229. Amsterdam: John Benjamins.

Edelman, S., Solan, Z., Horn, D. and Ruppin, E. 2004. "Bridging Computational, Formal and Psycholinguistic Approaches to Language." In *Proceedings of the 26th Annual Conference of the Cognitive Science Society*, K. Forbus, D. Gentner and T. Regier (eds.), 345–50. Mahwah NJ: Lawrence Erlbaum Associates.

Edwards, J. 1992. "Computer Methods in Child Language Research: Four Principles for the Use of Archived Data". *Journal of Child Language* 19:435–58.

Elman, J. 1993. "Learning and Development in Neural Networks: The Importance of Starting Small." *Cognition* 48:71–99.

Fanselow, G. 2004. "Fakten, Fakten, Fakten. " *Linguistische Berichte* 200:481–93.

Farmer, T., Christiansen, M., and Monaghan, P. 2006. "Phonological Typicality Influences Lexical Processing." *Proceedings of the National Academy of Sciences* 103:12203–12208.

Fenson, L., Dale, P., Reznick, J., Bates, E., Thal, D. and Pethick, S. 1994. "Variability in Early Communicative Development." *Monographs of the Society for Research in Child Development* 59:1–173.

Fenson, L., Dale, P., Reznick, J., Thal, D., Bates, E., Hartung, J., Pethick, S. and Reilly, J. 1993. *The MacArthur Communicative Development Inventories: User's Guide and Technical Manual.* San Diego CA: Singular Publishing Group.

Fernald, A. and McRoberts, G. 1996. "Prosodic Bootstrapping: A Critical Analysis of the Argument and the Evidence." In *Signal to Syntax: Bootstrapping from Speech to Grammar in Early Acquisition*, J. Morgan and K. Demuth (eds.), 365–88. Mahwah NJ: Lawrence Erlbaum Associates.

Fikkert, P. 1994. *On the Acquisition of Prosodic Structure.* Dordrecht: Holland Institute of Generative Linguistics.

Fisher, C. and Tokura, H. 1996. "Acoustic Cues to Grammatical Structure in Infant-Directed Speech: Cross-Linguistic Evidence." *Child Development* 67:3192–218.

Fitch, W., Hauser, M. and Chomsky, N. 2005. "The Evolution of the Language Faculty: Clarifications and Implications." *Cognition* 97:179–210.

Fletcher, P. 1985. *A Child's Learning of English.* Oxford: Blackwell.

Foisil, M. (ed.) 1989. *Journal de Jean Héroards. Publication du Centre de Recherche sur la Civilisation de L'Europe Moderne (2 Volumes: Vol 1, 1601–1608; Vol 2, 1609–1628).* Paris: Fayard.

Fretheim, T. and Gundel, J. (eds.) 1996. *Reference and Referent Accessibility.* Amsterdam: John Benjamins.

Freudenthal, D., Pine, J., Aguado-Orea, J. and Gobet, F. 2007. "Modelling the Developmental Patterning of Finiteness Marking in English, Dutch, German and Spanish Using MOSAIC." *Cognitive Science* 31:311–41.

Freudenthal, D., Pine, J. and Gobet, F. 2006. "Modelling the Development of Children's Use of Optional Infinitives in English and Dutch Using MOSAIC." *Cognitive Science* 30:277–310.

Fries, C. C. 1952. *The Structure of English: An Introduction to the Construction of English Sentences.* New York NY: Harcourt, Brace & Co.

Frigo, L. and McDonald, J. L. 1998. "Properties of Phonological Markers That Affect the Acquisition of Gender-Like Subclasses." *Journal of Memory and Language* 39:218–45.

Gallaway, C. and Richards, B. (eds.) 1994. *Input and Interaction in Language Acquisition.* Cambridge: Cambridge University Press.

Garrod, S. and Sanford, A. 1982. "The Mental Representation of Discourse in a Focused Memory System: Implications for the Interpretation of Anaphoric Noun Phrases." *Journal of Semantics* 1:21–41.

Gathercole, V. C. M., Sebastián, E. and Soto, P. 1999. "The Early Acquisition of Spanish Verbal Morphology: Across-the-Board or Piecemeal Knowledge?" *The International Journal of Bilingualism* 3:133–82.

Gazdar, G., Pullum, G. and Sag, I. 1982. "Auxiliaries and Related Phenomena in a Restrictive Theory of Grammar." *Language* 58:591–638.

Gerken, L.A. 1991. "The Metrical Basis for Children's Subjectless Sentences." *Journal of Memory and Language* 30:431–51.

Gerken, L.A. 1996. "Prosody's Role in Language Acquisition and Adult Parsing." *Journal of Psycholinguistic Research* 25:345–56.

Gerken, L.A., Jusczyk, P. and Mandel, D. 1994. "When Prosody Fails to Cue Syntactic Structure: Nine-Month-Olds' Sensitivity to Phonological VS Syntactic Phrases." *Cognition* 51:237–65.

Gillis, S. 1997. "The Acquisition of Diminutives in Dutch." In *Studies in Pre- and Protomorphology*, W. Dressler (ed.), 165–79. Vienna: Verlag der Österreichischen Akademie der Wissenschaften.

Gillis, S. and Ravid, D. 2006. "Typological Effects on Spelling Development: A Crosslinguistic Study of Hebrew and Dutch." *Journal of Child Language* 33:621–59.

Givón, T. (ed.) 1983. *Topic Continuity in Discourse: A Quantitative Cross-Language Study.* Amsterdam: John Benjamins.

Gleitman, L., Gleitman, H., Landau, B. and Wanner, E. 1988. "Where Learning Begins: Initial Representations for Language Learning." In *Linguistics: The Cambridge Survey*, F. Newmeyer (ed.), 150–93. Cambridge: Cambridge University Press.

Gleitman, L. and Wanner, E. 1982. "Language Acquisition: The State of the State of the Art." In *Language Acquisition: The State of the Art*, E. Wanner and L. Gleitman (eds.), 3–48. Cambridge: Cambridge University Press.

Gobet, F. and Pine, J. 1997. "Modelling the Acquisition of Syntactic Categories" In *Proceedings of the 19th Annual Meeting of the Cognitive Science Society.* Hillsdale NJ: Lawrence Erlbaum Associates.

Goldsmith, J. (ed.) 1995. *The Handbook of Phonological Theory.* Oxford: Basil Blackwell.

Goldwater, S. 2006. Nonparametric Bayesian Models of Lexical Acquisition. Brown University: Doctoral Dissertation.

Gómez, R. and Gerken, L. A. 2000. "Infant Artificial Language Learning and Language Acquisition." *Trends in Cognitive Sciences* 4:178–86.

Gordon, P., Grosz, B. and Gilliom, L. 1993. "Pronouns, Names, and the Centering of Attention in Discourse." *Cognitive Science* 17:311–47.

Greenfield, P. and Smith, J. 1976. *The Structure of Communication in Early Language Development.* New York NY: Academic Press.

Grice, H. 1975. "Logic and Conversation." In *Syntax and Semantics: Speech Acts*, P. Cole and J. Morgan (eds.), 41–58. New York NY: Academic Press.

Grinstead, J. 2000. "Case, Inflection and Subject Licensing in Child Catalan and Spanish." *Journal of Child Language* 27:119–55.

Grosz, B., Joshi, A. and Weinstein, S. 1995. "Centering: A Framework for Modeling the Local Discourse." *Computational Linguistics* 21:203–25.

Guasti, M., Thornton, R. and Wexler, K. 1995. "Negation in Children's Questions: The Case of English." In *Proceedings of the 19th Annual Boston University Conference on Language Development*, D. MacLaughlin and S. McEwen (eds.), 228–39. Boston MA: Cascadilla Press.

Guerriero, S., Cooper, A., Oshima-Takane, Y. and Kuriyama, Y. 2001. "A Discourse-Pragmatic Explanation for Argument Realization and Omission in English and Japanese Children's Speech." In *Proceedings of the 25th Annual Boston University Conference on Language Development*, A. Do, L. Dominguez and A. Johansen (eds.), 319–30. Somerville MA: Cascadilla Press.

Guerriero, S., Oshima-Takane, Y. and Kuriyama, Y. 2006. "The Development of Referential Choice in English and Japanese: A Discourse-Pragmatic Perspective." *Journal of Child Language* 33:823–57.

Gundel, J. 1985. "'Shared Knowledge' and Topicality." *Journal of Pragmatics* 9:83–107.

Gundel, J., Hedberg, N. and Zacharski, R. 1993. "Cognitive Status and the Form of Referring Expressions in Discourse." *Language* 69:274–307.

Gürcanlı, Ö., Nakipoglu, M. and Özyürek, A.. 2007. "Shared Information and Argument Omission in Turkish." In *Proceedings of the 31st Boston University Conference on Language Development*, H. Caunt-Nulton, S. Kulatilake and I. Woo (eds.), 262–73. Somerville MA: Cascadilla Press.

Haeseryn, W., Romijn, K., Geerts, G., De Rooij, J. and Van Den Toorn, M. 1997. *Algemene Nederlandse Spraakkunst.* Groningen: Martinus Nijhoff.

Hall, G. S. (ed.) 1907. *Aspects of Child Life and Education.* Boston MA: Ginn & Co.

Harbert, W. 2006. *The Germanic Languages.* Cambridge: Cambridge University Press.

Hart, B. and Risley, T.R. 1995. *Meaningful Differences in the Everyday Experience of Young American Children.* Baltimore MD: Brookes.

Hausser, R. 1999. *Foundations of Computational Linguistics: Man-Machine Communication in Natural Language.* Berlin: Springer.

Herslund, M. 2001. "The Danish s-Genitive: From Affix to Clitic." *Acta Linguistica Hafniensia* 33:7–18.

—. 2002. *Danish. Languages of the World: Materials 382.* München: Lincom.

Hickmann, M. and Hendriks, H. 1999. "Cohesion and Anaphora in Children's Narratives: A Comparison of English, French, German, and Mandarin Chinese." *Journal of Child Language* 26:491–52.

Hockema, S. A. 2006. "Finding Words in Speech: An Investigation of American English." *Language Learning and Development* 2:119–46.

Hoekstra, T. and Hyams, N. 1998. "Aspects of Root Infinitives." *Lingua* 106:81–112.

Holcomb, P., Coffey, S. and Neville, H. 1992. "Auditory and Visual Sentence Processing: A Developmental Analysis Using Event-Related Potentials." *Developmental Neuropsychology* 5:235–53.

Huddleston, R. 1980. "Criteria for Auxiliaries and Modals." In *Studies in English Linguistics for Randolf Quirk*, S. Greenbaum, G. Leech and J. Svartvik (eds.), 65–78. London: Longman.

Hughes, M. and Allen, S. 2006. "A Discourse-Pragmatic Analysis of Subject Omission in Child English." In *Proceedings of the 30th Annual Boston University Conference on Language Development*, D. Bamman, T. Magnitskaia and C. Zaller (eds.), 293–304. Somerville MA: Cascadilla Press.

Hyams, N. 1986. *Language Acquisition and the Theory of Parameters.* Dordrecht: Reidel.

—. 1994. "Non-Discreteness and Variation in Child Language: Implications for Principle and Parameter Models of Language Development." In *Other Children, Other Languages: Issues in the Theory of Language Acquisition*, Y. Levy (ed.), 11–40. Hillsdale NJ: Lawrence Erlbaum Associates.

Hyams, N. and Wexler, K. 1993. "On the Grammatical Basis of Null Subjects in Child Language." *Linguistic Inquiry* 24:421–59.

Ingram, D. 1989. *First Language Acquisition: Method, Description and Explanation.* Cambridge: Cambridge University Press.

Jacobs, R. A. 2002. "What Determines Visual Cue Reliability?" *Trends in Cognitive Sciences* 6:345–50.

Jäger, S. 1985. "The Origin of the Diary Method in Developmental Psychology." In *Contributions to a History of Developmental Psychology. International William T. Preyer Symposium*, G. Eckardt, W. Bringmann and L. Sprung (eds.), 63–74. Berlin: Mouton.

Jakobson, R. 1941. *Kindersprache, Aphasie und allgemeine Lautgesetze.* Uppsala: Almqvist & Wiksell.

Johnson, C. 2000. "What You See Is What You Get: The Importance of Transcription for Interpreting Children's Morphosyntactic Development." In *Methods for Studying Language Production*, L. Menn and N. Bernstein-Ratner (eds.), 181–204. Mahwah NJ: Lawrence Erlbaum Associates.

Johnson, E. and Jusczyk, P. 2001. "Word Segmentation by 8-Month-Olds: When Speech Cues Count More Than Statistics." *Journal of Memory and Language* 44:548–67.

Jones, M. 1996. A Longitudinal and Methodological Investigation of Auxiliary Verb Development. University of Manchester: Doctoral Dissertation.

Jordens, P. 2002. "Finiteness in Early Child Dutch." *Linguistics* 40:687–765.

Joseph, J. 1992. "Core and 'Periphery' in Historical Perspective." *Historiographia linguistica* 19:317–32.

Jusczyk, P. 1997. *The Discovery of Spoken Language.* Cambridge MA: The MIT Press.

—. 1999. "How Infants Begin to Extract Words from Speech." *Trends in Cognitive Sciences* 3:323–28.

Jusczyk, P. and Kemler-Nelson, D. 1996. "Syntactic Units, Prosody, and Psychological Reality During Infancy." In *Signal to Syntax: Bootstrapping from Speech to Grammar in Early Acquisition*, J. Morgan and K. Demuth (eds.), 389–408. Mahwah NJ: Lawrence Erlbaum Associates.

Karmiloff-Smith, A. 1979. *A Functional Approach to Child Language: A Study of Determiners and Reference.* Cambridge: Cambridge University Press.

—. 1985. "Language and Cognitive Processes from a Developmental Perspective." *Language and Cognitive Processes* 1:61–85.

—. 1986. "From Meta-Processes to Conscious Access – Evidence from Children's Metalinguistic and Repair Data." *Cognition* 23:95–147.

Kayama, Y. 2003. "L1 Acquisition of Japanese Zero Pronouns: The Effect of Discourse Factors." In *Proceedings of the 2003 Annual Conference of the Canadian Linguistic Society* S. Burelle and S. Somesfalean (eds.), 109–20. Montreal: University of Quebec at Montreal.

Kehoe, M. and Stoel-Gammon, C. 2001. "Development of Syllable Structure in English Speaking Children with Particular Reference to Rhymes." *Journal of Child Language* 28:393–432.

Kelly, M. 1992. "Using Sound to Solve Syntactic Problems: The Role of Phonology in Grammatical Category Assignments." *Psychological Review* 99:349–64.

—. 1996. "The Role of Phonology in Grammatical Category Assignment." In *Signal to Syntax: Bootstrapping from Speech to Grammar in Early Acquisition*, J. Morgan and K. Demuth (eds.), 249–62. Mahwah NJ: Lawrence Erlbaum Associates.

Kelly, M. and Bock, J. 1988. "Stress in Time." *Journal of Experimental Psychology: Human Perception and Performance* 14:389–403.

Kemler-Nelson, D., Hirsh-Pasek, K., Jusczyk, P. and Wright Cassidy, K. 1989. "How the Prosodic Cues in Motherese Might Assist Language Learning." *Journal of Child Language* 16:55–68.

Keuleers, E., Sandra, D., Daelemans, W., Gillis, S., Durieux, G. and Martens, E. 2007. "Dutch Plural Inflection: The Exception That Proves the Analogy." *Cognitive Psychology* 54:283–318.

Kilani-Schoch, M. and Dressler, W. 2005. *Morphologie naturelle et flexion du verbe Français.* Tübingen: Narr.

Kim, Y.-J. 2000. "Subject/Object Drop in the Acquisition of Korean: A Cross-Linguistic Comparison." *Journal of East Asian Linguistics* 9:325–51.

Klampfer, S. and Korecky-Kröll, K. 2002. "Nouns and Verbs at the Transition from Pre- to Protomorphology: A Longitudinal Case Study on Austrian German." In *Pre- and Protomorphology: Early Phases of Morphological Development in Nouns and Verbs*, M. Voeikova and W. Dressler (eds.), 61–74. München: Lincom.

Klima, E. and Bellugi, U. 1966. "Syntactic Regularities in the Speech of Children." In *Psycholinguistic Papers: The Proceedings of the 1966 Edinburgh Conference*, J. Lyons and R. Wales (eds.). Edinburgh: Edinburgh University Press.

Köpcke, K. 1982. *Untersuchungen zum Genussystem der deutschen Gegenwartssprache.* Tübingen: Niemeyer.

—. 1993. *Schemata bei der Pluralbildung im Deutschen: Versuch einer kognitiven Morphologie.* Tübingen: Narr.

Korecky-Kröll, K. and Dressler, W. In preparation. "The Acquisition of Number and Case in Austrian German Nouns." In *The Acquisition of Case and Number*, U. Stephany and M. Voeikova (eds.). Berlin: Mouton de Gruyter.

Koskenniemi, K. 1983. *Two-Level Morphology: A General Computational Model for Word-Form Recognition and Production.* Helsinki: University of Helsinki, Department of Linguistics.

Kuczaj, S. and Brannick, N. 1979. "Children's Use of the Wh-Question Modal Auxiliary Placement Rule." *Journal of Experimental Child Psychology* 28:43–67.

Kuczaj, S. A. and Maratsos, M. 1975. "What a Child Can Say before He Will." *Merrill-Palmer Quarterly* 21:89–111.

—. 1983. "Initial Verbs in Yes-No Questions: A Different Kind of General Grammatical Category?" *Developmental Psychology* 19:440–44.

Kuhl, P. 1999. "Speech, Language, and the Brain: Innate Preparation for Learning." In *Neural Mechanisms of Communication*, M. Konishi and M. Hauser (eds.), 419–50. Cambridge MA: The MIT Press.

Kuhl, P., Williams, K., Lacerda, F., Stevens, K. and Lindblom, B. 1992. "Linguistic Experience Alters Phonetic Perception in Infants by 6 Months of Age." *Science* 255:606–08.

Laaha, S. and Gillis, S. 2007. *Typological Perspectives on the Acquisition of Noun and Verb Morphology.* Antwerp: University of Antwerp.

Laaha, S., Ravid, D., Korecky-Kröll, K., Laaha, G. and Dressler, W. 2006. "Early Noun Plurals in German: Regularity, Productivity or Default?" *Journal of Child Language* 33:271–302.

Labov, W. 1973. "The Boundaries of Words and Their Meanings." In *New Ways of Analyzing Variation in English*, C. Bailey and R. Shuy (eds.), 340–73. Washington DC: Georgetown University Press.

Lakoff, G. 1987. *Women, Fire, and Dangerous Things: What Categories Reveal About the Mind.* Chicago IL: CSLI Publications.

Lee, J. 2006. "The Role of Joint Attention in Verb Learning." Paper presented at the *31st Annual Boston University Conference on Language Development*, Boston MA, USA.

Lee, L. 1974. *Developmental Sentence Analysis.* Evanston IL: Northwestern University Press.

Lehner, P. 1979. *Handbook of Ethological Methods.* New York NY: Garland.

Leopold, W. F. 1939–1949. *Speech Development of a Bilingual Child: A Linguist's Record (4 Volumes).* Evanston IL: Northwestern University Press (Reprint New York: AMS Press 1970).

Levelt, C., Schiller, N. and Levelt, W. 2000. "The Acquisition of Syllable Types." *Language Acquisition* 8:237–64.

Levy, Y. 1980. The Acquisition of Gender. The Hebrew University: Doctoral Dissertation.

—. 1988. "The Nature of Early Language: Evidence from the Development of Hebrew Morphology." In *Categories and Processes in Language Acquisition*, Y. Levy, I. Schlesinger and M. Braine (eds.), 73–98. Hillsdale NJ: Lawrence Erlbaum Associates.

Lew-Williams, C. and Fernald, A. 2007. "Young Children Learning Spanish Make Rapid Use of Grammatical Gender in Spoken Word Recognition." *Psychological Science* 18:193–98.

Lewis, M., Gerhard, S. and Ellis, H. 2001. "Re-Evaluating Age-of-Acquisition Effects: Are They Simply Cumulative-Frequency Effects?" *Cognition* 78:189–205.

Li, P., Zhao, X. and MacWhinney, B. 2007. "Self-Organizing Processes in Early Lexical Learning". *Cognitive Science* 31.

Lieven, E., Behrens, H., Speares, J. and Tomasello, M. 2003. "Early Syntactic Creativity: A Usage-Based Approach." *Journal of Child Language* 30:333–70.

Lieven, E., Pine, J. and Baldwin, G. 1997. "Lexically Based Learning and Early Grammatical Development." *Journal of Child Language* 24:187–219.

Lieven, E., Pine, J. and Dresner Barnes, H. 1992. " Individual Differences in Early Vocabulary Development: Redefining the Referential Expressive Dimension." *Journal of Child Language* 19:287–310.

Long, S. and Channell, R. 2001. "Accuracy of Four Language Analysis Procedures Performed Automatically." *American Journal of Speech-Language Pathology* 10:212–25.

López Ornat, S. 1994. *La Adquisición de la Lengua Española.* Madrid: Siglo XXI.

MacWhinney, B. 1975. "Pragmatic Patterns in Child Syntax". *Papers and Reports on Child Language Development* 10:153–65.

—. 1987a. *The CHILDES Project: Tools for Analyzing Talk.* Hillsdale NJ: Lawrence Erlbaum Associates.

—. 1987b. "The Competition Model." In *Mechanisms of Language Acquisition*, B. MacWhinney (ed.), 249–308. Hillsdale HJ: Lawrence Erlbaum Associates.

—. 1991. *The CHILDES Project: Tools for Analyzing Talk.* Hillsdale NJ: Lawrence Erlbaum Associates.

—. 1995. *The CHILDES Project: Tools for Analyzing Talk.* Hillsdale NJ: Lawrence Erlbaum Associates.

—. 2000. *The CHILDES Project: Tools for Analyzing Talk.* Mahwah NJ: Lawrence Erlbaum Associates.

—. 2004. "A Multiple Process Solution to the Logical Problem of Language Acquisition." *Journal of Child Language* 31:883–914.

—. 2005. "Item-Based Constructions and the Logical Problem". *ACL 2005*:46–54.
MacWhinney, B. and Leinbach, J. 1991. "Implementations Are Not Conceptualizations: Revising the Verb Learning Model". *Cognition* 29:121–57.
MacWhinney, B., Leinbach, J., Taraban, R. and McDonald, J. 1989. "Language Learning: Cues or Rules?" *Journal of Memory and Language* 28:255–77.
Malvern, D. and Richards, B. 1997. "A New Measure of Lexical Diversity." In *Evolving Models of Language*, A. Ryan and A. Wray (eds.), 58–71. Clevedon: Multilingual Matters.
Malvern, D., Richards, B., Chipere, N. and Purán, P. 2004. *Lexical Diversity and Language Development.* New York: Palgrave Macmillan.
Maratsos, M. 1983. "Some Current Issues in the Study of the Acquisition of Grammar." In *Handbook of Child Psychology*, P. Mussen (ed.), 707–86. New York NY: Wiley & Sons.
—. 2000. "More Overregularisations after All: New Data and Discussion on Marcus, Pinker, Ullman, Hollander, Rosen & Xu." *Journal of Child Language* 27:183–212.
Maratsos, M. and Chalkley, M. 1980. "The Internal Language of Children's Syntax: The Ontogenesis and Representation of Syntactic Categories." In *Children's Language*, K.E. Nelson (ed.), 127–214. New York NY: Gardner Press.
Marchand, H. 1969. *The Categories and Types of Present-Day English Word-Formation.* München: Beck.
Marcus, G. 1995. "Children's Overregularization of English Plurals: A Quantitative Analysis." *Journal of Child Language* 22:447–60.
—. 2000. "Children's Overregularization and Its Implications for Cognition." In *Models of Language Acquisition: Inductive and Deductive Approaches*, P. Broeder and J. Murre (eds.), 154–76. Oxford: Oxford University Press.
Marcus, G., Brinkmann, U., Clahsen, H., Wiese, R. and Pinker, S. 1995. "German Inflection: The Exception That Proves the Rule." *Cognitive Psychology* 29:189–256.
Marcus, G., Pinker, S., Ullman, M., Hollander, M., Rosen, T. and Xu, F. 1992. "Overregularization in Language Acquisition." *Monographs of the Society for Research in Child Development* 57:1–182.
Marslen-Wilson, W., Levy, E. and Tyler, L. 1982. "Producing Interpretable Discourse: The Establishment and Maintenance of Reference." In *Speech, Place, and Action: Studies in Deixis and Gesture*, R. Jarvella and W. Klein (eds.), 339–78. New York NY: Wiley.
Martin, P. and Bateson, P. 1993. *Measuring Behaviour: An Introductory Guide.* Cambridge: Cambridge University Press.
Maslen, R., Theakston, A., Lieven, E. and Tomasello, M. 2004. "A Dense Corpus Study of Past Tense and Plural Overregularization in English." *Journal of Speech, Language and Hearing Research* 47:1319–33.
Matthews, D., Lieven, E., Theakston, A. and Tomasello, M. 2006. "The Effect of Perceptual Availability and Prior Discourse on Young Children's Use of Referring Expressions." *Applied Psycholinguistics* 27:403–22.
McClure, C., Pine, J. and Lieven, E. 2006. "Investigating the Abstractness of Children's Early Knowledge of Argument Structure." *Journal of Child Language* 33:693–720.
McDonald, S. and Shillcock, R. 2001. "Rethinking the Word Frequency Effect: The Neglected Role of Distributional Information in Lexical Processing." *Language and Speech* 44:295–323.
Mehler, J., Jusczyk, P., Lambertz, G., Halsted, N., Bertoncini, J. and Amiel-Tison, C. 1988. "A Precursor of Language Acquisition in Young Infants." *Cognition* 29:143–78.

Meisel, J. 1986. "Word Order and Case Marking in Early Child Language. Evidence from Simultaneous Acquisition of Two First Languages: French and German". *Linguistics* 24:123–85.

Miikkulainen, R. and Mayberry, M. 1999. "Disambiguation and Grammar as Emergent Soft Constraints" In *The Emergence of Language*, B. MacWhinney (ed.), 153–76. Mahwah NJ: Lawrence Erlbaum Associates.

Miller, J. and Chapman, R. 1981. "The Relationship between Age and Mean Length of Utterance in Morphemes." *Journal of Speech and Hearing Research* 24:154–61.

—. 1983. *Salt: Systematic Analysis of Language Transcripts, User's Manual*. Madison: University of Wisconsin Press.

Mills, A. 1986. *The Acquisition of Gender: A Study of English and German*. Berlin: Springer.

Mintz, T. 2003. "Frequent Frames as a Cue for Grammatical Categories in Child Directed Speech." *Cognition* 90:91–117.

Mintz, T., Newport, E. and Bever, T. 2002. "The Distributional Structure of Grammatical Categories in Speech to Young Children". *Cognitive Science* 26:393–424.

Mishina, S. 1997. Language Separation in Early Bilingual Development: A Longitudinal Study of Japanese/English Bilingual Children. University of California, Los Angeles: Doctoral Dissertation.

Mishina-Mori, S. 2007. "Argument Representation in Japanese/English Simultaneous Bilinguals: Is There a Crosslinguistic Influence?" In *Proceedings of the 31st Annual Boston University Conference on Language Development*, H. Caunt-Nulto, S. Kulatilake and I. Woo (eds.), 441–50. Somerville MA: Cascadilla Press.

Miyata, S. 1995. "The Aki Corpus – Longitudinal Speech Data of a Japanese Boy Aged 1.6–2.12". *Bulletin of Aichi Shukutoku Junior College* 34:183–191.

Monaghan, P. and Christiansen, M. 2004. "What Distributional Information Is Useful and Usable in Language Acquisition?" In *Proceedings of the 26th Annual Conference of the Cognitive Science Society*, K. Forbus, D. Gentner and T. Regier (eds.), 963–68. Mahwah NJ: Lawrence Erlbaum Associates.

—. 2006. "Why Form-Meaning Mappings Are Not Entirely Arbitrary in Language." In *Proceedings of the 28th Annual Conference of the Cognitive Science Society*, R. Sun and N. Miyake (eds.), 1838–43. Mahwah NJ: Lawrence Erlbaum Associates.

Monaghan, P., Chater, N. and Christiansen, M. 2005. "The Differential Contribution of Phonological and Distributional Cues in Grammatical Categorisation." *Cognition* 96:143–82.

Monaghan, P., Christiansen, M. and Chater, N. 2007. "The Phonological-Distributional Coherence Hypothesis: Cross-Linguistic Evidence in Language Acquisition." *Cognitive Psychology* 55:259–305.

Morgan, J. 1986. *From Simple Input to Complex Grammar*. Cambridge MA: The MIT Press.

—. 1996. "Prosody and the Roots of Parsing." *Language and Cognitive Processes* 11:69–106.

Morgan, J. and Demuth, K. (eds.) 1996. *Signal to Syntax: Bootstrapping from Speech to Grammar in Early Acquisition*. Mahwah NJ: Lawrence Erlbaum Associates.

Morgan, J., Meier, R. and Newport, E. 1987. "Structural Packaging in the Input to Language Learning: Contributions of Prosodic and Morphological Marking of Phrases to the Acquisition of Language." *Cognitive Psychology* 19:498–550.

Morgan, J., Shi, R. and Allopenna, P. 1996. "Perceptual Bases of Grammatical Categories." In *Signal to Syntax: Bootstrapping from Speech to Grammar in Early Acquisition*, J. Morgan and K. Demuth (eds.), 263–83. Mahwah MA: Lawrence Erlbaum Associates.

Naigles, L. 2002. "Form Is Easy, Meaning Is Hard: Resolving a Paradox in Early Child Language." *Cognition* 86:157–99.

Narasimhan, B., Budwig, N. and Murty, L. 2005. "Argument Realization in Hindi Caregiver-Child Discourse." *Journal of Pragmatics* 37:461–95.

Newmeyer, F. 2003. "Grammar Is Grammar and Usage Is Usage." *Language* 79:682–707.

Newport, E. and Aslin, R. 2004. "Learning at a Distance I. Statistical Learning of Nonadjacent Dependencies." *Cognitive Psychology* 48:127–62.

Ninio, A. 1992. "The Relation of Children's Single Word Utterances to Single Word Utterances in the Input." *Journal of Child Language* 19:87–110.

Norris, J. and Ortega, L. 2000. "Synthesizing Research on Language Learning and Teaching Effectiveness of L2 Instruction: A Research Synthesis and Quantitative Meta-Analysis." *Language Learning* 50:417–528.

—. 2006a. "The Value of Practice of Research Synthesis for Language Learning and Teaching." In *Synthesizing Research on Language Learning and Teaching*, J. Norris and L. Ortega (eds.), 3–52. Amsterdam: John Benjamins.

—. 2006b. "Synthesizing Research on Language Learning and Teaching." Amsterdam: John Benjamins.

O'Grady, W. 1997. *Syntactic Development.* Chicago IL: The University of Chicago Press.

Ochs, E. 1979. "Transcription as Theory." In *Developmental Pragmatics*, E. Ochs and B. Schieffelin (eds.), 43–71. New York NY: Academic Press.

Office of Population Censuses and Surveys. 1970. *Classification of Occupations.* London: HMSO.

Onnis, L. and Christiansen, M. 2005. "Happy Endings for Absolute Beginners: Psychological Plausibility in Computational Models of Language Acquisition." In *Proceedings of the 27th Annual Meeting of the Cognitive Science Society*, B. Bara, L. Barsalou and M. Buchiarelli (eds.), 1678–83. Mahwah NJ: Lawrence Erlbaum Associates.

Onnis, L., Monaghan, P., Richmond, K. and Chater, N. 2005. "Phonology Impacts Segmentation in Speech Processing." *Journal of Memory and Language* 53:225–37.

Oshima-Takane, Y., Goodz, E. and Derevensky, J. 1996. "Birth Order Effects on Early Language Development: Do Secondborn Children Learn from Overheard Speech?" *Child Development* 67:621–634.

Pallier, C., Christophe, A. and Mehler, J. 1997. "Language-Specific Listening." *Trends in Cognitive Sciences* 1:129–32.

Palmer, F. 1965. *A Linguistic Study of the English Verb.* London: Longman.

Pan, B., Perlmann, R. and Snow, C. 2000. "Food for Thought: Dinner Table as a Context for Observing Parent-Child Discourse." In *Methods for Studying Language Production*, L. Menn and N. Bernstein-Ratner (eds.), 205–24. Mahwah NJ: Lawrence Erlbaum Associates.

Paradis, J. and Navarro, S. 2003. "Subject Realization and Crosslinguistic Interference in the Bilingual Acquisition of Spanish and English: What Is the Role of the Input?" *Journal of Child Language* 30:371–93.

Parisse, C. and Le Normand, M.-T. 2000. "Automatic Disambiguation of the Morphosyntax in Spoken Language Corpora". *Behavior Research Methods, Instruments, and Computers* 32:468–81.

Parker, M. and Brorson, K. 2005. "A Comparative Study Between Mean Length of Utterance in Morphemes (MLUm) and Mean Length of Utterance in Words (MLUw). *First Language* 25: 365–376.

Pearl, J. 2005. "The Input for Syntactic Acquisition: Solutions from Language Change Modeling." In *Proceedings of the 43rd Annual Meeting of the Association for Computational Linguistics (Acl'05)*, 12–18. Ann Arbor MI: Association for Computational Linguistics.

Peña, M., Bonatti, L., Nespor, M. and Mehler, J. 2002. "Signal-Driven Computations in Speech Processing." *Science* 298:604–07.

Pfau, R. and Steinbach, M. 2006. "Pluralization in Sign and in Speech: A Cross-Modal Typological Study." *Linguistic Typology* 10:135–82.

Piatelli-Palmerini, M. (ed.) 1980. *Language and Learning: The Debate between Jean Piaget and Noam Chomsky.* Cambridge MA: Harvard University Press.

Pine, J., Conti-Ramsden, G., Joseph, K., Lieven, E. and Serratrice, L. 2008. "Tense over Time: Testing the Agreement/Tense Omission Model as an Account of the Pattern of Tense-Marking Provision in Early Child English." *Journal of Child Language* 35:55–75.

Pine, J. and Lieven, E. 1997. "Slot and Frame Patterns and the Development of the Determiner Category." *Applied Psycholinguistics* 18:123–38.

Pine, J. and Martindale, H. 1996. "Syntactic Categories in the Speech of Young Children: The Case of the Determiner." *Journal of Child Language* 23:369–95.

Pine, J., Rowland, C., Lieven, E. and Theakston, A. 2005. "Testing the Agreement/Tense Omission Model: Why the Data on Children's Use of Non-Nominative 3psg Subjects Count against the ATOM." *Journal of Child Language* 32:269–89.

Pinker, S. 1984. *Language Learnability and Language Development.* Cambridge MA: Harvard University Press.

—. 1999. *Words and Rules: The Ingredients of Language.* London: Weidenfeld & Nicolson.

Pinker, S. and Prince, A. 1994. "Regular and Irregular Morphology and the Psychological Status of Rules of Grammar." In *The Reality of Linguistic Rules*, S. Lima, R. Corrigan and G. Iverson (eds.), 321–51. Amsterdam: John Benjamins.

Pinker, S. and Ullman, M. 2002. "The Past and Future of the Past Tense." *Trends in Cognitive Sciences* 6:456–63.

Pizzuto, E. and Caselli, M. 1992. "The Acquisition of Italian Morphology: Implications for Models of Language Development." *Journal of Child Language* 19:491–557.

Plunkett, K. and Marchman, V. 1991. "U-Shaped Learning and Frequency Effects in a Multi-Layered Perceptron: Implications for Child Language Acquisition." *Cognition* 38:43–102.

Popela, J. 1966. "The Functional Structure of Linguistic Units and the System of Language." *Travaux linguistiques de Prague* 2:71–80.

Pothos, E. and Chater, N. 2002. "A Simplicity Principle in Unsupervised Human Categorization." *Cognitive Science* 26:303–43.

—. 2005. "Unsupervised Categorization and Category Learning." *Quarterly Journal of Experimental Psychology* 58:733–52.

Preyer, W. 1882. *Die Seele des Kindes.* Leipzig: Grieben.

Prince, E. 1981. "Toward a Taxonomy of Given-New Information." In *Radical Pragmatics*, P. Cole (ed.), 223–55. New York NY: Academic Press.

—. 1985. "Fancy Syntax and 'Shared Knowledge'." *Journal of Pragmatics* 9:65–81.

Radford, A. 1990. *Syntactic Theory and the Acquistion of English Syntax: The Nature of Early Child Grammars.* Oxford: Blackwell.

Ravid, D. 1995. *Language Change in Child and Adult Hebrew: A Psycholinguistic Perspective.* Oxford: Oxford University Press.

—. 2006. "Word-Level Morphology: A Psycholinguistic Perspective on Linear Formation in Hebrew Nominals." *Morphology* 16:127–48.

Reali, F., Christiansen, M. and Monaghan, P. 2003. "Phonological and Distributional Cues in Syntax Acquisition: Scaling up the Connectionist Approach to Multiple-Cue Integration." In *Proceedings of the 25th Annual Conference of the Cognitive Science Society*, R. Alterman and D. Kirsch (eds.), 970–75. Mahwah NJ: Lawrence Erlbaum Associates.

Redington, M., Chater, N. and Finch, S. 1998. "Distributional Information: A Powerful Cue for Acquiring Syntactic Categories." *Cognitive Science* 22:425–69.

Rice, M., Wexler, K. and Hershberger, S. 1998. "Tense over Time: The Longitudinal Course of Tense Acquisition in Children with Specific Language Impairment." *Journal of Speech Language and Hearing Research* 41:1412–31.

Rice, S. 1997. "The Analysis of Ontogenetic Trajectories: When a Change in Size or Shape Is Not Heterochrony". *Proceedings of the National Academy of Sciences* 94:907–12.

Richards, B. 1990. *Language Development and Individual Differences: A Study of Auxiliary Verb Learning*. Cambridge: Cambridge University Press.

Rischel, J. 2003. "The Danish Syllable as a National Heritage." In *Take Danish – for Instance: Linguistic Studies in Honour of Hans Basbøll Presented on the Occasion of His 60th Birthday 12 July 2003*, G. Jacobsen, D. Bleses, T. Madsen and P. Thomsen (eds.), 273–82. Odense: University Press of Southern Denmark.

Rispoli, M. 1998. "Patterns of Pronoun Case Error." *Journal of Child Language* 25:533–54.

Rizzi, L. 1993/1994. "Some Notes on Linguistic Theory and Language Development: The Case of Root Infinitives." *Language Acquisition* 3:371–93.

Rose, Y., MacWhinney, B., Byrne, R., Hedlund, G., Maddocks, K. and O'Brien, P. 2005. "Introducing Phon: A Software Solution for the Study of Phonological Acquisition." In *30th Annual Boston University Conference on Language Development*, D. Bamman, T. Magnitskaia and C. Zaller (eds.), 489–500. Somerville MA: Cascadilla Press.

Rowland, C. 2007. "Explaining Errors in Children's Questions." *Cognition* 104:106–34.

Rowland, C. and Fletcher, S. 2006. "The Effect of Sampling on Estimates of Lexical Specificity and Error Rates." *Journal of Child Language* 33:859–77.

Rowland, C. and Pine, J. M. 2000. "Subject-Auxiliary Inversion Errors and Wh-Question Acquisition: What Children Do Know?" *Journal of Child Language* 27:157–81.

Rowland, C., Pine, J., Lieven, E. and Theakston, A. 2005. "The Incidence of Error in Young Children's Wh-Questions." *Journal of Speech, Language and Hearing Research* 48:384–404.

Rubino, R. and Pine, J. 1998. "Subject-Verb Agreement in Brazilian Portuguese: What Low Error Rates Hide." *Journal of Child Language* 25:35–59.

Rumelhart, D. and McClelland, J. 1986. "On Learning the Past Tense of English Verbs." In *Parallel Distributed Processing: Explorations in the Microstructure of Cognition*, J. McClelland and D. Rumelhart (eds.), 216–71. Cambridge MA: The MIT Press.

Sachs, J. 1983. Talking about the There and Then: The Emergence of Displaced Reference in Parent-Child Discourse. In *Children's Language. Volume 4*, K. E. Nelson (ed.), 1–28. Hillsdale NJ: Lawrence Erlbaum Associates.

Saffran, J. 2003. "Statistical Language Learning: Mechanisms and Constraints." *Current Directions in Psychological Science* 12:110–14.

Saffran, J., Aslin, A. and Newport, E. 1996. "Statistical Learning by 8-Month-Old Infants." *Science* 274:1926–28.

Sagae, K., Davis, E., Lavie, E., MacWhinney, B. and Wintner, S. 2007. "High-Accuracy Annotation and Parsing of *CHILDES* Transcripts." In *Proceedings of the Workshop on Cognitive Aspects of Computational Language Acquisition*, P. Buttery, A. Villavicencio and A. Korhonen (eds.), 25–32. Prague, Czech Republic: Association for Computational Linguistics.

Sagae, K., Lavie, A. and MacWhinney, B. 2005. "Automatic Measurement of Syntactic Development in Child Language" In *Proceedings of the 43rd Meeting of the Association for Computational Linguistics*, 197–204. Ann Arbor MI: ACL.

Sagae, K., MacWhinney, B. and Lavie, A. 2004a. "Adding Syntactic Annotations to Transcripts of Parent-Child Dialogs" In *LREC 2004*, 1815–18. Lisbon: LREC.

—. 2004b. "Automatic Parsing of Parent-Child Interactions". *Behavior Research Methods, Instruments, and Computers* 36:113–26.

Sahin, N., Pinker, S. and Halgren, E. 2006. "Abstract Grammatical Processing of Nouns and Verbs in Broca's Area: Evidence from fMRI." *Cortex* 42:540–62.

Santelmann, L., Berk, S., Austin, J., Somashekar, S. and Lust, B. 2002. "Continuity and Development in the Acquisition of Inversion in Yes/No Questions: Dissociating Movement and Inflection." *Journal of Child Language* 29:813–42.

Scarborough, H. 1990. "Index of Productive Syntax". *Applied Psycholinguistics* 11:1–22.

Schütze, C. and Wexler, K. 1996. "Subject Case Licensing and English Root Infinitives." In *Proceedings of the 20th Annual Boston University Conference on Language Development*, A. Stringfellow, D. Cahma-Amitay, E. Hughes and A. Zukowski (eds.), 670–81. Somerville MA: Cascadilla Press.

Schwarzwald, O. 1983. "Frequency and Regularity in Language." *Studies in Education* 35:163–74.

Scupin, E. and Scupin, G. 1907. *Bubis erste Kindheit.* Leipzig: Grieben.

—. 1910. *Bubi im 4.-6. Lebensjahre.* Leipzig: Grieben.

Sedlak, M., Klampfer, S., Müller, B. and Dressler, W. 1998. "The Acquisition of Number in Austrian German: A Case Study on the Early Stages." In *Studies in the Acquisition of Number and Diminutive Marking*, S. Gillis (ed.), 51–76. Antwerp: University of Antwerp.

Sells, P. (ed.) 2001. *Formal and Theoretical Issues in Optimality Theoretic Syntax.* Stanford CA: CSLI Publications.

Sereno, J. and Jongman, A. 1990. "Phonological and Form Class Relations in the Lexicon." *Journal of Psycholinguistic Research* 19:387–404.

Serratrice, L. 2002. "Syntax and Pragmatics in the Acquisition of Italian Subjects." Paper presented at the *Ninth International Congress for the Study of Child Language*, Madison WI, USA.

—. 2005. "The Role of Discourse Pragmatics in the Acquisition of Subjects in Italian." *Applied Psycholinguistics* 26:437–62.

Serratrice, L., Sorace, A. and Paoli, S. 2004. "Crosslinguistic Influence at the Syntax-Pragmatics Interface: Subjects and Objects in Italian-English Bilingual and Monolingual Acquisition." *Bilingualism: Language and Cognition* 7:183–205.

Shady, M. and Gerken, L. A. 1999. "Grammatical and Caregiver Cues in Early Sentence Comprehension." *Journal of Child Language* 26:163–75.

Shi, R., Morgan, J. and Allopenna, P. 1998. "Phonological and Acoustic Bases for Earliest Grammatical Category Assignment: A Cross-Linguistic Perspective." *Journal of Child Language* 25:169–201.

Shi, R., Werker, J. and Morgan, J. 1999. "Newborn Infants' Sensitivity to Perceptual Cues to Lexical and Grammatical Words." *Cognition* 27:11–21.

Shin, K. S. 2006. "Discourse Prominence in Korean Children's on-Line Processing of Nominal Reference." Paper presented at the *31st Annual Boston University Conference on Language Development*, Boston, MA, USA.

Shin, N. L. 2006. The Development of Null Vs Overt Subject Pronoun Expression in Monolingual Spanish-Speaking Children: The Influence of Continuity of Reference. City University of New York: Doctoral Dissertation.

Silverstein, M. 1976. "Hierarchy of Features and Ergativity." In *Grammatical Categories in Australian Languages*, R. Dixon (ed.), 112–71. Canberra: Australian Institute of Aboriginal Studies.

Siskind, J. 1999. "Learning Word-to-Meaning Mappings" In *Models of Language Acquisition*, P. Broeder and J. Murre (eds.), 121–53. Oxford: Oxford University Press.

Skarabela, B. 2006. The Role of Social Cognition in Early Syntax: The Case of Joint Attention in Argument Realization in Child Inuktitut. Boston University: Doctoral Dissertation.

—. 2007. "Signs of Early Social Cognition in Children's Syntax: The Case of Joint Attention in Argument Realization in Child Inuktitut." *Lingua* 117:1837–57.

Skarabela, B. and Allen, S. 2002. "The Role of Joint Attention in Argument Realization in Child Inuktitut." In *Proceedings of the Twenty-Sixth Annual Boston University Conference on Language Development*, B. Skarabela, S. Fish and A. Do (eds.), 620–30. Somerville MA: Cascadilla Press.

—. 2003. "Joint Attention in Argument Expression in Child Inuktitut." Paper presented at the *Georgetown University Roundtable in Linguistics*, Washington DC, USA.

—. 2004. "The Context of Non-Affixal Arguments in Child Inuktitut: The Role of Joint Attention." In *Proceedings of the 28th Annual Boston University Conference on Language Development* A. Brugos, L. Micciulla and C. Smith (eds.), 532–42. Somerville MA: Cascadilla Press.

Slobin, D.I. (ed.) 1985a. *The Crosslinguistic Study of Language Acquisition. Vol. 1: The Data.* Hillsdale NJ: Lawrence Erlbaum Associates.

—. 1985b. *The Crosslinguistic Study of Language Acquisition. Vol. 2: Theoretical Issues.* Hillsdale NJ: Lawrence Erlbaum Associates.

—. 1985c. "Crosslinguistic Evidence for the Language-Making Capacity." In *The Crosslinguistic Study of Language Acquisition. Vol. 2: Theoretical Issues*, D.I. Slobin (ed.), 1157–249. Hillsdale NJ: Lawrence Erlbaum Associates.

—. 1992. *The Crosslinguistic Study of Language Acquisition. Vol. 3.* Hillsdale NJ: Lawrence Erlbaum Associates.

—. 1997a. *The Crosslinguistic Study of Language Acquisition. Vol. 4.* Mahwah NJ: Lawrence Erlbaum Associates.

—. 1997b. *The Crosslinguistic Study of Language Acquisition. Vol 5: Expanding the Contexts.* Mahwah NJ: Lawrence Erlbaum Associates.

Smoczyńska, M. 2001. "Studying Jan Baudouin De Courtenay's Polish Child Language Data 100 Years Later." In *Cinquant'anni di Richerche Linguistiche: Problemi, Risultati e Prospettive per il terzo Millenio*, R. Finazzi and P. Tornaghi (eds.), 591–610. Alessandria: Edizioni dell' Orso.

Snedeker, J. and Trueswell, J. 2004. "The Developing Constraints on Parsing Decisions: The Role of Lexical-Biases and Referential Scenes in Child and Adult Sentence Processing." *Cognitive Psychology* 49:238–99.

Snow, C. 1986. "Conversation with Children." In *Language Acquisition*, P. Fletcher and M. Garman (eds.), 69–89. Cambridge: Cambridge University Press.

—. 1995. "Issues in the Study of Input: Finetuning, Universality, Individual and Developmental Differences, and Necessary Causes." In *The Handbook of Child Language*, P. Fletcher and B. MacWhinney (eds.), 180–93. Oxford: Blackwell.

Sokolov, J. and C., Snow (eds.) 1994. *Handbook of Research in Language Development Using CHILDES*. Hillsdale NJ: Lawrence Erlbaum Associates.

Solan, Z., Horn, D., Ruppin, E. and Edelman, S. 2005. "Unsupervised Learning of Natural Languages." *Proceedings of the National Academy of Sciences* 102:11629–34.

Song, H. and Fisher, C. 2005. "Who's She? Discourse Prominence Influences Preschoolers' Comprehension of Pronouns." *Journal of Memory and Language* 52:29–57.

—. 2007. "Discourse Prominence Effects on 2.5-Year-Old Children's Interpretation of Pronouns." *Lingua* 117:1959–87.

Song, J. Y. and Demuth, K. 2005. "Effects of Syllable Structure Complexity on Children's Production of English Word-Final Grammatical Morphemes." Paper presented at the *10th International Association for the Study of Child Language*, Berlin, Germany.

—. in press. "Compensatory Vowel Lengthening for Omitted Coda Consonants: A Phonetic Investigation of Children's Early Prosodic Representations". *Language and Speech.*

Stephany, U. 2002. "Early Development of Grammatical Number – A Typological Perspective." In *Pre- and Protomorphology*, M. Voeikova and W. Dressler (eds.), 7–23. München: Lincom.

Stern, C. and Stern, W. 1907. *Die Kindersprache.* Leipzig: Barth.

—. 1909. *Erinnerung, Aussage und Lüge in der ersten Kindheit.* Leipzig: Barth.

Stern, W. 1921. *Psychologie der frühen Kindheit.* Leipzig: Quelle & Meyer.

Steyvers, M. and Tenenbaum, J. 2005. "The Large Scale Structure of Semantic Networks: Statistical Analyses and a Model of Semantic Growth." *Cognitive Science* 29:41–78.

Stolcke, S. and Omohundro, S. 1994. "Inducing Probabilistic Grammars by Bayesian Model Merging." In *Grammatical Inference and Applications*, R. Carrasco and J. Oncina (eds.), 106–18. Berlin: Springer.

Stromswold, K. 1990. Learnability and the Acquisition of Auxiliaries. Massachusetts Institute of Technology: Doctoral Dissertation.

—. 1994. "Using Spontaneous Production Data to Assess Syntactic Development" In *Methods for Assessing Children's Syntax*, D. McDaniel, C. McKee and H. Cairns (eds.). Cambridge MA: The MIT Press.

Suppes, P. 1974. "The Semantics of Children's Language". *American Psychologist* 29:103–114.

Theakston, A. and Lieven, E. 2005. "The Acquisition of Auxiliaries Be and Have: An Elicitation Study." *Journal of Child Language* 32:587–616.

—. 2008. "The Influence of Discourse Context on Children's Provision of Auxiliary Be." *Journal of Child Language* 35:129–58.

Theakston, A., Lieven, E., Pine, J. and Rowland, C. 2001. "The Role of Performance Limitations in the Acquisition of Verb-Argument Structure: An Alternative Account." *Journal of Child Language* 28:127–52.

—. 2002. "Going, Going, Gone: The Acquisition of the Verb 'Go'." *Journal of Child Language* 29:783–811.

—. 2005. "The Acquisition of Auxiliary Syntax: Be and Have." *Cognitive Linguistics* 16:247–77.

Tiedemann, D. 1787. "Beobachtungen über die Entwickelung der Seelenfähigkeiten bei Kindern." *Hessische Beiträge zur Gelehrsamkeit und Kunst* 2:313–333,486–502.

Tomasello, M. 1992. *First Verbs: A Case Study of Early Grammatical Development.* Cambridge: Cambridge University Press.

—. 1999. *The Cultural Origins of Human Cognition.* Cambridge MA: Harvard University Press.

—. 2000a. "Do You Children Have Adult Syntactic Competence?" *Cognition* 74:209–53.

—. 2000b. "The Item-Based Nature of Children's Early Syntactic Development." *Trends in Cognitive Science* 4:156–63.

—. 2003. *Constructing a Language: A Usage-Based Theory of Language Acquisition.* Cambridge MA: Harvard University Press.

Tomasello, M. and Abbot-Smith, K. 2002. "A Tale of Two Theories: Response to Fisher." *Cognition* 83:207–14.

Tomasello, M., Akhtar, N., Dodson, K. and Rekau, L. 1997. "Differential Productivity in Young Children's Use of Nouns and Verbs." *Journal of Child Language* 24:373–87.

Tomasello, M., Kruger, A. and Ratner, H. 1993. "Cultural Learning." *Behavioral and Brain Sciences* 16:495–552.

Tomasello, M. and Stahl, D. 2004. "Sampling Children's Spontaneous Speech: How Much Is Enough?" *Journal of Child Language* 31:101–21.

Tyler, L. 1983. "The Development of Discourse Mapping Processes: The On-Line Interpretation of Anaphoric Expressions." *Cognition* 13:309–41.

Valian, V. 1986. "Syntactic Categories in the Speech of Young Children." *Developmental Psychology* 22:562–79.

—. 1991. "Syntactic Subjects in the Early Speech of American and Italian Children." *Cognition* 40:21–81.

Valian, V. and Aubry, S. 2005. "When Opportunity Knocks Twice: Two-Year-Olds' Repetition of Sentence Subjects." *Journal of Child Language* 32:617–41.

Valian, V. and Coulson, S. 1988. "Anchor Points in Language Learning: The Role of Marker Frequency." *Journal of Memory and Language* 27:71–86.

Valian, V. and Eisenberg, Z. 1996. "The Development of Syntactic Subjects in Portuguese-Speaking Children." *Journal of Child Language* 23:103–28.

Valian, V., Lasser, I. and Mandelbaum, D. 1992. Children's Early Questions. New York NY: Hunter College: Unpublished manuscript.

Valian, V. and Levitt, A. 1996. "Prosody and Adults' Learning of Syntactic Structure." *Journal of Memory and Language* 35:497–516.

Van de Weijer, J. 1998. Language Input for Word Discovery. Katholieke Universiteit Nijmegen: Doctoral dissertation.

Van Haeringen, C. 1947. "De Meervoudsvorming in het Nederlands." *Mededelingen der Koninklijke Nederlansche Akademie van Wetenschappen (afdeling letterkunde, nieuwe reeks)* 10:131–56.

Van Kampen, J. 1998. "Left Branch Extraction as Operator Movement: Evidence from Child Dutch" In *The Acquisition of Scrambling and Cliticization*, S. Powers and C. Hamman (eds.). Dordrecht: Kluwer.

Van Wijk, J. 2002. "The Dutch Plural Landscape." In *Linguistics in the Netherlands 2002*, H. Broekhuis and P. Fikkert (eds.), 211–21. Amsterdam: John Benjamins.

Vear, D., Naigles, L., Hoff, E. and Ramos, E. 2002. Grammatical Flexibility in Early Verb Use. University of Connecticut: Unpublished manuscript.

Vollmann, R., Sedlak, M., Müller, B. and Vassilakou, M. 1997. "Early Verb Inflection and Noun Plural Formation in Four Austrian Children." *Papers and Studies in Contrastive Linguistics* 33:59–78.

Warner, A. 1993. *English Auxiliaries: Structure and History.* Cambridge: Cambridge University Press.

Wegener, H. 1999. "Die Pluralbildung im Deutschen – Ein Versuch im Rahmen der Optimalitätstheorie." *Linguistik online* 4 (3/99).

Weissenborn, J. and Höhle, B. (eds.) 2001. *Approaches to Bootstrapping: Phonological, Lexical, Syntactic and Neurophysiological Aspects of Early Language Acquisition.* Amsterdam: John Benjamins.

Werker, J. and Tees, R. 1999. "Influences on Infant Speech Processing: Toward a New Synthesis." *Annual Review of Psychology* 50:509–35.

Wexler, K. 1998. "Very Early Parameter Setting and the Unique Checking Constraint: A New Explanation of the Optional Infinitive Stage." *Lingua* 106:23–79.

Wexler, K., Schütze, C. and Rice, M. 1998. "Subject Case in Children with SLI and Unaffected Controls: Evidence for the Agr/Tns Omission Model." *Language Acquisition* 7:317–44.

Wintner, S. 2007. "Finite-State Technology as a Programming Environment." In *Computational Linguistics and Intelligent Text Processing, 8th International Conference*, A. Gelbukh (ed.), 97–106. Heidelberg: Springer.

Wittek, A. and Tomasello, M. 2005. "Young Children's Sensitivity to Listener Knowledge and Perceptual Context in Choosing Referring Expressions." *Applied Psycholinguistics* 26:541–58.

Wright, H. F. 1960. "Observational Child Studies." In *Handbook of Research Methods in Child Development*, P. Mussen (ed.), 71–138. New York NY: Wiley.

Wykes, T. 1981. "Inference and Children's Comprehension of Pronouns." *Journal of Experimental Child Psychology* 32:264–79.

—. 1983. "The Role of Inferences in Children's Comprehension of Pronouns." *Journal of Experimental Child Psychology* 35:180–93.

Yu, C. 2006. "Learning Syntax-Semantics Mappings to Bootstrap Word Learning." In *Proceedings of the 28th Cognitive Science Society Conference*, R. Sun and N. Miyake (eds.), 924–29. Mahwah NJ: Lawrence Erlbaum Associates.

Yu, C. and Smith, L. B. 2006. "Statistical Cross-Situational Learning to Build Word-to-World Mappings." In *Proceedings of the 28th Cognitive Science Society Conference*, R. Sun and N. Miyake (eds.), 918–23. Mahwah NJ: Lawrence Erlbaum Associates.

Zevin, I. and Seidenberg, M. 2002. "Age of Acquisition Effects in Word Reading and Other Tasks." *Journal of Memory and Language* 47:1–29.

Ziesler, Y. and Demuth, K. 1995. "Noun Class Prefixes in Sesotho Child-Directed Speech." In *Proceedings of the 26th Child Language Research Forum*, E. Clark (ed.), 137–46. Stanford CA: CSLI Publications.

Zonneveld, W. 2004. "De Verwerving van een Morfologisch Proces: Nederlandse Meervoudsvorming." *Nederlandse Taalkunde* 90:1–28.

Index

In the series *Trends in Language Acquisition Research* the following titles have been published thus far or are scheduled for publication:

6 **BEHRENS, Heike (ed.):** Corpora in Language Acquisition Research. History, methods, perspectives. 2008. xxx, 234 pp.

5 **FRIEDERICI, Angela D. and Guillaume THIERRY (eds.):** Early Language Development. Bridging brain and behaviour. 2008. xiv, 263 pp.

4 **FLETCHER, Paul and Jon F. MILLER (eds.):** Developmental Theory and Language Disorders. 2005. x, 217 pp.

3 **BERMAN, Ruth A. (ed.):** Language Development across Childhood and Adolescence. 2004. xiv, 308 pp.

2 **MORGAN, Gary and Bencie WOLL (eds.):** Directions in Sign Language Acquisition. 2002. xx, 339 pp.

1 **CENOZ, Jasone and Fred GENESEE (eds.):** Trends in Bilingual Acquisition. 2001. viii, 288 pp.